FINDING GOD

WITHOUT GETTING LOST

JOHN T. DAVIS

To all who are searching for truth.

FAITH IS AN ADVENTURE BASED ON THE EVIDENCE

"One who claims that faith requires belief without evidence
or is contrary to fact does not know a biblical faith."

THE AUTHOR

*"…Always be prepared to give an answer to everyone
who asks you to give the reason for the hope that you
have. But do this with gentleness and respect"*

I PETER 3:15.

CONTENTS

WHY THIS BOOK?

This book is intended for both skeptics and believers: the former to be convinced of God's existence and identity, and the latter to be encouraged and strengthened by learning reasons for their faith. In addition, it is hoped the readers will find a fulfilling life of personal friendship with God if they do not have one already.

A lot has been written about God and religion over the centuries, some of which is confusing, contradictory, and inconsistent, while some is excellent and insightful. It is hoped that this writing will fall somewhere in the latter category.

This book will discuss the most important issues for the reader to consider when it comes to God's existence and identity. It uses a science- and evidence-based approach, using various scientific disciplines, history, theology, comparative religions, sound logic, etc., and brings them all together in an easy-to-read and understandable way. For the reader, this treatment is intended as a helpful roadmap to clarify the issues discussed, including God's plan for your life's fulfillment, meaning, and purpose.

This writing represents over 50 years of personal research, study, teaching, and writing; actually, it represents a lot more than that since it uses information gathered from many reputable and well-known experts—from both the past and the present. The list of Recommended

References at the end contains a small fraction of the material available to the public.

As an author and researcher, my natural inclination is to thoroughly discuss a subject so that an iron-clad case can be presented; thus, I tend to include every possible detail until the last nail is placed in the coffin when treating a subject. However, if that were done, this writing would become numerous books, resulting in the reading of the valuable information by fewer people.

Rather, this writing attempts to give the reader a relatively easy time of absorbing critical material by offering a somewhat high-level point-of-view, thus giving the reader a good bird's-eye view of the subject matter. In other words, the author does not want the reader to encounter the age-old problem of not seeing the forest because of all the trees. With that being said, more than enough supporting details and information are presented for those who love more than sufficient evidence.

The author humbly challenges the reader to think clearly and objectively when presented with the straightforward information. The reader is encouraged to dig in and investigate, as needed, the information presented in this book.

"Come now, and let us reason together"

Isaiah 1:18, KJV

SPECIAL NOTES

Under "Section II: God's Identity," chapters 13 and 14 show the scientific and prophetic evidence, respectively, for helping one determine who the true God is. The substance of these two chapters could have also been included in "Section I: God's Existence," since the information contained in the two chapters could also easily be utilized to support God's existence.

Almost all quotes of the Bible are indented and italicized to facilitate referencing when scanning through the text.

At the end of the book are Recommended References, listing valuable resources for readers to pursue at their leisure. Over the decades, the author has used many of these references in his personal research, even though they may not be specifically quoted herein.

SECTION I

GOD'S EXISTENCE

CHAPTER 1

IN THE BEGINNING...

"The big bang is how astronomers explain the way the universe began. It is the idea that the universe began as just a single point, then expanded and stretched to grow as large as it is right now..." ("What Is the Big Bang?" NASA; see E-Link Bibliography).

"If we accept the big bang theory, and most cosmologists now do, then a 'creation' of some sort is forced upon us." (science writer Barry Parker, *Creation—the Story of the Origin and Evolution of the Universe*, 1988, p. 202).

"The question is...whether there exists a Creator and Ruler of the universe; and this has been answered in the affirmative by some of the highest intellects that have ever existed." (Charles Darwin, *Descent of Man and Selection in Relation to Sex*, 1872, p. 63).

"...In my most extreme fluctuations I have never been an atheist in the sense of denying the existence of a God." (Charles Darwin, "Letter to John Fordyce." Darwin Correspondence Project, 'Letter no. 12041'; see E-Link Bibliography) [Note: Darwin fluctuated between theism and agnosticism].

When considering if God exists, we must start at *the* beginning of the universe. When the term *God* is used here, it refers to an all-powerful, eternal being (past and future) who is self-existent, with a

mind and personality. More information will be added to this definition later when we further specify exactly who God is (God's identity).
But first, let us see what kind of evidence there is for God's existence,
and then we will find out exactly *who* he/she/it is.

The Universe Had a Beginning

In science the beginning of the universe is known as the *big bang,*
or *singularity* (or *"a point of existence,"* if you will). Before the big bang/
singularity or "point of existence," the universe did not exist; its space,
matter, energy, and time (SMET) did not exist. Time is actually part of
the fabric of the universe, not separate from it. This beginning is commonly accepted by scientists today.

The big bang is **not** *a random explosion; it is the original creation
of SMET and its subsequent expansion, requiring a level of fine-tuning
(**design**) that is beyond imagination,* as this and the next chapter will
demonstrate. Design never happens by chance, but *always* requires a
designer. The universe's expansion has been ongoing for about 13.8 billion years, which is currently the most referenced age of the universe in
scientific circles. The results are what we see today: galaxies, stars, planets, novae, black holes, etc.

As the universe expands, it cools down and wears out, and entropy
increases. Entropy is *unusable or unavailable* energy. In an article by
Gordon W.F. Drake, professor of physics, he states:

> **Entropy**, the measure of a system's thermal energy per
> unit temperature that is unavailable [hence, not 'usable']
> for doing useful work. ("Entropy," *Britannica;* see E-Link
> Bibliography).

The second law of thermodynamics says entropy increases when
energy changes form or matter moves freely. Basically, everything gets
old and wears out, as any simple look in the mirror will tell you. There
are no exceptions to this law—ever.

This second law of thermodynamics, or increased entropy, means
that as time progresses, less and less usable energy exists in the universe

to keep things going. Energy is needed to produce *work*. *Work* is the flow of heat from hotter bodies to colder bodies of matter. Work encompasses everything from galaxy formation to cellular metabolism to the digestion of your last meal.

When all the *usable* energy runs out (and it will, given enough time), the universe will (per the above second law of thermodynamics) undergo several changes: (i) go dark and totally cold; (ii) have no more heat and motion; (iii) and have no life. But don't worry, as that is not about to happen yet.

For thousands of years the academic world thought the universe had always existed and always would. This paradigm has been called the steady-state theory. In 1915 the conventional thinking was challenged by Albert Einstein's general theory of relativity (the most proven theory in science, sometimes down to the fifteenth decimal place of certainty). Although his theory showed a beginning to the universe, Einstein, who disliked the idea of a beginning, inserted what was called a "cosmological constant" to avoid a beginning. However, he admitted his error in 1929 upon telescopically observing an expanding universe with astronomer Edwin Hubble. Subsequently, numerous astronomical observations and findings from scientific instruments, probes, and experiments have come to the same conclusion: the universe and all its SMET had a beginning.

In addition, **the second law of thermodynamics proves the universe had a beginning.** If the universe were infinitely old, it would mean an infinitely long time ago the second law of thermodynamics, the wearing out of the universe, would have been in operation. Therefore, the universe itself would have worn out a long, long time ago as well. We would not be here at this time (there would be no more usable energy for the magnitude of sustaining the stars or the monotony of digesting food). Therefore, there must have been a beginning. One could say, like with money, there is a limited amount of [usable] energy to go around.

What is the first law of thermodynamics? Simply put, once the universe was created, energy could not be created or destroyed, but it could change forms (energy to matter, usable to unusable energy).

The Verdict Is Final

Whether you want to call it the big bang or "the beginning of the universe" the reality that the universe and its SMET had a beginning is based on sound scientific findings. The evidence is too overwhelming. Some scientists may argue about what type of big bang occurred (such as inflationary vs. non-inflationary), but no one in scientific circles really debates the beginning of the universe (via the big bang event).

Are there any scientists still adhering to the steady-state theory or some version of an eternal universe? Of the thousands of astrophysicists, perhaps a handful or less do; the news media loves to give them occasional attention.

Due to the ubiquitous, widespread acceptance of the beginning of the universe in scientific circles, there is no need to show its acceptance by quoting such sources; it would be like quoting sources stating the earth is a sphere (although, believe it or not, there are a few who believe in a flat earth).

What about the Multiverse?

Faced with the theological implications of the big bang, the creation of the universe by a pre-existing agent (God), some have postulated what is called the *multiverse theory* (MVT). However, even if a MV could be true, it still ends up with the need for a pre-existing agent (God).

Essentially, the MVT proposes the idea that somewhere there exists something like a giant generator producing an infinite number of universes. Think of a bubble machine creating numerous bubbles. Using that analogy, each bubble is a universe with its own random collection of laws, physics, and so on. With enough universes popping into existence, at least one of them on a random basis was bound to get all the requirements right to bring life into being, and our universe was the lucky one. So goes the MVT argument.

This theory seems to be an attempt to explain away the need for a pre-existing agent and the clear design features of our universe, more specifically laid out for the reader in chapter 2. It is interesting to note that the MVT idea was floated after the big bang theory (and its inevitable theological implications) became entrenched in scientific circles.

While the MVT may sound interesting, it has no solid basis. There is *zero* evidence for multiple universes. It is commonly accepted in scientific circles that we cannot reach out beyond the space-time continuum of our universe; we cannot discover any such realities by any direct measurement, even if they were to exist. Since this theory cannot be falsified or verified, it is not, by definition, science. It is only an idea—a philosophical one. With absolutely no evidence at all to support the multiverse theory, reason can be used against it. Since the argument is for the possibility of an infinite number of universes (like our bubble machine's bubbles), every possibility becomes possible. In one universe, the laws of physics would enable you to be Superman and fly. In another one we can have flying toasters. Begin to see the logical, but absurd, implications?

In addition, where did the so-called generator or bubble machine come from? Such a "mechanism" would have to be a very complex one, requiring a beginning for itself and its intricate design (and design always requires a designer as the next chapter will show), so we are back to the need for a pre-existing agent. Remember, even if a MV were to exist, it can be argued that it too would be bound by cause and effect; it could not exist forever due to some version of the second law of thermodynamics (there can be no scenario where there is infinite energy), and thus would require its beginning from a pre-existing agent, which/who is outside of time and space.

As of the writing of this book, news articles have suggested the possibility of a parallel universe (singular, not multi), only to be followed soon after by an article in *Forbes* magazine where we find the following (boldfacing is this author's emphasis):

> In all the experiments we've ever performed, all the observations we've ever recorded, and all the measurements ever made, we've never yet discovered an interaction that demands the existence of something beyond our own, isolated Universe to explain....

> There's a remarkable story here that's all about good science. An experiment (ANITA) saw something unexpected, and

published their results. A much better experiment (IceCube) followed it up, and **ruled out their leading interpretation** [of a parallel universe]. It strongly suggested something was amiss with the first experiment, and more science will help us uncover what's truly occurring. For now, based on the scientific evidence we have, parallel universes will have to remain a science fiction dream." (Ethan Siegel, "Ask Ethan: Have We Finally Found Evidence for a Parallel Universe?" *Forbes Magazine*, May 22, 2020; see E-Link Bibliography).

Antony Flew, a world-renowned English philosopher and atheist until age 84, who became a believer in a Supreme Intelligence with a mind who created the universe based on the evidence, thought the postulation of multiple universes was a "truly desperate alternative." Flew writes (co-authored with Roy Abraham Varghese):

No matter how far you push back the properties of the universe as somehow "emergent," their very emergence has to follow certain prior laws. So multiverse or not, we still have to come to terms with the origin of the laws of nature. And the only viable explanation here is the divine Mind." (*There Is a God: How the World's Most Notorious Atheist Changed His Mind*, p. 122)

If the existence of one universe requires an explanation, multiple universes require a much bigger explanation: the problem is increased by the factor of whatever the total number of universes is….it seems a little like the case of a schoolboy whose teacher doesn't believe his dog ate his homework, so he replaces the first version with the story that a pack of dogs – too many to count – ate his homework. (*Ibid.*, p. 137)

What about the Quantum Gravity Era (Quantum Physics)?

I owe the summary information in this subsection to astrophysicist Dr. Hugh Ross, from his more detailed article "Does Quantum Gravity Avoid the Need for a Cosmic Creator?" (March 7, 2017)

(e-link: https://reasons.org/explore/blogs/todays-new-reason-to-believe/
read/todays-new-reason-to-believe/2017/03/07/does-quantum
-gravity-avoid-the-need-for-a-cosmic-creator).

Some may try to reference the world of quantum physics as a way of getting around the big bang origin of the universe and the need for a pre-existing agent (God). The entangling complexities of the highly theoretical world of quantum physics are beyond our discussion here (see referenced article and its references for more details). However, a few points should be made. For those who are not technically minded, they may wish to skip to the next subsection, "A Real Predicament for Atheists: Big Bang Theological Implications Are Clear."

Although there are effective rebuttals to the quantum physics attempts to circumvent the big bang, their complexities will not be specified here. Gravity dominates the working of the universe back to when the universe was 10^{-35} of a second old (that is just short of a trillionth, of a trillionth, of a trillionth of a second).

Due to technological limitations and other issues, we cannot "see" past the era ending at 10^{-43} of a second. At 10^{-43} the force of gravity becomes comparable to the strong nuclear force that holds protons and neutrons together. At this time gravity may possibly be modified by quantum mechanical effects, called the *quantum gravity era*. In this quantum era, speculations about what happened can run rampant. However, any theories about this era are only theories, mere speculations that are not subject to scientific observation, testing, etc. Thereby, such theories really are tantamount to the realm of the metaphysical.

However, many quantum gravity theories can be dismissed through the observations of distant quasars and gamma-ray sources. Over long distances, various quantum gravity models indicate that there will be increasing, small, individual space-time fluctuations (foam). These accumulated fluctuations should blur the images of the most distantly observed sources, especially at short wavelengths. However, these distant objects (such as quasars) are very clear, thereby overruling *random walk* (randomly varying quantum foam) *quantum gravity models* and *holographic quantum gravity models*. Dr. Ross points out that four European astrophysicists have concluded, "All the main QG [quantum gravity] scenarios are excluded." (F. Tamburini, et al., "No Quantum Gravity Signature from the Farthest Quasars," *Astronomy and Astrophysics 533* (September 2011): id. A71, doi:10.1051/0004-6361/201015808).

With the above said, could some sort of "quantum flux" be the cause of the universe? The evidence is against it. However, I would like to point out that a "quantum or gravitational flux" of some kind is still "something"; in this case, it is the "E" or "energy" in our SMET, which did not exist prior to the big bang. If our universe had its beginning via some kind of quantum flux, this flux in turn needed a pre-existing cause! It may have been simply part of the *created* "mechanism" God used to create the cosmos.

A Real Predicament for Atheists:
Big Bang Theological Implications Are Clear

The big bang, or beginning of all SMET, has clear theological implications; it requires the need for a pre-existing agent, which (or who) brought the universe into existence:

Something Cannot Come from Nothing

The universe could not bring itself into existence as it did not exist at one point! Therefore, prior to the beginning (big bang) of the universe, an agent had to exist, and it is this pre-existing agent that (or who) brought the universe into existence.

The Law of Cause and Effect

The universal law of "cause and effect" states that for every *effect* there has to be a *cause,* and the cause has to be greater than the effect.

Something cannot come out of nothing without cause, as stated, and this means the *effect* (the universe) had to have a pre-existing *cause* which is not found in SMET, and the pre-existing cause has to be greater than the result (the universe).

However, the logic of atheism contradicts the *law* of cause and effect and is contrary to the dictum that says something cannot create itself when that something did not exist. Since atheism denies God's existence, it must illogically contend that the universe created itself and popped into existence out of nothing without cause, even though it did not exist.

Unlike the atheistic position, the theistic (God) position as the answer to the need for a pre-existing agent does not violate the law of cause and effect, and it does not contradict the dictum that something cannot come out of nothing without any cause.

As a result, the majority of astronomers and astrophysicists (herein after referred to as "cosmologists") today believe an all-powerful Being with a mind created the universe. Some still refer to this Being or Supreme Intelligence as the Pre-existing Agent (some prefer not to use the term "God"). But as Shakespeare once said, "A rose by any other name smells just as sweet."

A *theist* is one who believes in the existence of an all-powerful being with a mind and personality. A *deist* is actually a theist, except the latter does not believe the pre-existing agent continued to be involved in the cosmos, especially not with humanity, after the initial creation of the universe, its laws, and physics.

The majority of cosmologists do not specifically believe in the Christian/biblical God; some do, some are just theists, and some are deists. However, for the most part in our discussion, the term *theist* will be utilized for convenience.

Who/What Created the Pre-Existing Agent (God)?

Seeing the logical dead end they are in, atheists often deflect the indefensibility of their position by asking the theist, "Who or what created God? Don't you have a problem similar to the atheist's position?"

A fair question, but it is one with a viable answer. Everything in this universe is limited to three spatial dimensions (height, width, depth) and one dimension of time. As pointed out, everything in this universe is limited by the law of cause and effect. And further, everything must have a beginning. This presents a conundrum for atheism, to be sure, since its only point of reference is the universe itself with its inherent limitations.

However, the theist position is not limited by these spatial/time dimensions/limitations. God created time and the three spatial dimensions; therefore, he is outside of, not bound by, any of them. Consequently, logically speaking, there is no reason why God has to have a beginning; a beginning only makes sense when something originates within the one dimension of time, like our universe.

A person may have difficulty grasping a reality where anything, including God, does not have a beginning. The difficulty is understandable, but is not necessarily a logical problem. Our finite thinking is limited by three spatial dimensions and one time dimension. It is hard to think outside of the box, if you will, to any other reality. More discussion will be given on extra-dimensional realities in the chapter on the Trinity (the triune God).

Where there is no time, there are no beginnings or endings, by definition. A beginning is nonsense in that kind of reality.

Therefore, it is not the theist with the problem; it is the atheist. He/she *is* bound by the laws of physics created in this universe.

A Real Problem for Many Religions

This need for our pre-existing agent (God) to create the universe is a problem for many religions. Most religions teach that their god or gods had a beginning within the dimension of time and in turn "created" their various realms within time and space (within this universe). Bottom line: they assume the universe in one form or another always existed.

> In light of this, the serious thinker should not give any further truth considerations to those religions teaching the universe always existed and always will; it violates solid, empirical scientific findings and the *laws of nature*.

But more on that later.

For Further Consideration:
The Bible Teaches the Big Bang

It is interesting to note that the Bible is the only religious text teaching what is now called *the big bang*, and the Bible has been proclaiming that idea for 3400 years (when Genesis was written); science only caught up to the Bible's teachings in the twentieth century on the subject at hand. The basics of the big bang in science include that the universe:

- had a beginning, including all SMET;

- is expanding; and

- will wear out (die from an entropic heat death).

The Bible teaches the above basics of the big bang:

- The universe had a beginning: Genesis 1:1; Genesis 2:3-4; Psalm 148:5; Isaiah 40:26, 42:5, 45:18, etc. Genesis 1:1 says God created the "heavens and the earth." The Hebrew word for "created" is *bara*, which means to create from nothing or that which did not exist before or something new. Only God does the bara-type of creation. The Hebrew for "heavens and the earth" is *hashamayin we ha erets*, meaning the entire universe.

- Time had a beginning: Titus 1:2 and II Timothy 1:9 state that time was created—had a beginning.

- The universe is expanding: in the past tense—Isaiah 45:12, 48:13, 44:24, 51:13; Jeremiah 51:15; in the present tense—Job 9:8; Ps. 104:2; Isaiah 40:22; Zechariah 12:1.

- The universe will wear out: Psalm 102:26; Romans 8:19-21.

Where did Moses (who penned Genesis) and the other biblical writers get their information? None of the cultures around them were teaching anything remotely similar but were instead promoting mostly scientific nonsense on cosmology. Some were good at tracking the movements of the constellations and visible planets, but that is not relevant here. So where did Moses and the other writers in the Bible get their data? One hint: It was not from space aliens. More on this later.

Summary Thoughts

Scientific evidence and laws require the creation of the universe by a pre-existent agent (as we shall see, this is God). The evidence for God is clear. There is no other viable, logical alternative. There are only two choices: (i) there is a pre-existing agent; or (ii) there is no pre-existing agent. Common sense, considering the evidence, comes to the same conclusion as the scientific evidence: there was a pre-existing agent.

Please note that we have not yet firmly identified exactly who or what this pre-existing agent is; we will get to that later. Chapters 1-8 prove the existence of a Creator God. Chapter 2 shows the universe has been designed. **Design requires a Designer!** This is another law there has never been an exception to.

At the end of chapter 2, you will read a series of quotes from noted scientists/astronomers: (i) concerning the evidence for a divine Designer based on the big bang theory and (ii) on the fine-tuning (showing design) of the universe.

THE DESIGNED UNIVERSE

"Here is the cosmological proof of the existence of God…
The fine tuning of the universe provides prima facie evidence of deistic design." (Cosmologist Edward Harrison, *Masks of the Universe*, pp. 252, 263)

This chapter will show the universe has been designed and, therefore, is not the result of random, purely natural processes.

Whenever design exists, there has to be a Designer (a being with a mind). Design never happens by chance.

If the universe has been designed, it has been designed by a designer, one who by necessity would be the pre-existing agent (see chapter 1), who this book will show is a self-existing divine Being with a mind and personality.

When the various parts or components or aspects of something are finely tuned to accomplish a given purpose or to convey information, we have design.

For example, let us say an electric motor has 50 parts/components. Each component is exactly shaped and precisely measured with the right materials in the right way to accomplish one purpose: to make a motor. No one would claim those parts and their synergistic actions happened by accident. Design is also involved when there is the conveyance of information, such as a language, software code, or even the words "I love you."

Similarly, think of the universe as a giant machine. There are currently over 1,000 known aspects (or *parts* as in our machine analogy) of the universe that are finely tuned for at least one purpose: to enable the existence of an earth-like planet capable of supporting life. *All these parts/aspects of our universe share at least one thing in common*—enabling at least one planet capable of supporting life! See the below internet link from Dr. Hugh Ross, astrophysicist; the information in this link is based on hundreds of sources from scientific literature supporting this number of over 1,000 designed aspects.

What is meant by *aspects* of the universe? "Aspects" refers to the universe's characteristics, nature, etc. For example, the size, shape, and age of galaxies; the age, size, and metallicity of stars; planetary and moon orbits; radiometric abundancies; size of electrons, etc.

The evidence is in, and it is very clear: each of the over 1,000 aspects or parameters of the universe is finely tuned to provide at least one planet capable of supporting life. Without these aspects being just right, there would have been no earth at any time in the history of the cosmos. Just a few of these parameters/aspects:

- Galactic level: location of galaxies, age, size, composition, shape, type, location of nearby small galaxies, etc.

- Stellar (star) level: color, metallicity, luminosity, size, age, composition, orbital location and pattern around the galactic center, etc.

- Planetary level: eccentricity and shape of orbit, orbital plane, composition, magnetic field(s), tectonic activity, atmospheric composition, surface/under surface composition, levels of soluble metals, levels of insoluble metals, planetary core size/content, etc.

- Moon level: size, distance from planet, shape of orbit, etc.

- Atomic level: size of electrons, number of electrons to protons, proton mass, neutrinos, etc.

- And so many more.

Following will be a discussion on numbers, exponents, statistical odds, etc. Such an analysis can get a bit tedious. However, as the saying goes, "The devil is in the details." Although perhaps a bit laborious to some, the following discussion on numbers is necessary for the reader to appreciate the design features of the universe and therefore its Designer.

First a brief tutorial on numbers and their exponents is needed to facilitate understanding of the enormous size of the numbers to be given. Scientists often use what is called "scientific notation," which is the use of exponents, to describe how big a number is; it is a shorthand way of expressing larger numbers. An exponent tells how many zeroes follow the base number (often "1"). For example, 10^2 means 10x10 or the number 1 with two zeroes, or the number 100. 10^4 means 10x10x10x10 or the number 1 with 4 zeroes after it, or 10,000. And so on. If we say something has a random chance of 1 in 10^3 of happening, we are saying it has one chance in a thousand (1000) of happening.

Lastly, each increment of one in the exponent means an increase of 10-fold. For example, 10^4 (or 10,000) is ten times greater than 10^3 (1000) or is a hundred times greater than 10^2 (100). Compare 10^{12} to 10^6, for example. The first number is 1,000,000 times greater than the second, *not* two times.

Just how finely tuned is the universe? We could get into each of the over 1,000 items here, but only a few will be mentioned to make the point. Without going into the various "mechanisms" involved and how these precise measurements affect the possibility of an earth-like planet, let it be said here that many of them involve the force of gravity, the strong and weak nuclear forces, and electromagnetism.

The universe has about 10^{78} protons and neutrons. The numbers to be presented here are either stated specifically in scientific literature or can be calculated from information in the scientific literature. **Dr. Hugh Ross, astrophysicist and president of the organization** *Reasons to Believe*, **has a website explaining the above and below numbers, based on over 1,000 references from published scientific literature (see the three applicable e-linked articles in the E-Link Bibliography under "Ross, Hugh").**

As of 2006, science was aware of 676 aspects of the universe that would have to be finely tuned to enable at least one planet to be capable of supporting bacterial life on a prolonged basis in the entire universe. The total of 676 cosmological, galactic, terrestrial, and other features must be fine-tuned to support permanent simple life. The odds of this happening by random chance, rather than by design, was calculated out to 1 chance out of 10^{556} (see *Why the Universe Is the Way It Is*, pages 121-124, by astrophysicist Dr. Hugh Ross). Also as of 2006, the number of finely-tuned features needed to enable high-tech humans was 824 with a random chance of their happening being 1 out of $10^{1,050}$ (*Ibid*). Today scientists are aware of over 1,000 finely-tuned factors (over the 676 identified in 2006) needed to enable permanent simple life (bacteria) on a planet. *Note: this is not the odds of finding life itself, but only the odds of a planet happening by random chance that could support simple life.*

The odds of 1 out of 10^{556} would be like saying the following:

- Take all the atoms in our universe, which is 10^{78}; (Vishal Thakur, "How Many Atoms in the Universe?" *Science ABC,* updated 13 Jan 2020; see E-Link Bibliography)

- Then multiply our universe (or multiply all the atoms in our universe) by 39.8 trillion times, and

- Then if you took one atom out of all those universes (or 10^{556} atoms), there would never be even one earth-like planet capable of supporting life in the entire cosmos in its complete history!

These numbers are way beyond human comprehension. It has been said that if something has a random chance of only 1 in 10^{50} it is impossible; that is nothing compared to our 10^{556}.

Now you can see that the universe is obviously designed and certainly not a random chance accident. As of 2017, the 676 aspects mentioned above had grown to over 1000. The odds of the 1000 aspects happening by random chance have not yet been calculated.

Let us consider just a few examples of how finely tuned things are (otherwise you might be fighting the sandman to stay awake).

At the beginning of the universe, just after the big bang event, all matter in the universe was tightly compacted together. The amount of matter back then was the same as it is now, only now it is more spread out (the universe is expanding). The amount of visible, ordinary matter (the stuff we can see) in the universe is equal to about 10^{60} dimes; that was the amount of matter upon/just after the big bang and is currently still the same amount. This is called the cosmic mass density ratio, finely tuned to 1 out of 10^{60} (astrophysicist Dr. Hugh Ross, *Creation as Science*, p. 94).

So to fill all the galaxies of the cosmos would take about 10^{60} dimes. Just after the big bang (at about one trillionth, of one trillionth, of one trillionth, of one millionth of a second, or 10^{-43} of a second), if one would have taken out the equivalent of one dime's worth of matter, there would never have been a planet capable of supporting life anywhere at any time. That is how finely tuned the amount of matter is. Some people ask why all that "stuff" is out there if life exists only on earth: they have their answer.

If the force of gravity were off by more than 1 out of 10^{60}, there would be no stars and planets. A little less gravity and the heavenly bodies would have never formed (their atoms would be spreading out without coalescing); a little more gravity and we would have nothing but black holes and neutron stars.

Only spiral galaxies with symmetrical arms (about 5% of all galaxies) are capable of harboring planets containing theoretical life due to shape and gravimetric issues.

If the expansion rate at the beginning of the universe were off by more than 1 out of 10^{57}, no life would be possible: at a faster rate only light elements (hydrogen, etc.) would exist; any slower there would be too many heavy elements. This would be like saying, take all the grains of sand on earth's beaches (about 10^{23}), multiply that by one trillion, by one trillion, by ten billion times, and if one removed one grain of sand that would eliminate all possibility of life.

Doing this later in the universe's existence would not have had the same effect on the universe's matter since the same amount now would be more spread out and therefore have less gravimetric effect on other matter.

Another example: the fine-tuning of dark energy is 1 out of 10^{120} just after the big bang. Aforementioned astrophysicist Dr. Hugh Ross of *Reasons to Believe* has described that dark energy is the "self-stretching property of the universe causing its expansion."

"Dark energy is the name given to the force that is believed to be making the universe larger" ("Dark Energy," *Simple English Wikipedia;* see E-Link Bibliography). The universe is actually accelerating in its expansion rate. Theoretical physicist Lawrence Krause affirms the fine-tuning of dark energy as 1 out of 10^{120} (Lawrence M. Krauss, "The End of the Age Problem and the Case for a Cosmological Constant Revisited," *Astrophysical Journal* 501 (July 10, 1998): p. 461).

Remember from above, the amount of matter was finely tuned to 1 out of 10^{60}; we saw the meaning of those odds. For dark energy, if its amount were off by only 1 out of 10^{120}, no planet capable of supporting life would ever happen! The figure of 1 out of 10^{120} is one trillion, one trillion, one trillion, one trillion, one trillion times more precise than the 1 out of 10^{60} given earlier.

The proof for design is overwhelmingly clear. With these kinds of odds, random chance could never result in a planet capable of supporting life. Bottom line: a random chance scenario producing life would require an irrational faith.

Only a few of the possible parameters have been specifically mentioned, and they were applicable to the time just after the big bang. Most of the parameters (such as galaxy size, location, age, solar metallicity, etc.) are applicable for timeframes *after that time and up to the present.*

Who would ever stake their life on something like NASA's space shuttle coming together via a chance hurricane tearing through a junk yard? Well, such an occurrence is almost infinitely more likely than all the aforementioned 676 aspects/parameters happening by random chance to produce a planet capable of life.

No one would knowingly risk his life on odds like 1 in 1000. Why, he would not even bet a dollar with those kinds of odds, yet millions of people are betting their lives that God (our Designer) does not exist, as they are assuming planet Earth happened by random chance.

The fine-tuning of the universe is sometimes referred to as the *anthropic principle*. It means the universe is designed for life.

Mentioned earlier, one of the world's most ardent and well-known atheists, Antony Flew, remained an atheist up to the age 84. He finally became a theist (really upset a lot of atheists). Why? His change of heart was due to more recent scientific evidence, in part the big bang and the fine-tuning of the universe.

> In summary, the universe is a giant machine of sorts, with over 1000 parts having been finely tuned to allow at least one planet capable of supporting life. This is design of the highest order. And design always comes from a Designer, never from random chance.

Consider what scientists are saying as the result of their research into the physics of the universe:

- Albert Einstein, famous astrophysicist and an apparent deist (again a "deist" believes God created the universe but after that has remained silent), stated the following:

    » God does not play dice [with the universe].

    » In view of such harmony in the cosmos, which I, with my limited human mind, am able to recognize, there are yet people who say there is no God. But what really makes me angry is that they quote me for the support of such views. (*The Expanded Quotable Einstein*, p. 214)

» I am not an atheist… (Einstein quoted by Walter Isaacson, *Einstein: His Life and Universe*, p. 390)

- Famous astrophysicist, Stephen Hawking, also an apparent deist but quite possibly later became an atheist:

  » It would be very difficult to explain why the universe should have begun in just this way; except as the act of a God who intended to create beings like us. (*A Brief History of Time*, p. 127)

- Edward Harrison, cosmologist (quoted earlier):

  » Here is the cosmological proof of the existence of God… The fine tuning of the universe provides prima facie evidence of deistic design. (*Masks of the Universe*, p. 252, 263)

- Famous NASA astrophysicist, Robert Jastrow, concerning the big bang and the fine tuning of the universe:

  » For the scientist who has lived by his faith in the power of reason, the story ends like a bad dream. He has scaled the mountains of ignorance: he is about to conquer the highest peak; as he pulls himself over the final rock, he is greeted by a band of theologians who have been sitting there for centuries. (*God and the Astronomers*, p. 116)

- Geoffrey Brubridge, UCSD (University of California San Diego) astronomer, complained of his fellow astronomers:

  » [They were rushing off to the] First Church of Christ of the Big Bang. (Stephen Strauss, "An Innocent's Guide to the Big Bang Theory: Fingerprint in Space Left by the Universe as a Baby Still has Doubters Hurling Stones," *The Globe and the Mail* [Toronto, 25 April 1992, p. 1])

- Famous British astronomer/mathematician, Sir Frederic Hoyle, although he apparently never became a theist per se, made the following comment:

  » A super intellect has monkeyed with physics, as well as with chemistry and biology (*The Intelligent Universe*, p. 16).

- Allan Sandage, astronomer, winner of the Crawford Prize in Astronomy (equivalent to a Nobel Prize) is quoted as saying:

  » I find it quite improbable that such order comes out of chaos. There has to be some organizing principle. God to me is a mystery but is the explanation for the miracle of existence, why there is something instead of nothing. (John Noble Wilford, "Sizing up the Cosmos: An Astronomer's Quest," *New York Times*, p. 89)

- Robert Griffiths, winner of Heinemann prize in mathematical physics, is quoted:

  » If we need an atheist for a debate, I go to the philosophy department. The physics department isn't much use. (Tim Stafford, "Cease-fire in the Laboratory," *Christianity Today*, p. 18)

- Paul Davies, physicist, stated:

  » The laws [of physics]…seem themselves to be the product of exceedingly ingenious design. (*Superforce*, p. 243)

  » [There] is for me powerful evidence that there is something going on behind it all…It seems as though somebody has fine-tuned nature's numbers to make the

Universe…impression of design is overwhelming. (*The Cosmic Blueprint*, p. 203; "The Anthropic Principle," *Science Digest* 191, No. 10, p. 24)

- George Greenstein, astronomer, asks:

  » As we survey all the evidence, the thought instantly arises that some supernatural agency – or, rather, Agency – must be involved. Is it possible that suddenly, without intending to, we have stumbled upon scientific proof of the existence of a Supreme Being? Was it God who stepped in and so providentially crafted the cosmos for our benefit? (*The Symbiotic Universe*, p. 27)

- Roger Penrose, distinguished mathematician (colleague of Stephen Hawking), says the following:

  » I would say the universe has a purpose. It's not there somehow by chance. (from the Stephen Hawking-related movie *A Brief History of Time*)

CHAPTER 3

THE ULTIMATE CODE

"...And now the announcement of Watson and Crick about DNA. This is for me the real proof of the existence of God." (quote of Salvador Dali, found in Alan Lindsay Mackay's *A Dictionary of Scientific Quotations*, 1991, p. 66)

"...a live reading of that [DNA] code at a rate of three letters per second would take thirty-one years, even if reading continued day and night." (Francis S. Collins, director of the Human Genome Project, *The Language of God*, 2006, p. 1)

Any type of coding shows design and requires a coder with a mind and intelligence. Some examples of coding are Morse code, encrypted coding, computer software coding, and languages. If a code exists, it was designed by a coder(s). Computer simulations and reality have shown that random processes never result in any extent of organized coding.

So why do some people deny that the greatest, most complex code ever devised was designed by a designer/coder? What code is that? It is the genetic code of any of earth's millions of species. It was initially discovered by scientists Watson and Crick.

The genetic code, or genome, is more complex than one can really imagine. In each human cell, this code is three billion letters long, utilizing various combinations of four chemicals, abbreviated A, T, C, and G, plus attendant phosphates and sugars.

Who would ever think the Encyclopedia Britannica could result from a random explosion in a print factory?

The genome of animals and plants is much more complex than any book or books. The genetic code is billions of times more complex than the entire Encyclopedia Britannica, which consists of thousands of pages.

According to a doctor (in biology) friend of mine, if the genetic code in each cell of a human body were to be straightened out and put end to end, it would reach from earth to Pluto and back 3.5 times! Granted, this involves repetition of the human genome, but it illustrates how wonderfully complex we are.

If we saw the words *I love you* in the sand on a beach, no one would ever propose that those words were the result of the random working of water and sand.

In *Searching for the Mind,* an article by Jon Lieff, M.D., entitled "New Studies Reveal Higher Levels of Genetic Complexity," dated April 2014, the author illustrates only one aspect of the genetic code's complexity:

> From the messenger RNA, the protein is built into a row of amino acids that forms the protein. The three-dimensional folding of this row of amino acids is so complex that currently, all the supercomputers in the world would take 2,000 years to calculate the folding of one average-sized protein (approximately 400 amino acids). Especially neurons have many much larger proteins, each in an exact shape. We simply cannot know how these many amino acids, each with a complex 3D shape, will fold when put in a row.

A singular supercomputer is capable of trillions of calculations *per second.* Imagine combining ALL the supercomputers in the world (some estimate that to be about 500) to perform the above calculations (to get the correct folding structure of one protein consisting of 400 amino acids and it taking 2,000 years to calculate the mere correct folding of ONE set of the amino acids into a single three-dimensionally shaped protein. In other words, it would take 165,000,000,000,000,000,000 (1.65×10^{18}) calculations per second for 2,000 years.

Pure common sense and logic dictate the creation of the genetic code of life by a Supreme Intelligence. It reminds me of a software engineer highlighted in one of Illustra Media's DVDs on God and creation who walked into the office of an associate after looking at the human genome's coding ability for correcting any errors. He said, "Someone has been here before." He, of course, was referring to the Divine Coder. Want to insult software engineers or coders? Tell them that their coding was a mere accident or that they got really lucky. Similarly, don't people insult God when they consider the genetic code a mere accident?

In addition, the information content of the genetic code (in addition to the coding itself) cannot be contained in pure matter, as information is the result of intelligence; it is a non-material attribute. By definition, information must come from a non-material (non-matter) source. Always has, always will. Pure matter cannot contain "information."

The information in the genetic code tells the thousands of parts of each cell to perform various functions so the cell can survive and gives instructions on how to construct the thousands of molecular machines found in each cell. A molecular machine is "merely" a combination of proteins performing the functional equivalent of a lever, truck, conveyer belt, etc.

In the famous Scopes Monkey Trial of the 1920s, where evolutionists were debating creationists, one of the evolutionists said, "If you could prove the cell is a machine, we evolutionists would lose our argument." At that time, scientists thought the cell was only a simple gelatinous type of substance (sort of like Jello) with electricity going through it. Today, based on their own logic, the evolutionists have lost their argument since we now know that each cell has thousands of molecular machines. And machines are never the result of random processes. The necessity of God's existence is again shown.

CHAPTER 4

LIFE'S ORIGIN

"The odds of a single bacterium re-assembling by chance are 1 in $10^{100,000,000,000}$."!(Yale University physicist Harold Morowitz, *Energy Flow in Biology*)

The discussion of life's origin actually began with chapter 3 on the genetic code and the origin of information.

Other aspects of life's origin will be examined in this chapter, with an emphasis on prebiotic chemicals (*prebiotic means "chemicals that are basic to life, existing before life began"*). According to evolutionists, these prebiotic chemicals progressively became more complex and eventually resulted in the first living cell.

Dr. Hugh Ross, previously mentioned, has reported that his visits to origin of life researchers' periodic conferences show that these researchers are not an optimistic group. Over the last sixty years, the news has not been good when it comes to showing how life could have theoretically arisen by natural random processes. It has become increasingly difficult for these researchers to come up with a naturalistic (i.e., without God) origin-of-life scenario.

The more research performed, the less and less likely, if not impossible, a naturalistic solution to the origin of life seems, given the available science and data.

What About the Miller-Urey Experiment (Prebiotic Soup)?

Many may recall from their schooling the famous Miller-Urey test tube experiments of the 1950s, wherein Miller (the student) and Urey (professor) created in a laboratory what they thought were the early conditions of the earth with a hydrogen, ammonia, methane and water vapor atmosphere. They then ignited an electrical charge into the mixture. The result was the formation of a few amino acids (prebiotics) essential to life. This was heralded as a major advance in understanding how life may have eventually begun.

That experiment's findings were invalidated when it was later discovered that the wrong chemicals representing earth's atmosphere were used. Note the following:

> But the **Miller-Urey** results were later questioned: It turns out that the gases he used (a reactive mixture of methane and ammonia) did not exist in large amounts on early Earth. Scientists now believe the primeval atmosphere contained an inert mix of carbon dioxide and nitrogen— a change that made a world of difference. (Douglas Fox, "Primordial Soup's On: Scientists Repeat Evolution's Most Famous Experiment," *Scientific American*, Mar 28, 2007)

In spite of this error, people still can find the Miller-Urey Project listed in college textbooks as a valid experiment relevant to life's beginning. In addition, the toxins formed were artificially separated from the amino acids. In reality, the toxins would tend to counteract/negate the amino acids. There are further problems with this experiment that we will not go into here.

No Primordial Soup

The so-called primordial soup of chemicals that Miller, Urey, and others postulated, where chemical reactions supposedly became increasingly complex until the first living cell was the result, has now been determined not to have existed before life began.

What's the proof? The earliest carbonaceous (carbon) evidence eliminates the famous primordial soup paradigm as the precursor of life. At that point in earth's history (about 3.8 bya), and at some level of complexity, one could encounter one or two variations of the ratios of carbon-13 to carbon-12. One set of ratios would indicate some sort of *nonliving* primordial soup of prebiotic chemicals, as explained above; the other carbon ratio would come from life's processes. Evolutionists contend the prebiotic chemical soup preceded the advent of life. However, it is now known that the carbon ratios from life processes came first; therefore, there was no prior prebiotic soup eventually leading to life. Quoting astrophysicist Dr. Hugh Ross in his book *Creation as Science*:

> Timing of the Late Heavy bombardment compels researchers to conclude that life's origin on Earth occurred within a geological instant. Carbon-13 to carbon-12 ratio analysis of ancient carbonaceous material along with abundant analysis of certain uranium oxide precipitates establishes that life was abundant on earth as far back as 3.8 billion years ago. Carbon-13 to carbon-12 ratio analysis, plus nitrogen-15 to nitrogen-14 ratio analysis, on ancient carbonaceous material further establishes that a primordial soup or mineral subcontract of prebiotic molecules never existed on earth (p. 116).

Science currently knows the earliest indicators (about 3.80 billion years ago) consist of the ratio of carbon-13 to -12, which resulted from life's processes and were *not* of the carbon ratio coming from a nonliving primordial soup. Therefore, life did not result from a primordial soup.

The Time Factor

The evidence that life had its origins on earth at least as far back as 3.8 bya is isotropic (chemical) in nature. Fossil evidence goes back to 3.7 bya (as of the time of this writing). That presents an insurmountable problem for any naturalistic pathway to life, as the earth did not have a set of conditions for permitting ongoing life until about 3.8 bya. In other words, in a *geological* instant, life started as soon as it was possible. This does not leave any time for any theoretical chemical progression to reach the level of life. As stated, the carbonaceous evidence shows life did not occur as the result of a so-called prebiotic soup.

However, for the moment, let us assume that the carbonaceous evidence indicated a prebiotic soup existed, which could lead to the first living cell.

The below numbers are commonly known in biology. Their calculations are purely mathematical in nature.

The cell is made largely of proteins. Proteins are made up of chains of amino acids (there are 20 different amino acids in living organisms). These chains range in complexity from about 50 to over 1,000 amino acids. Today's bacteria have about 2,000 types of proteins. The human body has about 200,000.

Take a relatively simple protein of 100 amino acids. The random chances for this specific simple protein to form would require 20^{100} tries (the "20" being the number of amino acids in living organisms, the "100" being the number of different amino acids in our simple protein). This 20^{100} is equal to 10^{130}.

Let us consider the above-discussed number of 1 chance in 10^{130} as the odds of getting the specified one simple protein that is found in a simple bacterium by chance. Note that we are not talking about the bacterium at this point, but about a single protein found in a bacterium.

Given the rough estimate of about 10^{78} atoms in the entire universe, and assuming 1,000,000,000,000 chemical interactions for each atom per second, and assuming they always produce unique molecules (both are totally absurd scenarios), and assuming the universe is 30 (not 13.8) billion years old (i.e., 10^{18} seconds = 30 billion years, rounded), it would still take a universe one hundred billion billion times longer than a 30 billion year old universe just to get this one simple protein by chance! — that's a 3,000,000,000,000,000,000,000,000,000,0 00 year old universe.

All of this would be necessary for only one simple protein to form. A relatively simple bacterium (a living, one-cell creature) has up to 2000 proteins, with the earliest and simplest bacterium containing somewhere between almost 300 to about 500.

Peter Tompa and George D. Rose state:

> Nobody knows how a viable cell emerges from the massive combinatorial complexity of its molecular components. And of course nobody has ever synthetically mimicked it. An interactome is the whole set of molecular interactions in a particular cell. If one merely considers all protein-protein interactome combinations in just a single yeast cell, the result is an estimated $10^{79,000,000,000}$. (*Protein Science* 2011, 20, 2074-2079. Dept. of Structural Biology, Vrije Universiteit Brussel, Belgium, and the Dept. of Biophysics, Johns Hopkins University, Baltimore, Maryland)

The universe is about 4.36×10^{15} seconds old. Compare that to the above $10^{79,000,000,000}$ possibilities! That would require about $10^{78,999,999,985}$ combinations (or attempts) *per second* for 13.82 billion years to get all the possible protein to protein interactome combinations in just a single yeast cell! The above shows that the possible number of wrong combinations is beyond comprehension and that there is no time for chemical reactions to result in a living cell. And remember, these are just protein to protein interactions, which does not include all the non-protein to non-protein interactions.

World Famous British astronomer, mathematician, and Nobel laureate, Sir Frederick Hoyle, along with a group of graduate students, calculated the probability of generating by chance just the proteins (enzymes) of a single bacterium. The result: 1 chance in $10^{40,000}$. That is the number 1 followed by 40,000 zeroes. (*The Intelligent Universe*, by Fred Hoyle, p. 17).

Dr. Hoyle, up to that point, believed life arose by chance on earth. However, upon these findings, he turned 180 degrees. *Nature* quoted him as saying life arising by chance has the same likelihood that "a tornado sweeping through a junk yard might assemble a Boeing 747 from the materials therein" (*Nature*, Vol. 294, No. 5837, Nov. 1981).

One cannot even begin to comprehend a number like $10^{40,000}$.

Remember the entire universe is estimated to have about 10^{78} atoms. Fred Hoyle's calculations only considered the approximate 2,000 proteins in a simple one-cell bacterium. The human body uses about 200,000 proteins.

Still, we have not even begun to understand the immensity of the problem. Sir Frederick Hoyle's calculations dealt only with the proteins found in a one-cell bacterium, not the whole bacterium. What do you think would be the odds of the *entire* bacterium forming by chance? This would include its peptides, phosphates, DNA, RNA, cell wall, etc.

Yale University physicist Harold Morowitz thought about that issue. He assumed a scenario wherein one simple bacterium was melted down into all its basic building blocks. Then, after cooling the mixture, he calculated what the odds would be of the single bacterium's re-assembling by chance. The odds are: one chance in $10^{100,000,000,000}$! (Harold Morowitz, *Energy Flow in Biology*).

In light of the above, one need not even calculate how old the universe would have to be in order to accommodate the 1 in $10^{100,000,000,000}$ chance of a simple bacterium forming.

Bottom line: a 13.8-billion-year-old universe is much too short a time period for life to arise by random processes, let alone within the limited timeframe of 4.5 bya (earth's creation) to about 3.8 bya (when life first started). The timeframe from 4.4 – 3.85+ bya has been called the *Hadean* (as in hades, or hell) *era* or *eon* due to inhospitable conditions. The most intense period of comet and asteroid bombardment on earth is called the late heavy bombardment (LHB), which occurred from about 3.9 to 3.8 bya, with the peak at 3.87.

During the LHB, as of 2006, "Astronomers estimate that roughly 17,000 collisions scattered a total of 200 tons of extraterrestrial material per square yard over the entire surface of Earth…"! (Dr. Hugh Ross, *Creation as Science*, p. 115). Many planetary scientists believe the LHB was so intense that it volatilized earth's oceans and liquefied the crust hundreds of meters deep. This situation nearly or completely sterilized the planet, making life virtually impossible, if not impossible. Amazingly, as stated, we have evidence of life back to 3.8 bya.

In light of the above, as soon as it was possible for life to arise, it did.

It arose in a *geological moment in time*. In addition, this life was metabolically and biochemically complex, contrary to an evolutionary paradigm requiring the first life to be very simple in nature.

But even given an infinitely old universe, the case for a random chance scenario for life's formation would still be impossible in the opinion of this author (and the opinions of others).

Chemical Predestination?

In the late 1960s and into the 1970s a theory called "chemical predestination" was proposed. This was explained in a book in 1969 entitled, *Chemical Predestination* by Dean H. Kenyon and G. D. Steinman. What this term means is this: perhaps chemicals innately (or automatically) form increasingly complex molecules, and this could have accounted for how life eventually resulted.

This approach was relatively short-lived. Several years after the book's publication, Dean H. Kenyon encountered too many problems with the theory, and he subsequently abandoned it. His journey through this process is documented in a DVD/film by Illustra Media (illustramedia.com; see Recommended References) entitled *The Mystery of Life*. A good book on this subject, although admittedly a complex one, is entitled *A Cybernetic Approach to Evolution* by A.E. Wilder Smith (holder of three doctorates), showing how the more complex molecules do not form by some innate, built-in natural laws, among other issues.

The Oxygen Paradox: To Be or Not to Be

A naturalistic, evolutionary source for the origin of life faces yet another intractable problem: the presence of atmospheric oxygen or the lack thereof before life first occurred. This is called the *oxygen paradox*:

- If there was no oxygen, there would not be any ozone in the early earth's atmosphere to prevent lethal doses of radiation from outer space, as well as any advancing prebiotic (prelife) chemical reactions.

- Conversely, if there was oxygen, the chemical itself would destroy any prebiotic chemical reactions.

Either way, no life could result. This is a job for a divine Creator.

Transpermia (It Came from Outer Space)

Due to the above issues and many others, some scientists have now turned to the stars, proposing that life, or its essential building blocks, came from outer space.

This proposal does not solve the problem, only pushing it back one step: how did life originate in outer space? Physics, and therefore chemistry, is the same throughout the cosmos. In addition, the transpermia theory (life or its basic chemical elements coming from outer space) suffers from a myriad of additional problems in its attempt to explain how such materials moved from outer space to earth, such as lethal doses of radiation, etc. However, these problems will not be elaborated on here.

Quick Reappearance of New Life after Major Extinction Events

Earth has experienced about five major extinction events in its history, wherein a good percentage of life forms existing at the time went extinct. Typically, the cause of these events was volcanic and/or meteorite impacts.

After these major extinction events occurred, thousands of new species appeared for the first time within a very short period of time, a time period much too short for any theoretical evolution to occur. For example, after the Permian extinction event about 251 mya, which destroyed up to about 95% of all life on earth, thousands of new life forms suddenly appeared within about 100,000 years. Evolution cannot account for the rapid appearance of new life forms after these extinction events.

Other Naturalistic Problems

Although many other scientific issues and problems exist in the theoretical path from chemicals to life on a naturalistic basis, they will not be discussed here for brevity's sake. Biochemistry is an exceedingly complex and varied field of study and one that can be shown not to favor a naturalistic pathway to life.

However, the issue of homochirality should be briefly mentioned. This means that in biological systems, the molecules making up DNA, RNA, and other nucleic acids are "right-handed," or they all face the same direction. The case with amino acids is just the opposite; nineteen out of twenty amino acids found in living systems are left-handed. This is homochirality.

However, nature's *nonliving* chemical reactions inevitably favor a 50/50% balance. All attempts to show how nature went from a 50/50% ratio (or close thereto) to a 100/0% ratio have failed. Scientists have simply not been able to produce homochirality. No homochirality, no life.

Summary

No primordial soup prior to life. Impossible time issues. No innate chemical "predestination." The oxygen paradox. Invalidity of transpermia. The issue of extinction events. The homochirality issue. In fact, for many scientific reasons, it is argued that chemical evolution reaching the level of life would not be possible, regardless of how much time was allowed.

So if chemical evolution is not feasible then what is left? Divine creation. The appearance of life has to come about by either naturalistic (random) means or divine means. It has been shown that the former was not possible according to the scientific evidence.

CHAPTER 5

THE CAMBRIAN EXPLOSION

Regarding the Cambrian Explosion, Charles Darwin stated: "The case at present must remain inexplicable; and may be truly urged as a valid argument against the [evolutionary] views here entertained." *(On the Origin of Species by Means of Natural Selection,* 1869 ed., p. 381)

The *Cambrian Explosion* (CE) provides further evidence for a divine Creator. The CE occurred about 539–542 million years ago and took anywhere from an instant in time up to under a 410,000-year span (out-of-date earlier estimates had ten to fifteen million and then down to three million). Current technology limits our measuring of under a 410,000 year span that long ago.

The CE period is one where there was a sudden burst of new life forms on earth. Before the CE, only very simple animal-type life forms existed: unicellular types, some simple worms, etc. However, upon the CE, up to 85% of all life's phyla forms suddenly appeared in the fossil record. These new life forms were very complex– articulated limbs, compound eyes, complex discreet organs, and so on. A phylum is simply a man-made taxidermic classification of life's forms; for example, the phylum *Chordata* has several classes of animals, with mammals being one of them.

The next chapter gives details regarding the problems associated with the lack of transitional forms in the *entire* fossil record, and how these missing forms are a fatal situation for evolution and further proof of a Creator God.

Transitional forms (before, during, and after the CE) in evolutionary theory are clearly required. For evolution to progress from one type of animal to another, there had to have been multiple small transitions, slowly changing the former animal into the latter one. In evolutionary theory, moving from just one type of animal to another would have required up to thousands, if not millions, of transitional forms between two animal types. When considering the entire fossil record, there should be multiple millions of transitional forms. However, according to many evolutionists, such as those quoted in this and the next chapter, there are no real transitional forms.

No such needed transitional forms existed prior to the CE. This is impossible if evolution were to be true. The complex life forms of the CE suddenly appear in the fossil record with no record of any transitional forms preceding them. Darwin admitted this presented a major roadblock to his theory. See the last part of this chapter for his observations.

Some may respond by saying the pre-CE transitional forms have not been found yet; Darwin hoped they would be found in the future. However, the "they have not been found" response is not valid.

Since Darwin's time, many more fossils have been found in the fossil record before, during, and after the CE. The result: sudden appearance of the animals of the CE without preceding transitional forms is even more clearly delineated in the fossil record than in Darwin's time. Plus, there is fossil evidence of very simple life forms prior to the CE. We even have fossil evidence of mere spores existing prior to the CE, which, being more fragile than fossils, were less likely to have been preserved. So the argument that they haven't been found or could not be preserved does not agree with the observable scientific evidence.

It is important to note that instead of Cambrian life forms starting from the simple and progressing to the more complex, as evolution would demand, we see some of the most complex forms in the earlier stages of the CE.

Bottom line: evolutionary theory is absolutely dependent on the existence of millions of transitional forms – on millions of life forms before the CE, and they don't exist. If they had existed, there would be evidence. Consequently, the most logical conclusion is that evolution did not occur, and the only other alternative, divine creation, must be responsible.

Evolutionists and the Cambrian Era

Let us look at a few quotations from evolutionists:

- Darwin himself observed:

  » There is another and allied difficulty, which is much more serious. I allude to the manner in which many species in several of the main divisions of the animal kingdom suddenly appear in the lowest known fossiliferous rocks....

  To the question why we do not find rich fossiliferous deposits belonging to these assumed earliest periods, I can give no satisfactory answer...the difficulty of assigning any good reason for the absence beneath the Upper Cambrian formations of vast piles of strata rich in fossils is very great....

  The case at present must remain inexplicable; and may be truly urged as a valid argument against the [evolutionary] views here entertained. (Chapter IX, "On the Imperfection of the Geological Record," *On the Origin of Species by Means of Natural Selection,* 1869 ed., pp. 378, 379, 381)

- The famous Richard Dawkins, atheist, evolutionist and biologist, stated:

  » The Cambrian strata of rocks, vintage about 600 [now we know it to be about 539–542] million years ago, are the oldest in which we find most of the invertebrate groups. And we find many of them already in an advanced state of evolution the first time they appear. It is as though they were just planted there, without any evolutionary history. Needless to say, this appearance of sudden planting has delighted creationists. (*The Blind Watchmaker*, p. 229)

- N. Eldredge, paleontologist:

  » Then there was something of an explosion. Beginning about six hundred million years ago [we now know it was about 539–542 million years ago] and continuing for about ten to fifteen million years [now we know it was sometime under 410,000 years], the earliest known representatives of the major kinds of animals still populating today's seas made a rather abrupt appearance. This rather protracted 'event' shows up graphically in the rock record: all over the world, at roughly the same time, thick sequences of rocks, barren of any easily detected fossils, are overlain by sediments containing a gorgeous array of shelly invertebrates: trilobites (extinct relatives of crabs and insects), brachiopods, mollusks. All of the typical forms of hard-shelled animals we see in the modern oceans appeared, albeit in primitive, prototypical form, in the seas of six hundred million years ago.

  Creationists have made much of this sudden development of a rich and varied fossil record where, just before, there was none…

  Indeed, the sudden appearance of a varied, well-preserved array of fossils which geologists have used to mark the beginnings of the Cambrian Period (the oldest division of the Paleozoic Era) does pose a fascinating intellectual challenge. (American Museum of Natural History, N. Eldredge, *The Monkey Business: A Scientist Looks at Creationism*, p. 44)

- Swedish paleontologist and evolutionist, Stefan Bengtson stated:

  » If any event in life's history resembles man's creation

myths, it is this sudden diversification of marine life when multicellular organisms took over as the dominant actors in ecology and evolution. Baffling (and embarrassing) to Darwin, this event still dazzles us and stands as a major biological revolution...the animal phyla emerged out of the Precambrian mists with most of the attributes of their modern descendants. (*Nature* 345.765, 1990)

- D. Axelrod said:

  » One of the major unsolved problems of geology and evolution is the occurrence of diversified, multi-cellular marine invertebrates in Lower Cambrian rocks on all the continents and their absence in rocks of greater age. (*Science* 128:7, 1958)

- Douglas Futuyma comments:

  » It is considered likely that all the animal phyla became distinct before or during the Cambrian, for they all appear fully formed, without intermediates connecting one form to another. (*Evolutionary Biology*, 2nd ed., 1986, p. 325)

It is interesting to note that in recent years, since the latter half of the twentieth century, the above problems outlined by scientists still persist; in fact, they are more pronounced.

The next chapter will go into further detail about the lack of transitional forms and the admissions of evolutionists to that effect.

CHAPTER 6

LACK OF TRANSITIONAL FORMS

"Why is not every geological formation and every stratum full of such intermediate links? Geology assuredly does not reveal any such finely graduated organic chain: and this, perhaps, is the most obvious and gravest objection which can be urged against my theory." (Charles Darwin, *Origin of Species*, 1860 ed., p. 280)

As discussed in the previous chapter, the lack of transitional forms prior to the Cambrian Explosion (CE) shows the need for a divine Creator. Even more so, the lack of transitional forms *throughout* the fossil record shows the need for a divine Creator.

Darwinian Evolution Requires Transitional Forms

To reiterate from the last chapter, a transitional form (TF) or intermediate form in Darwinian evolutional theory is a fundamental requirement if the theory is to be valid. According to evolutionary theory, there must exist numerous TFs between any two types of animals. Charles Darwin admitted to the lack of the necessary innumerable transitional forms. (Refer to the quotations of his material in the below section entitled "Charles Darwin Admits to Lack of Transitional Forms.")

For example, going from a reptile to a bird would require thousands, perhaps millions, of TFs. Also, going from just one type of reptile to another type of reptile could require up to thousands of TFs. Consequently, in the entire fossil record, there should be millions of TFs.

The purported changes are the result of random genetic variations where on rare occasions a change can supposedly give the new organism a competitive advantage in its environment. These mutations must be minute each time they occur, as any degree of real change would almost certainly kill the animal. Very slight genetic changes in humans, for example, almost always result in significant deformities or death; this is why Darwinian evolution requires each "generation" of a change(s) to be very small, maintaining the viability of the resulting life form. However, rarely do genetic mutations (changes) produce positive results, and they have never been shown in the fossil record to eventually result in a different type of animal.

Micro- vs. Macro-Evolution

Neither science nor the Bible has a problem with what is called "micro-evolution," which is a term referring to small changes *within* a genotype, an animal type, typically within a species or genus level. For example, there are varying breeds of cats and dogs.

However, what the Bible and the facts of nature (including the fossil record) have a problem with is what is called "macro-evolution." That term refers to a process when a genotype (or type) of animal (such as a cat) *gradually* becomes a different type of animal (such as a dog, for illustration purposes).

These macro-evolutionary changes and their required TFs are regularly missing between "animal types" in the fossil record, and this is devastating to Darwinian evolution.

Charles Darwin Admits to Lack of Transitional Forms

Charles Darwin admitted to the lack of TFs in the fossil record:

> [Since] innumerable transitional forms must have existed, why do we not find them imbedded in countless numbers in the crust of the earth? (*Origin of Species*, 1860 ed., p. 172)

> Why is not every geological formation and every stratum full of such intermediate links? Geology assuredly does not reveal any such finely graduated organic chain: and this,

perhaps, is the most obvious and gravest objection which can be urged against my theory. (*Ibid.*, 1860 ed., p. 280)

Why, if species have descended from other species by fine gradations, do we not everywhere see innumerable transitional forms? (*Ibid.*, 1902, 6th ed., p. 233)

Darwin had hoped the TFs would be found in the future. They have not.

A Clear Description of What Constitutes a Transitional Form

Before proceeding, a clear definition or picture is needed of what a TF actually is. Some say any animal is a TF as it is between the first living cell and modern human beings. Thus, using that line of thought, an elephant would be defined as a transitional form as it is between the first living cell and modern human beings.

However, this is not a correct definition of a TF. A TF is any intermediary specimen sharing traits from both its ancestral origins and its descendent group (the form into which it is ultimately evolving), with each generation of a given TF being a single link in a long chain of inter-generational micro-transformations. With enough time and TFs, per evolutionary theory, a reptile could evolve into a bird.

A correct picture of what is a TF would be something like this: Let us take for our example *Animal Type A*, which we shall say is a crocodile. *Animal Type B* will be a bird. Evolutionists have often said birds evolved from reptiles. A crocodile is referenced here as our reptilian candidate only for illustrative purposes, as most evolutionists would pick another reptile as being in the ancestry of birds.

TFs in our above example would be numerous small changes, starting with the crocodile. Eventually the descendants of the crocodile would start forming small nodules or bumps on their backs or sides (after thousands of generations of TFs, these would be wings). Over time, the forelegs would gradually shorten to the point of disappearing since the eventual result, a bird, would not have forelegs. The snout would shorten over many thousands of generations, with the crocodile losing its teeth and the snout hardening into a beak as the end result. Of course, the crocodile's skeletal and muscular structures would have to totally change, as would its organs, respiratory system, etc. You get the picture. These are what are called TFs.

In the entire fossil record, we have not found animals fitting the above definition of TFs. Darwin himself admitted that without these TFs, evolution as a theory cannot stand; TFs are a fundamental part of the theory. Of course, any theoretical TFs that would be preserved are typically those affecting morphological changes, especially skeletal structures.

> What we consistently find in the fossil record are fully complete animals that suddenly appear in the fossil record and are fit for their purpose and environment, not transitional forms.

Transitional Forms Not Competitive

Another problem with TFs is that they would not be competitive for survival in the wild. Take our crocodile, for example. With shortened forelimbs, it could not maneuver on either land or water very well, presenting definite survival problems. An ever shortening of its snout and forelegs would present obvious defensive problems for our crocodile, not to mention the loss of its teeth. Eventually the newly forming creature would have two appendages flapping around on its back (i.e., proto-wings), which were not yet functional for any purpose, slowing the animal down and getting in the way. And so on. It should be pointed out that such proto-wings would be eliminated by any so-called evolutionary processes, as anything short of a fully-developed wing would be a disadvantage to the animal in question, thereby eliminating chances of getting to the bird stage in the first place; any theoretical intermediate stages would almost always not work.

Most TFs by nature would not pass the survival test and therefore would die out, preventing any so-called theoretical progression or evolution. The fossil record per evolutionary doctrine should be littered with these. But it is not. Plus, allowing for a little humor, for each TF of our crocodile, the other crocodiles would be laughing at their poor fellow crocodile(s) suffering from their "weird" genetic maladies.

But What About...?

Some may try to give a few examples of TFs. There are three problems with these examples: (i) there would have to be thousands of TFs before and after the claimed TF; however, there are none; (ii) these are really not TFs as needed and defined above; and (iii) some evolutionists claim a few TFs have been found, but they are essentially nothing since the fossil record should contain millions of them. If the evolutionary theory and the few examples cited were correct, they would not be contested so often, even among evolutionists.

One alleged example would be the so-called transition of lobe-finned fishes (living in shallow waters) to amphibians (tetrapods). These so-called transitions are sometimes called "fishapods," with a species called *Tiktaalik* being the first of the hoped-for intermediates.

However, more recent discoveries have presented some problems with this evolutionary perspective (Fazala Rana, "Tetrapod Transition: Evidence for Design," January 1, 2010; see E-Link Bibliography). A creature called *Ventastega* has been found living about 365 mya and is believed to be about the "half-way point" between Tiktaalik and amphibians (tetrapods). However, its skeletal features are out of sequence, as older or previous fishapods show more advanced features than those of *Ventastega*. Another fishapod, called *Panderichtys,* has been found, which lived at about 385 mya, making it closer to the lobe-finned fish than an amphibian. However, it has digits at the end of its fins, whereas *Tiktaalik*, which comes later, does not. This is contrary to the evolutionary paradigm.

Another example is the ancient bird called archaeopteryx, which appears in the fossil record about 150 million years ago with full flight capability and fully developed feathers (a very complex organic structure). However, as evolutionists like to point out, it has teeth in its

beak and a claw under each wing, which they contend infer a reptilian ancestry. However, famous zoologist and evolutionist Stephen J.
Gould, along with biologist Niles Eldredge, noted:

> Although Archaeopteryx is often proposed as a transitional
> form, 'its fossils do not count.' ("Punctuated Equilibria:
> The Tempo and Mode of Evolution Reconsidered," *Paleo-*
> *biology*, Vol. 3, No. 2 [Spring, 1977], pp. 115-151)

Some evolutionists point to theropod dinosaurs (some apparently
had feathers) as predecessors to Archaeopteryx. However, the problem
is that the fossil record shows these feathered dinosaurs all come *after*
Archaeopteryx (but you do not hear about that in the news).

Reasons to Believe scholar and biochemist, Fazala Rana, PhD, comments on the so-called feathered dinosaurs (theropods):

> These new dates place the Yixian Formation within the
> early Cretaceous period, making archeopteryx at least 20
> million years older than the so-called 'intermediates' [the-
> ropods] leading up to it. The theropods from the Yixian
> Formation, like all theropods, now fall within the 'tempo-
> ral paradox.' That is, all theropods, despite their declared
> status as progenitors of birds, show up in the fossil record
> well *after* the first appearance of birds. (Fazala Rana, "New
> Challenge to the Bird-Dinosaur Link," April 1, 2000; see
> E-Link Bibliography, which in turn references Alan Feduc-
> cia, *The Origin and Evolution of Birds*, 2nd ed., p. 382)

Further problems include the fact that there should be up to thousands of TFs between Archaeopteryx and whatever reptile it supposedly came from. However, there are no TFs. There are one or two
examples of birds today with claws under their wings while in their
juvenile state, and the existence of teeth does not necessarily indicate
non-avian ancestry since there are reptiles with no teeth.

Major gaps exist between the various types of animals throughout
the fossil record. This is not what should occur if evolution were true.

However, if divine creation activity as described in the Bible's book of Genesis chapter one is true, then these gaps should be expected: Genesis states each "type" of animal would reproduce after its own kind (see chapter 1 of Genesis).

What About the "Cave Men?"

No discussion of TFs would be complete without some reference to the subject of "cave men" or the more technically correct "bi-pedal primates" that one would expect between apes/monkeys and modern man (called homo sapiens sapiens). This subject could span multiple volumes. A more cursory treatment will be given here as is appropriate to this discussion.

Yes, there is generally an increasing size in cranial capacity from the various species of apes/monkeys to modern humans. In terms of when obligatory bipedalism (mandatory upright walking on two legs) started, there is much debate. Some scientists think this took place anywhere from about 5-6 mya to 3.3 mya or later.

The bipedal primate fossil record can sometimes be confusing, with new discoveries sometimes throwing a monkey wrench (no pun intended) into making sense of it all. Plus, the issues of genetic variability within species, the age and sex of a fossil, and even sometimes the philosophical perspectives of the paleontologist add to the confusion amongst interpretations of the findings of evolutionists.

If macro-evolutionary forces were at work, we should then see gradual changes in each of the various species of bipedal primates, from their first appearance to when they go extinct. However, we do not see this. For example, *homo erectus* looks the same from its advent at about 1.8 mya to its extinction perhaps as late as 100,000 years ago. Also, we see a step-like or jump-like progression from one species to the next, which would not be expected in an evolutionary scenario's demand for gradual change.

Recent mtDNA (mitochondria DNA) evidence shows the 6.5% difference between Neanderthals and modern humans to be almost as much of a difference as the 8.9% between man and chimpanzees. This and other evidence show that the Neanderthals were not our ancestors.

(M.A. Krings, et al., "Neanderthal DNA Sequences and the Origin of Modern Humans," *Cell* 90 (1997), pp. 19-30).

On this subject, the following quotes from scientific literature show *it is a real jungle out there* (pun intended) regarding this area of the fossil record:

> Amid the bewildering array of early fossil hominoids, is there one whose morphology [shape] marks it as man's hominid ancestor? If the factor of genetic variability is considered, the answer appears to be no. (Robert Eckhardt, *Scientific American* 226 [1]: 94 [1972])

> In the present state of our knowledge, I do not believe it is possible to fit the known hominid fossils into a reliable pattern. (Mary Leakey, *Disclosing the Past*, 1984, p. 214)

> There is no clear-cut and inexorable pathway from ape to human being. (David Pilbeam, "Rearranging Our Family Tree," *Human Nature* [6/78], p. 44)

On whether man evolved from gibbons, chimps, or orangutans:

> The fossil record has been elastic enough, the expectations sufficiently robust, to accommodate almost any story. (David Pilbeam, "Patterns of Hominoid Evolution," *Ancestors: The Hard Evidence*, 1985, p. 53)

> One is forced to conclude that there is no clear-cut scientific picture of human evolution. (R. Martin, "Man Is Not an Onion," *New Scientist* 4 [8/77]: 285)

> The human fossil record is no exception to the general rule that the main lesson to be learned from paleontology is that evolution always takes place somewhere else. (J. S. Jones, S. Rouhani, "How Small Was the Bottleneck?" *Nature* 319 [6 February 1986]: 449)

Comments from Evolutionists on Lack of Transitional Forms

Most people would be surprised at many of the candid observations and comments by leading evolutionists about the lack of TFs.

A casual review of what is on the internet will show some sources trying to explain away the lack of numerous TFs by giving various explanations, which really do not fit the scientific research or the facts of nature. We have seen from previous quotes, including those of Darwin himself, numerous transitional forms are indeed required. One argument often presented is that we haven't found the TFs yet. On a statistical basis alone, this argument cannot stand. For example, we have found a vast majority of the non-transitional forms (established forms) in the fossil record. To say we have not found any or only a few of the many more millions of TFs that must have existed is not a viable position.

The following will provide several more quotes of what some noted evolutionists are really saying:

- E.J.H. Corner of Cambridge University:

  » But I still think that to the unprejudiced, the fossil record of plants is in favor of special creation. (*Contemporary Botanical Thought*, p. 97)

- A. H. Clark states:

  » Since we have not the slightest evidence, either among the living or the fossil animals, of any intergrading types [transitional forms] following the major groups, it is a fair supposition that there never has been any such intergrading types. (*The New Evolution; Zoogenesis*, p. 196)

  » No matter how far we go in the fossil record of previous animal life upon earth, we find no trace of any animal forms which are intermediate between the various major groups or phyla. (*Ibid.*, p. 189)

- D.B. Kitts, Professor in Geology Dept., University of Oklahoma:

  » Despite the bright promise that paleontology provides a means of 'seeing' evolution, it has presented some nasty difficulties for evolutionists, the most notorious of which is the presence of 'gaps' in the fossil record. Evolution requires intermediate forms between species, and paleontology does not provide them. (*Evolution* 28:467 [1974])

- S. J. Gould pronounced:

  » The extreme rarity of transitional forms [note: many evolutionists would say 'no' transitional forms] in the fossil record persists as the trade secret of paleontology. The evolutionary trees that adorn our textbooks have data only at the tips and nodes of their branches; the rest [i.e., the branches and trunk] is inference, however reasonable [per the evolutionary paradigm], not the evidence of fossils. We fancy ourselves as the only true students of life's history, yet to preserve our favored account of evolution by natural selection, we view our data as so bad that we never see the very process we profess to study. ("Evolution's Erratic Pace," *Natural History*, Vol. 86, p. 14.)

- R.B. Goldschmidt observed:

  » The facts of greatest general importance are the following. When a new phylum, class, or order appears, there follows a quick, explosive (in terms of geological time) diversification so that proactively all orders or families known appear suddenly and without any apparent transitions. ("The Material Basis of Evolution, "*American Scientist* 40:97 [1952])

- N. Macbeth:

  » Darwinism has failed in practice. The whole aim and purpose of Darwinism is to show how modern forms descended from ancient forms, that is, to construct reliability phylogenies (genealogies or family trees). In this he has utterly failed. (*American Biology Teacher* [November 1976], p. 495)

- In his review of the book by Steven Stanley, *Macroevolution Pattern and Process*, David Woodruff states:

  » But fossil species remain unchanged throughout most of their history, and the record fails to contain a single example of a significant transition. (*Science* 208:716 [1980])

- In *Newsweek* magazine, November 3, 1980, in an article entitled "Is Man a Subtle Accident?":

  » The more scientists have searched for the transitional forms that lie between species, the more they have been frustrated.

What About Punctuated Equilibrium?

Because of the lack of TFs, a few evolutionists have tried to circumvent Darwinian evolution with its lack of innumerable TFs by hypothesizing that life forms every now and then took quick bursts of fewer TFs.

The extreme version of this theory is posited by R. B. Goldschmidt and is sometimes called the *Hopeful Monster* hypothesis of how life changes through macro (very large) changes. For example, some reptile supposedly gave birth to an anomaly, say a chicken for illustration purposes. One wonders what animal the chicken would then reproduce with? Other, more moderate versions of punctuated equilibrium propose that small, localized populations of animals would undergo rapid genetic changes producing new life forms with fewer TFs.

Most evolutionists have totally rejected these punctuated equilibrium versions of evolution. Genetically, both versions are simply not viable, especially the *Monster Theory* version. The other more moderate version is still stuck with the need for up to thousands, if not millions of TFs that do not exist.

CHAPTER 7

CHEMICAL ROBOTS WITH NO FREE WILL OR LOVE

"Free will is an illusion. Our wills are simply not of our own making." (Neuroscientist, philosopher, and atheist Sam Harris, *Free Will*, 2012, p. 5)

"**DNA neither cares nor knows**. DNA just is. And we dance to its music." (Atheist Richard Dawkins, *River out of Eden: A Darwinian View of Life*, 1995, p. 133) [boldfacing is this author's emphasis]

"**We are machines** built by DNA whose purpose is to make more copies of the same DNA. …This is exactly what we are for. **We are machines for propagating DNA**, and the propagation of DNA is a self-sustaining process. **It is every living object's sole reason for living**." (Richard Dawkins in a Royal Institution Christmas Lecture, "The Ultraviolet Garden," no. 4, 1991, quoted in Vinoth Ramachandra, *Subverting Global Myths: Theology and the Public Issues Shaping Our World*, 2008, p. 187) [boldfacing is this author's emphasis]

"Unless you assume a God, the question of life's purpose is meaningless." (ultimate source is letter to Hugh Moorhead from philosopher Bertrand Russell, January 10, 1952, Rick Warren, *The Purpose Driven Life*, 2002, p. 17)

Before leaving the hard sciences and information of Chapters 1-6, the author wishes to emphasize that "Section I: God's Existence" could also include, in essence, the contents of Chapters 13 and 14, which contain additional hard evidence of both scientific considerations and prophetic fulfillment that show God's existence. However, those two chapters are strategically positioned for reasons mentioned in those chapters.

Now we will shift gears from the hard sciences and information to discuss in this and the next chapter some non-material considerations.

> Atheism at its core and its very fabric teaches that matter and energy (hereinafter referred to as just matter) are all there is, was, or ever will be. Atheism, therefore, automatically precludes the existence of any non-material (or non-matter) issues and/or existence of any kind, such as love, free-will, ultimate meaning, purpose, moral absolutes, and beauty. For any so-called appearances of such, atheism would contend they are simply the result of only chemical reactions to external stimuli. Again, matter is it. Period. Of course, energy is acknowledged but is the result of only some sort of materialist conditions.

In atheism, the universe and our existence amount to a complex combination of "Lego" blocks (i.e., atoms, molecules). What happens when you have even more complex combinations of building blocks? You just have more of the same stuff, and this stuff cannot ever become greater than itself.

Many atheists do not readily admit to the cold, hard logic of their philosophical position as given above. Some fully acknowledge it, while others try, consciously or unconsciously, to insert some aspect of spirituality (which is a non-material aspect) into human existence in one form or another (such as finding so-called purpose or meaning in political, humanitarian, and relational endeavors). However, when it comes down to it, per atheistic doctrinal logic any such temporary activities are only driven/formed by chemical reactions to external stimuli. Regardless of how complex matter may become, it cannot be more than itself or become more than itself.

Regardless of how complex the Lego set of molecules becomes, it is still just valueless matter or stuff, knowing NO love, free-will, purpose, meaning, morals, etc. which are outside the chemical reactions of matter.

> True or ultimate love, free will, purpose, meaning, morals, and so on are not found inside the prevue of inanimate matter and its chemical reactions; that is axiomatic. They are truly found in something beyond matter's limitations. The "more" being our spiritual nature, a non-material reality.

Perhaps it is belaboring the point, but the result of something cannot be greater than its cause. According to the universal law of cause and effect, matter (the cause) cannot produce an effect (such as love, etc.) that is greater than itself. Matter cannot produce consciousness and self-awareness, no matter how complex it may become.

I recall a discussion with an atheist whose wife was nearby. I asked him, "Does your wife love you?"

Of course he answered, "Yes."

I responded, "Oh, no she doesn't. And you don't love your wife." Needless to say, I got their attention and went on to explain that if matter is all there is, then there is no such thing as a free-will attribute like love.

My point in all of the above is this: Since human free will obviously exists and since love obviously exists, then atheism, which cannot truly explain them, does not stand up to reality; therefore, atheism is invalid; it cannot explain reality.

Conversely, the existence of non-material realities such as free will, love, etc. show the need for a God, as these things are only possible if God exists; nothing else or no one else can truly explain their existence.

Some may try to argue that the presence of love, free will, etc. does not prove God. My response is this: the ultimate answer for their existence has to belong to either the "natural" (only material/matter) or the "supernatural" (non-material/non-matter) realm. There are no other realms possible. The natural realm cannot explain things like love, free will, appreciation of beauty, etc. as discussed. Therefore, like it or not, one is logically "stuck" with the supernatural (non-material) realm in which to find viable answers. Additionally, the supernatural realm (made possible by God) does provide very good reasons for things like love, free will, and so on.

Some people may say everything is illusionary, including love, free will, etc. Really? Then there is no reason to pay attention to such an argument, which itself has to be illusionary!

Some may respond that there are no such things as love, free will, and so on, emphasizing that we are nothing but chemical robots. Not only is that answer unsatisfying, but the first six chapters of this book clearly demonstrate why such a naturalistic view of nature is not viable.

Concerning moral absolutes, ultimate right and wrong, an atheist may try to object to God's existence by saying, "If there was a God, he would not allow so much evil and suffering in the world."

The atheist's argument against God due to so much evil and suffering has its own irony since it contradicts the logic of the very argument the atheist is trying to propose.

If there is no God, then there would be no ultimate good or evil because, as the atheist often likes to point out, the universe consists of only matter, and that's all there is, ever was, or ever will be. Again, purely inanimate matter cannot contain or create good, evil, love, meaning, or purpose. Therefore, there can be no such things as *ultimate, objective* right or wrong, good or evil, only the subjective opinions of individual people or groups.

It can be further pointed out that the atheist's "evil and suffering" argument has other problems. For example, if an atheist admits to such a thing as evil in his argument (which does not exist in an atheistic paradigm), the atheist will need to do the following:

• Logically admit that there must be an opposing good by which evil is determined or measured.

- Further admit that if there is good, then there has to be some objective standard by which good can be determined.

- Acknowledge that since a moral, objective standard is impossible in a purely material universe, the fact that we all agree there is/are such things as truly good (or evil) shows atheism to be inadequate and deficient in explaining reality.

- Logically concede that if there is absolute good, then there has to be an absolute lawgiver (God), as there is no other possible candidate as its source since matter is incapable of producing moral absolutes.

Ignoring the above obvious, inescapable logic, some might try to say: "There are no absolutes. It is only what the culture or individual determines to be right. There are no absolute rights or wrongs."

First I would ask, "Is that an absolute statement you are promoting?" It is bad when one's argument (no moral absolutes) promotes the very idea (an absolute such as "there are no absolutes") he is trying to oppose.

Secondly, I would state, "I did not know you believed Hitler's killing six million Jews could be okay." The reaction is typically, "I didn't say that!" Then my rejoinder is, "Maybe that was not your intent, but the clear logic of your statement supports it. The logic of what you are saying is that Hitler and the Nazis had their own cultural imperative to kill six million Jews, and no other culture or person has the right to say they are wrong since you are contending that everything is relative."

Do you see the problems we get into when trying to deny moral absolutes? Moral and spiritual anarchy is typically the logical result, as has been shown by many past evil rulers who have bought into the paradigm that moral absolutes do not exist.

Yes, it may be good for society's continued existence not to murder its occupants, but for a person who does not believe in moral absolutes that person can't say such a massacre is ultimately right or wrong since absolutes do not exist in their mind. Plus, how can a person who denies absolutes say it is a good thing that society itself exists. Such a statement presupposes some objective standard by which it can be determined that it is good for society to exist and be healthy. Now we are back to the absolute lawgiver again.

I also often ask a person who denies moral absolutes, "Could it ever be okay to senselessly torture and kill a two-year-old child for the sheer enjoyment of it?" The obvious answer is "No" (an *absolute* response).

"What would you do if someone stole your car?" is another question I might ask of the one who denies moral absolutes. Of course, this person would think such an act was wrong and would report it to the police, hoping to get his car back. If he truly believed everything was only relative, then it could be argued that the person who stole his car thought the act of stealing was okay, and thus the victim could not say anything against the person's relative moral position on stealing. Moral relativism destroys any reason to hold people accountable for their actions in terms of ultimate right/wrong and good/bad. If moral relativism and atheism were true, the ultimate basis (ultimate moral and ethical values) for our entire court system and sense of justice would fall apart. The above data leads to the following quote:

> From this simple analysis, surely it follows that individuals cannot logically be held responsible for their behavior. (Anthony R. Cashmore, biologist, in an article "The Lucretian Swerve: The Biological Basis of Human Behavior and the Criminal Justice System" in *PNAS [Proceedings of the National Academy of Sciences of the United States of America*], March 9, 2010 (10) 4499-4504)

The idea of moral relativism is an unrealistic intellectual exercise in a fantasy world; when it is rigorously applied to reality/real life, it simply does not work, despite any attempted fanciful, philosophical exercises to the contrary.

Much more could be offered in the discussion of the existence of moral absolutes (good, evil), but the above makes a short, simple (not simplistic) argument that absolutes do exist, and they can only truly exist if there is a God, an Absolute Law Giver.

In closing, no one can deny there are physical/scientific absolutes:

- Gravity exists

- Earth revolves around the sun

- The sun exists

- And so on

One can argue that since physical absolutes exist, moral and spiritual absolutes can (and do) also exist. Some might say that in the physical word there are absolutes, but there are no moral/spiritual absolutes. This is only an opinion with no evidence; plus the statement itself assumes an absolute. The evidence, as briefly shown, is that the moral/spiritual realm also has absolutes.

In closing, the author fully realizes there are volumes of books written by philosophers on the issues of free will, love, etc. This book does not pretend to be a comprehensive treatise of these areas but contends that the information contained herein does indeed stand up to logical examination and presents a good argument that scientific materialism is an inadequate "mechanism" to explain reality, physical or otherwise.

CHAPTER 8

THEN THERE'S BEAUTY...

[1]*"The heavens declare the glory of God; the skies proclaim the work of his hands. [2]Day after day they pour forth speech; night after night they reveal knowledge. [3]They have no speech, they use no words; no sound is heard from them. [4]Yet their voice goes out into all the earth, their words to the ends of the world"* (Psalm 19:1-4).

"For since the creation of the world God's invisible qualities—his eternal power and divine nature—have been clearly seen, being understood from what has been made, so that people are without excuse" (Romans 1:20).

This chapter in favor of God's existence is shorter and simpler than the previous chapters. However, in some sense, it may be the most important one of all.

As discussed in more length in the last chapter, atheism argues that matter is the only reality of the universe; according to atheism, matter is the only thing that has existed, does exist, and ever will exist. That being the case, the universe would be devoid of non-material realities such as love, free will, ultimate right and wrong, etc. Matter cannot produce non-matter realities. However, since such realities as love, free-will, etc. do exist, they argue against atheism.

Another non-material reality is the ability to experience beauty. If there were no spirit, only stuff or matter, beauty and its appreciation would not be among our abilities, since pure matter is incapable of experiencing beauty. The fact that we experience it shows we are more than just matter. And being more than just matter indicates the existence of God, who gave us this spiritual capacity to recognize and enjoy beauty.

I have heard it said most atheists tend to live in cities, cut off from nature and its attendant beauty. However, people living closer to nature have a much less difficult time saying "God did this!"

This reaction is not surprising as Scripture itself says the created order, nature, reveals God's truth, righteousness, and glory. For example, see Psalm 19:1-4; 50:6; 97:6; Job 12:7-8. In urban living, much of the created order is not readily observed.

Not to belabor the point, but can you imagine a chunk of matter (no matter how complex it might be in a living system/animal) enjoying the beauty of a sunset/sunrise or an awe-inspiring scene of a beautiful lake in the mountains? Or how about the beauty of a pretty flower or rose?

Of course, we laugh at such a possibility. But for living beings who have a spirit and soul, the appreciation of beauty is within our capacity. Truly, although it is not quantifiable, this experience and the enjoyment of beauty itself is a sign of the existence of a non-material aspect of our nature, a spiritual side if you will, which in turn evidences the need for a Creator God as its source.

SECTION II

GOD'S IDENTITY

CHAPTER 9

LAW OF
NON-CONTRADICTION

Logical Thinking

The previous eight chapters have shown proof, mostly scientific, for the existence of a Creator God. Beginning in Section II, the issue of identifying *who* the one true God is will be examined.

Because we have not yet identified the true God, this god could theoretically be a he, she, it, or even a "they." For purposes of reading convenience, we will simply use the word "God" (singular, capital) for the most part in this chapter and the first part of the next.

Some people respond by contending that people can worship the same God but call God by different names. Is this possibly true? Does this happen?

If this were true, the god(s) of each of the different religions do not support such an idea. Each god of the various religions of the world claims he/she/it is the true God, while claiming the god(s) of other religions are false/nonexistent.

If this is the same God talking in the various religions, "he" has done a mighty poor job of identifying himself and a great job of contradicting himself.

The simple truth of the matter is that each of the world's religions teaches its god(s) is the true one. These various gods differ from one another in their basic nature/makeup (their identity) and/or in their primary messages. Therefore, their contradictory claims could not originate from the same Intelligent Being (God).

In the real world, different gods means different identities and not just different names/labels referring to the same god(s). In fact, sometimes contradictory religions use the same names/labels but redefine the nature of the deity being referenced; they refer to a different deity with similar labels.

For example, in Christianity, there is only one God, existing everywhere in the eternal past and eternal future, therefore existing prior to the universe's creation. The god who is the father of Mormonism is one of three gods for this and other planets; he only reorganizes pre-existing matter, which Mormonism claims is eternal (an eternal universe).

Outside of that there are trillions of gods and goddesses over their own organized planets in Mormonism. Each of the gods and goddesses of Mormonism came into being from the sexual union of their respective god the father with one of his goddess wives. Then each of these gods was born a spirit, then took on a physical body on a planet in a mortal state as a physically born baby, obeyed the Mormon gospel, and physically died. Eventually a few became their own gods and goddesses. They then start the process over again, and so on. Mormons call this *The Law of Eternal Progression.*

So although Mormons often call the head god for Earth their "God the Father," it is in no way the same as Christianity's (the Bible's) God the Father. Mormonism's god the father has his god the father; his god the father has his god the father; and so on infinitely into the past in a universe with no beginning or end. These teachings of Mormonism can be verified in many authoritative Mormon sources, including the following:

- *Mormon Doctrine* from Mormon Apostle Bruce R. McConkie

- *Doctrines of Salvation*, Vols. I, II, and III from Mormon President Joseph F. Smith

- *The Articles of Faith* by Mormon Apostle James E. Talmage

- *Journal of Discourses* by President Brigham Young, 26 vols.

- *History of the Church of Jesus Christ of Latter-Day Saints*, Vols. I-VII

- *The Seer* by Apostle Orson Pratt

- *The Pearl of Great Price*

- *The Doctrine of Covenants of the Church of Jesus Christ of Latter-Day Saints*

The Book of Mormon, Mormonism's first publication, does not teach most of the later-created Mormon core doctrines given above.

The god of Islam is also very different from the God of the Bible. The god (Allah) of Islam denies the major teachings of the Bible: the triune God (Trinity) of the Bible, the deity of Jesus Christ, Christ's death by crucifixion and resurrection from the dead, salvation through faith alone by the grace of Jesus and his atonement, as well as other major doctrines. No supporting references are needed here as Islam universally teaches and acknowledges its Islamic doctrines contradict orthodox Christianity's fundamental doctrines given above. The same God simply could not be the originator of both Islam and biblical Christianity. Numerous examples of other religions could be cited to show their gods and messages to be contradictory to the Christian God.

Each of the major (and minor) religions contradict each other on who (or what) God is and/or how one is saved (or other similar terms). Logic clearly prohibits the Creator God from being the author of contradictory theologies/

> views, especially those concerning WHO he actually is and HOW our souls are eternally saved.

As a consequence, the true God (whomever/whatever he/she/it/ they may be at this point in our discussion) cannot be the originator of contradictory religions – and each of the religions are contradictory, as stated earlier. Yes, they may have some common moral or ethical precepts (e.g., thou shalt not murder), but this is clearly not the concern here: it must be determined WHO God is and HOW one is supposed to react to that God (involves salvation). All this brings us to…

The Law of Non-Contradiction (LNC)

When *Idea A* contradicts (or is different from) *Idea B,* the Law of Non-Contradiction (LNC) prohibits their both being true at the same time in the same way. For our search, this means:

> ### THE LAW OF NON-CONTRADICTION (LNC)
>
> The **LNC** states that opposing ideas or positions cannot both be true at the same time in the same way. Therefore, since the various religions of the world contradict each other on WHO God is and/or WHAT his primary message is, the LNC (and just plain logic) prohibits more than one of them from being true.

The following chapters will show there is indeed one true God and the identity of this God.

CHAPTER 10

NARROWING OUR GOD CHOICES

Remember from the last chapter and its Law of Non-Contradiction (LNC), logic clearly prohibits the true God from being the author of contradictory theologies/views, especially those concerning the two most important subjects: (1) WHO God is and (2) HOW our souls are eternally saved.

As previously stated, the God(s) of each of the various religions of the world contradict each other on their teachings of who he/she/it is. This matter is not trivial but is critical indeed.

> Ascertaining the one true God *is not an issue of simply using different names for the same deity, but is a core matter of identity.* If a person wants to have a relationship with the real God, then one must have that God's identity correct. To have any kind of relationship with another personality/entity, a person first has to accept who the person/entity is.

For example, when I first met my future wife (Gloria), if I had insisted that she was a *different* woman (not just a different name, but a different person), let us say "Kathy" (with Kathy's lifetime experiences and temperament/personality), I would not have been able to establish a relationship with the real Gloria. I could not have imposed my "imaginary Kathy" onto the real Gloria and could not have had any chance at a relationship with the real, actual Gloria. Bottom line, I had to accept Gloria for who she was/is. The same logic applies to God.

> If we are to determine who the true God is, then we have to find the one who precedes all space, time, energy, and matter (SMET) in order for that God to create SMET (the universe).

Caution!

This line of sound reasoning eliminates most religions, as we shall see. Nonetheless, a word of caution is needed here. One must be careful in jumping onto the scientific bandwagon, proclaiming as false anything contrary to a given scientific finding. There have been times when the so-called findings of science have changed over the years. The facts of nature do not change, but sometimes science's interpretation of the facts of nature can change based on new evidence and discoveries.

So great care must be taken in declaring a religious position as false if it contradicts the big bang, for example. However, and this cannot be stressed enough, the science of the big bang is so thoroughly researched and backed up by factual findings and photographs one can be confident this is one finding of science (among others, like gravity) that will not change.

When astronomers view objects deep into space, they are viewing those objects as they appeared in the past. For example, when we look at and photograph the Andromeda galaxy, we are seeing it as it appeared 2 mya, since it is 2 million light years distant; it took that light 2 million years to reach our telescopes. Also, when we view the sun, we are seeing it as it appeared eight minutes ago, since it takes its light eight minutes to reach Earth. Therefore, astronomers can see "back into time" to see what the universe looked like, and therefore what was happening, back to about 13 bya.

Regardless of what we call it, whether it is called the big bang or simply the beginning of the universe, the universe had to have a beginning, as previously shown. There is no such thing as infinite energy, which requires a beginning per the second law of thermodynamics. And this requires a pre-existing agent to the universe who brought the universe into existence.

Whatever choices we make in our search for the true God, they must be in agreement with reality. We should not consider any theological system (and its god or gods) that denies such a fundamental reality regarding the origin of our universe! If that religion's god (or gods) gets that wrong such a deity or deities are not true and real. Therefore, such a theological system is not a reliable source of truth, and does not warrant further consideration.

Polytheism, pantheism, and monotheism will be discussed below; these are our only theoretical possibilities for finding our true God, as we shall see. Although an emphasis is placed here on the issue of the necessity of a beginning to the universe, many more issues could be addressed in analyzing the various religions, such as other scientific issues, history, logic, internal inconsistencies, false prophecies, etc. Some of these later issues will be briefly touched on (some more than others), but presently the emphasis will be on the necessity of a beginning to the universe and that such requires a pre-existing agent or Creator. Again, if a religion cannot get such a basic issue right, why consider it any further? To use an analogy, if a person does not know the alphabet that person cannot be trusted to write a novel!

Polytheism, Pantheism, or Monotheism?

In searching for God's true identity, we can start at a higher level of logic. The word *theism* literally means "the study of God." A *theist* is a person who believes in God. Typically, however, the terms *theist* and *theism* are used in relation to the belief in one true God, and they will be used primarily that way in subsequent chapters.

The only three possible "general" alternatives where we can find our true God(s) are as follows (terms used: *poly* = many, *pan* = all, and *mono* = one):

- **Polytheism** teaches there are two or more gods.

- **Pantheism** teaches everything is god, and the universe never had a beginning but always was and always will be. It teaches that god is not a being with personality but rather a nonpersonal, omnipresent force manifested in all things: trees, grass, cows, stars, etc. More specifically, pantheism often teaches these things (such as trees) are actually an illusionary manifestation of some sort of omnipresent force (not a person) called god. This force does not love, forgive, or have personality. Here, god is an *it*. Panentheism is similar to pantheism except it does not limit this inanimate god force to the universe. The eastern religions and the New Age Movement are classic examples of pantheism/panentheism, primarily the former.

- **Monotheism** teaches there is only one God for this universe and the heavenly realm. This one God created the universe and has a mind and personality.

Whichever approach is valid, it is clearly evident that the others cannot be true since each approach to who God is (and how a person is saved) contradicts the others. Remember the LNC from the last chapter.

POLYTHEISM VS. PANTHEISM VS. MONOTHEISM

The one true God has to be found within the realms of polytheism, pantheism, or monotheism. Since each of the three clearly contradicts the position of the other two concerning who God is and his primary message, only one of these three areas can be true per the Law of Non-Contra-diction (or just plain logic).

Polytheism?

Any consideration of the many polytheistic religions of the past and present (such as the mythical, mystery, and pagan religions, as well as Greek mythology) shows their contents to be obviously fictional and fanciful, not based in reality and/or history. Here one finds gods/god-desses coming into existence *within* space and time, fighting each other and having petty affairs with other gods' wives (remember the gods of Greece/Rome). One could also find the earth existing on the back of a turtle, gods fighting with their blood forming the seas and their bones forming the land, etc. Therefore, further investigation is simply not warranted. Today the most well-known polytheistic religion is likely Mormonism. The last chapter briefly described its gods and goddesses.

Polytheistic religions, including Mormonism, all basically teach that the universe has always existed. The gods/goddesses of polytheistic religions come into existence within time and space. Aside from their obvious mythical associations, their teaching of an infinitely existing universe (past and future) contradicts known scientific laws as shown earlier in this writing.

> *Based on the scientific evidence of the universe's beginning and eventual end, polytheism should be discounted: (i) since it teaches that the universe has always existed and always will, and (ii) since its gods began within time and space.*

Creation (as we have previously seen) exhibits an order of complex-ity and precision beyond imagination, which certainly did not result from the actions of a variety of different, often competing, pagan gods/goddesses who came into existence at different times and had different agendas; they all came into being *during* the universe's existence and, therefore, could not bring it into existence.

Pantheism?

Pantheism basically teaches that "god" is:

- a nonpersonal, inanimate force or principle that permeates everything, which does not love or care; usually called the "Brahman." The universe and god (force or principle) are typically one and the same, and/or the former is a manifestation (of some sort) of the latter.

- monistic: everything is god, *god is everything*; everything is a manifestation of god, which includes good, evil, stars, plants, cow dung, rape, murder, compassion, etc. For example, this author heard a prominent teacher on eastern mysticism state "the whole Nazi thing" was a negative manifestation of god.

Some teach a "pan<u>en</u>theistic" god where this nonpersonal force is not limited to the universe. For our purposes, the term "pantheism" shall also include "panentheism." Eastern spiritual philosophy is the main source for pantheistic theology, with Hinduism and Buddhism being the two main areas of thought.

Getting into the particulars of eastern spiritual pantheistic teachings can be a real jungle of information of differing opinions/teachings that have also varied over time, and can have self-contradictions and can sometimes be ambiguous. There are differing "spiritual" texts, schools of thought, etc. What one Hindu or Buddhist may believe the other may not in some of the details. They are not monolithic. The information here is a general, valid representation.

In pantheism the universe is eternal and infinite in one form or another; typically the belief is that it *has* gone through, and *will* go through, an infinite number of repetitive "rebirths and deaths" (oscillations). In astronomy we can go back about 13 billion years in our observations, and these observations clearly show one beginning, as do all other scientific findings. An ever-oscillating universe would require infinite energy, which we do not have, as previously shown. It is now known there is not enough matter in the universe to stop it expanding and subsequently contract.

A major view in pantheism is that all of physical reality is merely an illusion or *maya*, which is just not tenable for many obvious reasons. For example, multiple people at different locations experience the same "event" or "condition." This is simply not consistent with the nature of illusions.

A logical analysis of reincarnation/transmigration, a major teaching in pantheism, suffers from a host of logistical problems and internal inconsistencies, which will not be looked at here.

Hinduism comprises a large portion of pantheistic teaching. In *theory* Hinduism is largely (and perhaps 100%) pantheistic; but in *practice* it sometimes mixes in polytheistic views. In various Hindu traditions there is a cumulative total of over 300 million gods/goddesses, often including the three main Hindu gods (Brahma, Vishnu, and Shiva), *each god/goddess having a beginning* of some sort, coming from the eternal Brahman, the universal, inanimate force or principle of reality mentioned above. The goal is to get rid of individuality and to merge into the "oneness" of the Brahman; analogous to like a drop of water (self) into the ocean.

According to some Hindu traditions, Brahma (not to be confused with "Brahman") came from a golden egg (as did this current universe); later teachings claimed Brahma came from a lotus flower from Vishnu's belly button. Various Hindus may worship these so-called gods, and in this sense are polytheistic *in practice. However, since it is largely taught they came from the one universal force (Brahman), Hinduism is ultimately pantheistic.*

In Hinduism there are even some so-called "monotheists." For example, the God Krishna is often claimed to be a (or "the") Supreme God, but he came, had a start, from the Brahman. Krishna is said to be the eighth incarnation of the god Vishnu, and Vishnu is a manifestation of Brahman! *This hardly fits the definition of monotheism* (see next section). Many or all of the few so-called "Supreme Gods" of Hinduism are merely manifestations of the Brahman.

The other major eastern religion, Buddhism, depending on the source consulted, can range from a sort of pantheism, or even panentheism, to an "atheist-like" view. Belief in any "god" or "gods" or "doctrine" is not important; one finds truth in oneself. In some of Buddhism's teachings there are higher-level spiritual entities, but they ultimately are temporary. Buddhism has sometimes been called more "philosophical" rather than "religious." The goal is annihilation of individuality and self.

> *Based on science's findings, the universe had one beginning and will end and is finite; therefore, pantheism (including panentheism) should be discounted from consideration for the reasons discussed above.*

Monotheism

The above leads us to only one logical, viable conclusion: monotheism is the area where we need to limit our search for the true God:

> In light of the fact that the universe had a beginning, only monotheism should be examined in a search for the true God; only monotheism has the candidates for a God Who preceded the universe and created it.

The question is this: "**Who** is the one true God?" The question is not "**Whom** (plurality of gods) are the true gods?" The question is not "**What** (pantheism/panentheism) is the true god?" But our question must be: "**Who** (singular) is the one true God?"

The previous evidence and the above discussion narrow our search for the true God to somewhere within monotheism. Therefore, our discussion is limited to three remaining monotheistic possibilities: Islam, Judaism, or Christianity, the three main monotheistic religions on planet Earth, composing about 99% of all monotheistic possibilities. The succeeding chapters will show which of these choices is right.

Other Considerations?

The reader might ask, "What about some of the smaller, polytheistic/pantheistic religious systems like Scientology (tends toward pantheism) and variants of the New Age movement (mostly pantheistic), etc.?" Further investigation is not warranted since they hold to an eternal, uncreated universe. Further, these systems have other problems, such as grave historical issues, false prophecies, and other aspects. What has been discussed here represents approximately 99% of polytheistic/pantheistic adherents for all intents and purposes.

Of the monotheistic religions, Christianity, Judaism, and Islam make up about 99% of monotheistic-believing people and will be examined in the next chapter. But what about some of the smaller monotheistic religions? Time does not permit going into all the possible details, issues, and lack of evidence regarding such systems (not to mention the evidence *against* them), nor their other problems. No one book, including this one, could cover all possibilities.

However, let us take the Jehovah's Witnesses as an example. This group teaches there is one God yet also teaches that Jesus is a god; to them Jesus is a created being, the archangel "Michael." Therefore, they are against Christ's deity, as well as the Trinity, the physical resurrection of Christ, and salvation through faith alone in Christ (see Chapter 20). Most of their major tenets contradict the major doctrines of the Bible as agreed upon by thousands of scholars over the centuries.

Further, their organization, the Watchtower Society, has many grave historical problems and errors (such as erroneously predicting—*in print*—Armageddon in the name of God twenty-five times) since their beginning in the 1880s. Their own bible, called the New World Translation (NWT), was translated by seven people: at least five of their names have been discovered, and these five did not even know Greek or Hebrew. The NWT was approved by two people (Franz and Knorr), who also did not know Greek or Hebrew. They translated from languages they did not know. No disrespect is intended toward Jehovah's Witnesses, who are generally very sincere, well-meaning people; however, facts are facts.

The point is this: to examine every monotheistic religion that has ever existed would not be of any real value here and would not be practicable.

Conclusion

This writing is not basing the search for the true God only on the scientific evidence, although that has been the primary basis thus far. Of course, there are considerations other than scientific, such as logic, history, non-material realities (as previously discussed), etc.

Again, no disrespect is intended to any adherents of any of the referenced belief systems mentioned, but it is wished to treat this subject objectively with facts. People can be sincere and well-meaning but also wrong. It is also a matter of simple logic that not more than one paradigm of contradictory paradigms can be correct (and all may be incorrect, depending on the subject matter!). Or as Joe Friday in the old TV series *Dragnet* used to say, "Just the facts, ma'am, just the facts."

CHAPTER 11

ONLY TWO POSSIBLE GODS LEFT

The information in the preceding chapter narrowed down our search for the true God. Our possible choices must reside somewhere within polytheism, pantheism, or monotheism as there are no other alternative theologies/possibilities. Further, polytheism, pantheism, and monotheism each contradict the others on the identity of God. Therefore, potentially only one of these ideologies can get it right when it comes to who God is; remember the Law of Non-Contradiction (LNC).

Additionally, the last chapter showed that, due to scientific and other reasons, polytheism and pantheism are not viable choices, leaving only some version of monotheism as being true.

MONOTHEISM'S POSSIBILITIES

Within the realm of monotheism, there are basically two candidates for our true God search. They are:

- Islam's God (Allah)

- The Bible's God (Yahweh or Jehovah) – Christianity argues the biblical God is triune (three persons in one God) in both the Old Testament (OT) and New Testament (NT), while Judaism contends the OT God is totally singular or one God – one person.

Both Allah and Yahweh are claimed to have existed before the universe.

The God of Islam (Allah)

Quite possibly Muhammad (died 632 AD; Islam's founder and Prophet) borrowed from the Bible in the Qur'an's teaching that the universe had a beginning and was created by a divine being; he certainly had exposure to Christians and Jews.

However, for the moment, Islam's Allah will remain in consideration as a possibility for the true God (later we will see why this is not a feasible option). The Qur'an does not specifically teach a cosmology akin to the big bang, but it does teach that Allah created the universe. Therefore, Islam's Allah will remain as a theoretical candidate for consideration up to this point, even though various scientific and historical errors are believed to exist in the Qur'an, which would disqualify it from further consideration, not to mention its doctrinal issues.

Islam's Allah undoubtedly has origins in Arabian paganism (which was polytheistic), but that would entail too much detail to give it adequate treatment here. Of course, many uninformed Muslims would deny such origins, but a number of Muslim scholars and others have presented strong evidence that before Muhammad started teaching Allah was the one true God, pagan Arabian teachings contended Allah was a chief god among other gods. In fact, the supreme god of the Quraish tribe (from which Muhammad came) was Allah. Muhammad's father's name was Abd-Allah, which means "slave of Allah."

Some scholars contend that Allah came from the chief Arabian pagan moon god, who had three daughters. For our purposes here, the moon-god theory will not be analyzed any further. However, it is interesting that the symbol of Islam is the crescent moon with three smaller stars, and Muslims use a lunar calendar. However, again, to facilitate our discussion, we will simply consider Islam a monotheistic religion, regardless of its origins, due to its long-standing teachings (since the seventh century) of one God, Allah.

Judaism vs. Christianity

What about Judaism vs. Christianity? As noted earlier, Judaism says the OT teaches that God is a singular unity or just singular: one person or entity/being (*yachid* in Hebrew for a singular unity). Christianity views the one true God of the OT and NT as a composite unity (*echad* in Hebrew, meaning a composite unity) or in this case "trinity," meaning that the one God is actually three persons (Father, Son [Jesus Christ] and Holy Spirit) in one, wherein each of the three persons is fully the one same true God.

It is interesting to note that the OT's Deuteronomy 6:4 says, *"Hear, O Israel: The LORD our God, the LORD is one,"* using the Hebrew word *echad* for a composite unity. More on this in the chapter on the Trinity.

The Bible (Old and New Testaments) is abundantly clear that there is only one true God. In this treatise we will refer to him as the God of the Bible or the Bible's God. Whether he is triune or not will be discussed in the chapter on the Trinity.

Our immediate discussion will concentrate on the God of Islam (Allah) vs. the God of the Bible (Yahweh or Jehovah), wherein both are taught to have eternally existed in the past and where both are said to have created the universe.

CHAPTER 12

DO THE BIBLE AND QUR'AN TEACH THE SAME GOD?

Before looking at other considerations in searching for the one true God, a basic question needs to be addressed: Could the God of the Bible also be the God of the Qur'an, though referenced by different names?

Response 1: The answer is easy if one assumes the Bible's God is (i) the triune God of Christianity (the one true God who manifests himself in three distinct personages [Father, Son, Holy Spirit], each one being equally and fully the one true God, and (ii) this one God took on human flesh as Jesus Christ to die for the sins of the world. The answer is also easy if one considers Christianity's salvation through faith in who Jesus Christ is (God), in his blood atonement (death) for man's sins on the cross, and his subsequent physical resurrection from the dead.

Islam vehemently denies the Trinity, denies God had a son, denies Jesus Christ is God (or the Son of God, a term of deity), denies Jesus Christ died on the cross and physically rose three days later, and also denies salvation through faith in Jesus Christ.

Bottom line: If Christianity's God is correct, Islam's God cannot be correct...or vice versa. Both cannot be true since they contradict one another on fundamental issues of who God is and how one experiences eternal life, etc.

Response 2: This response assumes, for the moment, orthodox Judaism's perspective: the one true God of the Bible is not triune, and he did not come as Jesus Christ, and that salvation is by works (human effort). Orthodox Judaism and Islam are very similar on God's nature, meaning both teach God is not triune but is only a singular unity (one person, one God). *However, the message of Judaism's God is vastly different from the message of Islam.* What is required for salvation in one is vastly different and contradictory from the other. Therefore, Judaism's message and Islam's message cannot be from the same divine source. God would not contradict himself. Also, the character of Judaism's God is vastly different from that of Islam's Allah, while the character (behavior, ethics, morals, etc.) of Christianity's God is the same as Judaism's, except for the critical issues of the Trinity and Jesus's deity.

Salvation in both orthodox Judaism and Islam is by works, by trying to be good enough, although they differ on what those works or deeds must be. Thus, the one God could not be the source for both.

Other differences between the Bible and the Qur'an also help illustrate that these are two separate sources of information. In the Bible, the garden of Eden is on earth, with its location given in the Middle East. In the Qur'an, the garden of Eden is not on earth. In the Bible, Abraham lived about 2,000 years before Christ and Mary, the earthly mother of Christ. However, in the Qur'an Mary was living at the same time as Abraham. The list could go on, but the point is obvious—the Bible and the Qur'an are two different, contradictory sources of information. Therefore, the God of the Bible (triune or not) cannot also be the God of Islam.

CHAPTER 13

SCIENTIFIC EVIDENCE

Just as scientific considerations can be used in determining that a Creator God exists, such considerations can also be employed to help determine the specific identity of God.

As noted earlier, the contents of this chapter could have easily been placed under "Section I: God's Existence," since the scientific information herein could also be used to help show God's existence.

Of all the major religions, *only* the Bible teaches all the basics of big bang cosmology: (i) everything (space, matter, energy, and time) had a beginning; (ii) the universe's subsequent expansion; and (iii) the aging/death of the universe. In fact, the Bible taught such thousands of years ago, long before the findings of more modern science.

Thus, from the perspective of the above cosmological proof, it can be argued that the Bible clearly shows the most evidence of divine inspiration since such knowledge was not known by any human source at the time it was written. Therefore, this points to the God of the Bible as being the true God we seek.

A Muslim might argue that the Qur'an teaches its God, Allah, created the universe, and therefore he existed before it (Surah 7:54). He might also argue that the Qur'an states that the universe is expanding: "And the heaven, We built it with craftsmanship and We are still expanding" (Surah 51:47). Who the "We" is referring to is difficult to ascertain, and "are still expanding" seems to refer to a "who" and not a "what" (universe) in this context, so the Qur'an only clearly teaches Allah created the universe.

As mentioned before, it could be argued that Muhammad borrowed from the earlier-written text of the Bible that states God preceded and created the universe. The book of Genesis was written sometime during the period of 1446-1406 BC, and some scholars maintain the book of Job was composed before that, perhaps during the patriarchal period.

The Qur'an also mentions Abraham, Mary, and others but contains at least one blatant historical error in reference to them, having Abraham and Mary living at the same time in history (Abraham actually lived about 2,000 years before Mary). The Qur'an has the flood ending just before Abraham shows up, which has so many problems we won't get into that one, except to ask how the world could have had a population of millions, part of which was including the fully mature Egyptian empire, if the flood had just ended with only eight survivors.

More Scientific Evidence

So far we have concentrated on the biblical verses in relation to the big bang (e.g., Genesis 1:1, Titus 2:9, I Timothy 1:9, etc.). Now we need to examine additional amazing "scientific-related" information in the Bible, such as in the remainder of Genesis 1 (i.e., Genesis 1:2 – 1:27).

Genesis chapter one accurately gives ten events and three conditions the earth went through, all in their proper order. Only in the twentieth century did modern science finally come to agree with this information. Genesis was written between 1446-1406 BC (the time of the Exodus). No other religious text, including the Qur'an, contains such information – nowhere close.

The above-referenced ten events and additional three conditions are discussed in detail later in this chapter. However, for now, the referenced three conditions refer to the three phases the earth's atmosphere went through from the point of view (POV) of earth's surface:

- opaque (light cannot penetrate - Genesis 1:2)
- translucent (light can get through, but the heavenly bodies cannot be seen - Genesis 1:3; like a cloudy day), and
- transparent or clear (Genesis 1:14-21).

Further, when any details of the subject matter of creation are brought up in other religious texts, the information presented is often highly fanciful and clearly in contradiction to sound, solid facts of nature. This further strengthens the case for the Bible's God being the true God (Moses, the writer of Genesis, could not have obtained such astounding information from any earthly sources because the latter were teaching scientific nonsense at the time). Therefore, the source for the information in Genesis had to be a divine one and from the God of the Bible. By the way, it definitely would not have come from so-called space aliens trying to delude the entire human race!

Astrophysicist Dr. Hugh Ross was raised an atheist. Because of the big bang, he had to concede the existence of some type of God. At one point in his life, he considered putting God to the test. He reasoned that if God were the source of any of the main religious books of the world, those texts would not contain any fundamental scientific errors in them.

After going through all the major religious texts (except the Bible), he found major scientific errors in all of them. Lastly, he examined the Bible. Expecting to find errors there too, he began by reading Genesis chapter one, and what he read astounded him. To his amazement, the ten events in Genesis one, plus the three conditions the earth went through, and the sequence of those events and conditions were all correct. As we will see, it took modern science until the twentieth century to come to agree with the Bible's ancient statements. Dr. Ross chronicles his findings in a book entitled *Navigating Genesis,* as well as in other writings. Dr. Hugh Ross is the president of the Christian think tank *Reasons to Believe* (see *https: www.reasons.org*).

Someone may say at this point, "But wait a minute. What about those 24-hour days in Genesis one? Modern science certainly contradicts that." For the answer to this question, refer to the next subsection: "Are There Scientific Errors in the Bible?"

Peter W. Stoner, chairman of Mathematics and Astronomy at Pasadena City College and Robert C. Newman, STM, PhD. in astrophysics, co-authored a book entitled *Science Speaks*. They estimated the odds of Moses's guessing all the details and the sequence of events given in Genesis one as 1 chance in 31,135,104,000,000,000,000,000 (*Science Speaks*, chapter 1; book is no longer in print, but is available online at sciencespeaks.dstoner.net).

Peter Stoner adds: "This is an extremely small chance. Let us try to visualize it. Suppose we decide to have a drawing and have this number of tickets printed. In order to get them printed, let us engage more than 8,000,000 presses, each capable of printing 2,000 tickets per minute. And then they would have to run day and night for 5,000,000 years to print this number of tickets. Now let one ticket be marked and the whole mass thoroughly stirred. Then we will blindfold you and let you draw one ticket. Will you get the right one? Your chance is better than Moses' chance would have been of writing this one chapter from the information known in his day" (*Ibid*).

In other words, one could rightly say it would take more faith to believe in a series of random guesses than to believe the information of Genesis one came from a divine being.

Note the following endorsement of the above-referenced book, *Science Speaks*:

> The manuscript for *Science Speaks* has been carefully reviewed by a committee of the American Scientific Affiliation members and by the executive council of the same group and has been found, in general, to be dependable and accurate in regard to the scientific material presented. The mathematical analysis included is based upon

principles of probability which are thoroughly sound, and Professor Stoner has applied these principles in a proper and convincing way.

American Scientific Affiliation
H. HAROLD HARTZLER, PhD
Secretary-Treasurer
Goshen College, Ind.

Now let us proceed to the events, earth's conditions, and their sequence to show that the information contained in Genesis chapter one had to be from God. Again, Moses surely did not glean this information from any human sources of the time since they were teaching scientific nonsense.

Preceding Day 1: *Genesis 1:1-2 - ¹In the beginning God created the heavens and the earth. ²Now the earth was formless and empty, darkness was over the surface of the deep, and the Spirit of God was hovering over the waters.*

BIBLE/SCIENCE COMMENTS: The Hebrew word for create used here is *bara*, which can mean "to create out of nothing, or to create something which did not exist before." This fits perfectly with the big bang, as discussed previously in this book. The expression "heavens and the earth" in the Hebrew is *hashamayin we ha erets*, which means the entirety of the cosmos (everything in it – galaxies, stars, our sun, planets, moons, etc., with *erets* referring to the earth). The Hebrew language when Genesis was penned did not have a singular word for the "universe" or "cosmos."

People often miss the importance of the point-of-view (POV) of the writer/narrator of Genesis one. In Genesis 1:1 *("In the beginning God created the heavens and the earth")*, the POV is a heavenly one, looking at the universe, including the earth, as a whole; in other words, the POV is from outside the created realm (from the heavenly realm) as a whole.

In Genesis 1:2 something critical occurs: the POV changes to the surface of the earth: *"Now the earth was formless and empty, darkness was over the surface of the deep."* The POV is now from earth's surface and remains there for the rest of the chapter. *"The surface of the deep"* is referring to earth's surface waters. This POV is further reinforced by Genesis 1:2, where it says *"And the Spirit of God was hovering over the waters."* Again, the POV remains the same for the rest of Genesis one. As we shall see, this is critical in the proper interpretation of the events of Day 4 (Genesis 1:20-21).

At this point in Genesis 1:2, the earth was enveloped with a thick cloud layer like Venus, plus dust and debris from the newly created earth and solar system. The earth was eventually totally covered in water. Light could not penetrate the opaque atmosphere, leaving the surface so dark the POV from the surface would show no forms and it appeared void. The term *void* can also refer to lack of organization.

Day 1: *Genesis 1:3-5 - ³And God said, "Let there be light," and there was light. ⁴God saw that the light was good, and he separated the light from the darkness. ⁵God called the light "day," and the darkness he called "night." And there was evening, and there was morning – the first day.*

SCIENCE COMMENT: Science concurs. From the POV of the surface of the earth, light finally appears. Science has determined that this is when the previous opaque atmosphere (of Genesis 1:2) has thinned out enough to allow light to penetrate to the surface (it is now translucent, like a cloudy day), but the heavenly bodies cannot yet be seen.

Day 2: *Genesis 1:6-8 - ⁶And God said, "Let there be a vault between the waters to separate water from water." ⁷So God made the vault and separated the water under the vault from the water above it. And it was so. ⁸God called the vault "sky." And there was evening, and there was morning – the second day.*

SCIENCE COMMENT: Science concurs. This is the event where the water vapor in the atmosphere was separated from the water in the oceans; i.e., air or sky appeared between the two.

Day 3: *Genesis 1:9-11, 13 – ⁹And God said, "Let the water under the sky be gathered to one place, and let dry ground appear." And it was so. ¹⁰God*

called the dry ground "land," and the gathered waters he called "seas."...
[11]*Then God said, "Let the land produce vegetation...*[13]*And there was evening, and there was morning–the third day.*

BIBLE/SCIENCE COMMENTS: Science concurs. The main growth in land mass occurred about 2.5–1.5 bya. The Hebrew word for vegetation, *ets,* could include just about anything of a plant-type nature, including the very primitive plants. Evidently, the latter is being referred to at this point in Genesis. Early plant spores dating 1.2 bya have been found on land.

Day 4: *Genesis 1:14-19 -* [14]*And God said, "Let there be lights in the vault of the sky to separate the day from the night...* [15]*and let them be lights in the vault of the sky to give light on the earth." And it was so.* [16] *God made two great lights—the greater light to govern the day and the lesser light to govern the night. He also made the stars.* [17] *God set them in the vault of the sky to give light on the earth,* [18] *to govern the day and the night, and to separate light from darkness. And God saw that it was good.* [19] *And there was evening, and there was morning—the fourth day.*

BIBLE COMMENT: Remember that based on Genesis 1:2, the POV of the narrator is from the surface of the earth, not from somewhere in outer space.

God did not create the lights (sun, moon, stars) on Day 4, but actually created them on Day 1, as discussed. The lights only became visible ("let there be lights") on Day 4 *from the POV of earth's surface.* Notice these lights were/are to give light to the earth's surface and to separate day and night—such first occurred on Day 1, but only now have they become visible from the earth's surface. Verses 16 and 17 say, *God made two great lights—the greater light to govern the day and the lesser light to govern the night. He also made the stars.* The Hebrew word for "made" is *asah,* which is in the past tense (sort of like "had made"). When was that? Day 1.

SCIENCE COMMENT: Science concurs. We now know earth's atmosphere changed at this time from a translucent one (like a cloudy day) to enough of a transparent or clear one that from the earth's surface one could see the sun, moon, and stars. This is significant since many of the animals created on Day 5 would need to *see* the sun, moon, and stars to regulate their biological clocks, migration, etc.

Day 5: *Genesis 1:20-21, 23 -* [20]*And God said, "Let the water teem with living creatures, and let birds fly above the earth across the vault of the sky."* [21]*So God created the great creatures of the sea and everything which the water teams and moves about in it, according to their kinds, and every winged bird according to its kind....* [23]*And there was evening, and there was morning– the fifth day."*

BIBLE COMMENT: The emphasis here is on ocean life and the birds; both are very relevant (food, etc.) to everyday life. During this period, dinosaurs, insects, and earlier mammals were created. They are not mentioned here since they are not relevant to the main intention of Genesis, specifically the information about the main types of animals people experience and are of most importance to humans. We can be sure Moses knew about insects…remember the ten plagues of Egypt? Also, to mention dinosaurs would have served no purpose here since man has only known about their existence since about the mid-nineteenth century.

SCIENCE COMMENT: Science concurs. This fifth "day" undoubtedly emphasizes, in part, the Cambrian Explosion of about 539–542 million years ago, and subsequently Day 5 proceeds down to about 50 mya (creation of whales). As noted earlier in this book, the Cambrian Explosion is a period when complex ocean life suddenly burst on the scene out of nowhere; up to about 85% of all animal phyla first appeared at this time. Birds first appeared at about 150 mya.

Day 6: *Genesis 1:24-31 -* [24]*And God said, "Let the land produce living creatures according to their kinds: the livestock, the creatures that move along the ground, and the wild animals, each according to its kind." And it was so.* [25]*God made the wild animals according to their kinds, the livestock* *according to their kinds, and all the creatures that move along the ground according to their kinds. And God saw that it was good.* [26]*Then God said, "Let us make mankind in our image…*[27]*So God created mankind in his own image, in the image of God he created them; male and female he created them….*[31]*And there was evening, and there was morning–the sixth day.*

SCIENCE COMMENT: The animals referred to here are three types of mammals that did appear in the fossil record *after* the whales and birds of Day 5 (other types of land mammals appeared before the whales during the time of Day 5 but were not the topic of concern by Moses for that "day"). The three types of mammals mentioned here are those most important to humanity. The reference to creatures that crawl upon the ground refers to a type of mammal, not insects, etc., since the Hebrew word for creatures at the beginning of verse 24 is "nephesh," which typically refers to birds and mammals.

What About Scientific Errors in the Bible?

The reader may be saying, "Okay, the Bible gets the basics of big bang cosmology correct, and it is the only religious text to do so, and it's really hard to explain the other information in Genesis 1 without the revelation of God. However, what about the scientific errors in the Bible?"

This is a valid question with some very good answers. First, there are no demonstrable scientific errors in the Bible. Considering the size and scope of this writing, we cannot address each of the alleged errors, which are not many to begin with. Many other books, by scientists and others, have been written to provide satisfying explanations to show the Bible is without error, scientifically or otherwise. Further sources are listed in the bibliographies and Recommended References sections of this book. Three examples will be referenced here for illustrative purposes.

First Example: Does Genesis teach that God created the cosmos/earth, including man, in six 24-hr. days?

An excellent book on this subject is *A Matter of Days,* written by astrophysicist Dr. Hugh Ross. It presents a thorough analysis of the biblical position of the "days" of Genesis, and of the scientific findings supporting a multi-billion-year-old universe (currently estimated at about 13.8 billion years). The book fully addresses arguments for a 24-hr. interpretation of the "days" in Genesis, showing such a position to be biblically erroneous, and demonstrates how the Bible supports an "old" universe rather than one of several thousand (6-10,000) years.

In short, regarding the days of Genesis listed in chapters 1–2, the Hebrew word for "day" is *yom.* At the time of the writing of Genesis the Hebrew word *yom* had four literal definitions: 24 hrs., 12 hrs., daylight, and a longer period of time (such as an era, eon, or epic). Checking any Hebrew dictionary concerning that timeframe will confirm this. Context dictates which of the four literal definitions applies. Also at that time, Hebrew had only one word for "era, eon, or epic," and the word was, you guessed it, *yom.*

Without getting into all the biblical details of Genesis 1–2, the context clearly shows *yom* (or day) refers here to a long period of time. Just four issues will be given here:

A. On Day 3 early vegetation is created (Genesis 1:11). However, subsequently in Day 3, Genesis 1:12 talks about the vegetation bearing or growing seeds and fruit, which takes longer than one day; no hint other than natural growth processes are in play.

B. On Day 6 all of the following takes place:
- God creates three types of mammals
- God creates Adam
- God plants a garden (garden of Eden)
- God puts Adam into the garden
- Adam takes care of the garden

- God has Adam name all the animals (at least the birds and mammals),

- Adam is lonely and wants a mate, and then

- God creates Eve, with Adam expressing in the Hebrew "at long last" (paraphrase of the Hebrew) when he sees her.

- *Do the above sound like they occurred within one 24-hour period? Hardly.* Note that God could have created the universe in a few minutes if he had so wished. Rather, the issue is: what does the evidence and text say?

C. *Genesis 2:4* (KJV) states: *These are the generations* [*toledoth* in Hebrew] *of the heavens and of the earth when they were created, in the day* [*yom* in Hebrew] *that the Lord God made the earth and the heavens.* Notice here that *yom* refers to the six days of Genesis 1.

D. According to the Bible, God is still in his seventh day of rest (he is not creating, which ended on Day 6) – the seventh day started just after the creation of Adam and Eve. We are still in the Bible's seventh day, which by anyone's figuring is a long period of time and not 24 hours. Refer to Dr. Ross's book *Navigating Genesis* for further details or go to the *Reasons to Believe* website: www.reasons.org.

Second Example: Doesn't Genesis teach that the sun, moon, and stars were created on Day 4 since Genesis 1:20 says, "…let them [sun, moon, stars] appear"?

Although previously mentioned, the information on point of view below bears repeating.

People often miss the importance of the point of view (POV) of the writer/narrator of Genesis 1. As stated before, in Genesis 1:1 ("*In the beginning God created the heavens and the earth*") the POV is a heavenly one, looking at the universe as a whole, including the earth; in other words, the POV is from outside the cosmos, including the earth (POV is from the heavenly realm).

Then in Genesis 1:2 something very critical occurs: the POV changes to the surface of the earth: *Now the earth was formless and empty, darkness was over the surface of the deep.* The POV is now from earth's surface and remains there for the rest of the chapter. *The surface of the deep* is referring to earth's surface waters. This POV is further reinforced by the second part of the verse, where it says, *And the Spirit of God was hovering over the waters.* Again, the POV remains the same for the rest of Genesis 1. This is critical in the proper interpretation of the events of Day 4 (Genesis 1:20-21).

Notice Genesis 1:14-19 (Day 4) does not say God created the sun, moon, and the stars but only that they "appeared." Further, it states that God had made (*asah*, Hebrew past tense) the sun, moon, and stars. When was that? The answer is found in Genesis 1:1; they were created before Day 1.

From the POV of earth's surface, the sun, moon, and stars were first made to appear on Day 4 of Genesis 1. This is scientifically correct, as shown previously, since at this stage in earth's development the atmosphere changed from being translucent (like a cloudy day) to at least a partially clear one.

From the POV of the surface the sun, moon, and stars could be seen for the first time on Day 4. Plus, Genesis 1:1 is very clear that the sun, moon, and stars were actually created at the beginning (before the first day), and they existed on Day 1 (in Genesis 1:3 there was day and night on earth [which we know to be a round sphere], thus meaning the light [the sun] had to be coming from a central point). Back in Genesis 1:1 the Bible says God created the heavens and the earth, which in Hebrew means the entire universe – everything including the sun, moon, and stars. The expression in Hebrew is *hashamayin we ha erets.*

Third example: Doesn't Day 6 of Genesis have it wrong by having the mammals created after the whales of Day 5?

The fossil record shows some land mammals were created before the whales of about 50 million years ago. However, the three types of mammals indicated in Genesis on Day 6 did indeed first appear *after* the whales. These are the type of mammals most important to humans for food, agriculture, etc., and therefore specifically referenced by Moses.

The above three examples illustrate some of the many things people say about the Bible that are not true. Always check what you have been told, using good research and facts.

In summary, only the Bible has been shown to stand up to the test of science. Yes, some claims in the Bible cannot be tested scientifically, such as the virgin birth (a virgin birth miracle would be no big feat for God who created the universe), but those things that can be checked out have passed the test. This cannot be said of other religious books.

The Qur'an and Science

The Qur'an states Allah created the universe and therefore existed before it.

On the point of Allah creating the universe, the Bible said God created the universe over 2,000 years before the Qur'an said it. Therefore, it is quite possible Mohammed borrowed these ideas from the Bible since he had access to the Bible's teachings/statements; ultimately, one cannot say for certain that such borrowing took place.

The author has read pro-Islamic literature on the supposedly scientific statements in the Qur'an, few as they are. Some Muslims claim such statements show that the Qur'an is divinely inspired, contending that such knowledge did not exist from secular sources at the time they were written in the seventh century.

In reading the above Islamic claims, I believe any careful, objective examination would come to the following conclusion: they show no scientific knowledge outside of humanity's knowledge at the time they were written in the seventh century; also, they show no particularly keen scientific insights.

Since the main focus of this book does not include an extensive review of the claimed scientific-related Islamic passages, they will not be examined here in any detail. However, the reader is encouraged to objectively check them out for themselves.

One must be careful in the discussion of any errors in the Qur'an.

A lot of information on the topic of science and the Qur'an being supposedly at odds is readily available. However, in some of the cases, the Qur'an may intend for the descriptions to be only metaphorical in nature, not literal. I have attempted to avoid the opportunity for such criticisms here, with no desire to misrepresent the Qur'an's intended meaning on any subject.

Are there scientific errors in the Qur'an? Consider the following quotes from the Qur'an (a few examples of the total that could be listed; boldfacing is this author's emphasis):

- Errors on human reproduction/fetus development:

  » He [man] was created from a fluid, ejected, Emerging from between the backbone and the ribs. (Qur'an 86:6-7).

  » Narrated by 'Abdullah bin Mus'ud: "Allah's Apostle, the true and truly inspired, said, '(The matter of the Creation of) a human being is put together in the womb of the mother in forty days, and then he becomes a clot of thick blood for a similar period, and then a piece of flesh for a similar period. Then Allah sends an angel who is ordered to write four things. He is ordered to write down his (i.e. the new creature's) deeds, his livelihood, his (date of) death, and whether he will be blessed or wretched (in religion). Then the soul is breathed into him.'" (Sahih Bukhari 4:54:430).

  » When We made the sperm into a clot of congealed blood; **then** of that clot We made a (fetus) lump; **then** we made out of that lump bones, then [not *and*] clothed the bones with flesh; **then** we developed out of it another creature. So blessed be Allah, the best to create! (Qur'an 23:14)

  » "Was he [man] not a drop of fluid which gushed forth? **Then** he became a clot; **then** (Allah) shaped and fashioned and made of him a pair, the male and female." (Qur'an 75:37-39).

COMMENTS: The male semen is located in the testicles between a man's legs, NOT between the backbone and ribs. Also, at no point during a fetus's development is there anything anywhere like a stage of congealed blood or a clot. Lastly, the sex of the fetus is determined from the very beginning, not sometime later as the fetus has either "XX" (male) or "XY" (female) chromosomes at the beginning.

- Cosmos-Related:

  » "The hour drew nigh and the moon did rend asunder" (Qur'an 54:1-3).

  » Narrated Anas: "That the Meccan people requested Allah's Apostle to show them a miracle, and so he showed them the splitting of the moon." (Sahih Bukhari 4:56:831; also see *4:830-832; 5:208-211; 6:387-390*)

  » "We have adorned the lowest heaven with lamps and We have made them [the lamps] a means of bombardment on the devils" (Qur'an 67:05).

  COMMENTS: In theory, an almighty Creator could split the moon or any planet or star if he wished to do so. However, there is no evidence of this happening and no recording of such an incredible event by any other culture. And obviously, heavenly bodies are not used, even in part, as a means of bombardment of devils.

- Concerning earth's mountains:

  » "And He has set up on the earth mountains standing firm, lest it [the earth] should shake with you; and rivers and roads; that ye may guide yourselves" (Qur'an 16:15)

  COMMENTS: Mountains are formed by colliding tectonic plates (which causes shaking), and in no way,

shape, or form do they (the mountains) help the earth
not to shake.

Conclusion

Compared to any other religious texts, the Bible wins when it comes
to scientific accuracy and scientifically-related information that could
not have come from human sources at the time the text was written.

Further, there are demonstratable scientific errors in the Qur'an
and *not* in the Bible. Although not discussed, other religious texts contain real problems when it comes to science. For example, in Buddhism
the universe oscillates every 4.2 billion years (expands/contracts). All
the scientific and photo evidence soundly contradicts that statement.

But we now shift the emphasis primarily to the God of the Bible vs.
the God of the Qur'an. In conclusion, the scientifically-related information of religious texts strongly points to the God of the Bible as the
true God.

CHAPTER 14

PROPHETIC EVIDENCE

Isaiah 44:7 – *Who then is like me [God]? Let him proclaim it. Let him declare and lay out before me what has happened... and what is yet to come – yes, let them foretell what will come.*

The issue of prophetic accuracy can help determine who the true God is. Since the prophetic information in this chapter could also be used to help prove God's existence, as only God has the ability to be 100% accurate in prophetic announcements, the contents of this chapter could have easily been placed as one of the chapters in "Section I: God's Existence."

Time is something that is part of the fabric of our universe, not separate from it. If the universe were to be destroyed, our one dimension of time would also be destroyed. Einstein's theory of relativity and its implications show this to be true.

Our universe (our space-time continuum) is limited to one dimension of time plus three physical dimensions – height, width, and depth. Man cannot reach outside the space-time continuum of this universe. Therefore, man cannot have access to more than one dimension of time. In our one dimension of time, events only occur in sequence: event A, then event B, and so on.

In order to foretell the future, one would have to have the ability to access at least two dimensions of time, which is impossible in our universe. The only alternative is for an individual to have access to Someone who *is* outside of time and therefore can see any point in time at any given time.

Consequently, if it can be shown that a particular religious system is capable of 100% accuracy in predicting the future and all other religious systems have not shown this ability, the one true God must be the God of that religious system. Clearly, man does not have the ability to foretell the future.

Over the millennia, many people have claimed to foreknow the future. However, upon closer examination, we find they really do not. Either their so-called prophecies are so general one could drive a Mac truck through them, or they were written after the event they supposedly prophesied, or they proved to be wrong. These problems apply to psychics such as Jean Dixon, Nostradamus, etc.

However, in the Bible the test for a prophet of the true God was that a person had to be 100% accurate 100% of the time. If he spoke a prophecy in the name of the God of the Bible and it did not come true the penalty would be quite severe. It should also be mentioned that such false prophets typically promoted false gods: a grievous error. How many psychics today or in the past would survive the 100% test rule? Answer: *None.* However, all the Bible's prophets survived the test. In Deuteronomy 18:22 the Bible states,

> *If what a prophet proclaims in the name of the* LORD *does not take place or come true, that is a message the* LORD *has not spoken. That prophet has spoken presumptuously, so do not be alarmed.*

The God of the Bible also uses prophecy as a means of challenging false gods:

> Isaiah 42:8-9 – [8]*I am the* LORD; *that is my name! I will not yield my glory to another or my praise to idols.* [9]*See, the former things have taken place, and new things I declare; before they spring into being I announce them to you.*

Isaiah 41:22-23 – [22] *Tell us, you idols, what is going to happen. Tell us what the former things were, so that we may consider them and know their final outcome. Or declare to us the things to come,* [23] *tell us what the future holds, so we may know that you are gods.*

Isaiah 46:10 – *I* [God] *make known the end from the beginning, from ancient times, what is still to come.*

John 13:19 – *I* [God] *am telling you now before it happens, so that when it does happen you will believe that I am who I am.*

Only the Bible's God makes such claims and challenges. This writer (for whatever that is worth) and other scholars are not aware of any such claims and challenges in any other religious system or book; indeed, something to consider.

To handle this subject objectively, and factually, only "*fulfilled prophecies*" (FPs) will be used. In this treatise, for a prophecy to be called a "fulfilled prophecy," it has to meet the following criteria:

- BEFORE: it can be shown it was written BEFORE the predicted event;

- AFTER: can be shown from history the predicted event occurred *after* the written date of the predictive prophecy;

- DETAIL: must have a good level of detail in what it says; vague generalities are not allowed;

- FUTURE: prophecies concerning events still in *our* future (as of the 2020s) cannot be considered, since they could not yet have been fulfilled;

- SELF-FULFILLMENT: the prophecy is outside the power of the prophet's ability to manipulate history so it fulfills his prophecy.

Where Should We Begin?

What major religions of the world have prophecies written in their scriptures? Many do not even attempt it, and for good reason: only the true God can accurately predict future events. Actual FPs (*fulfilled prophecies* per our definition) are really only found in the Bible.

Remember, each of the major religions contradict each other on who God is and what he is saying to the world. At best, only one of them can be true. The last chapter on scientific evidence showed the God of the Bible is the strong choice so far.

Although Mormonism is not a major world religion, its founder Joseph Smith issued about 55 false prophecies. A check on the internet can provide multiple good sources for the details, such as:

- Dick Bear and Jim Robertson. *False Prophecies of Joseph Smith*; see E-Link Bibliography

- J. Warner Wallace, *Cold-Case Christianity*; see *E-Link Bibliography*

- Plus many more.

Over the years (since the 1880s), the Watchtower Society of the Jehovah's Witnesses has predicted Armageddon about 25 times in print—obviously, all of them false. Refer to a good article by well-known Dr. John Weldon concerning the false prophecies of the Jehovah's Witnesses, entitled "False Prophecy in the Watchtower Society"; see E-Link Bibliography. The internet can provide numerous viable sources detailing these false prophecies. Also, refer to the Recommended References at the end of this book.

Of the major religions in the world, only one stands out as having FPs: the Bible. We will look at the proofs of this later, as well as Qur'anic/Islamic attempts at prophecy and how they compare to those in the Bible.

Islam's Qur'an

The number of claimed prophecies in the Qur'an is about 22. This number comes from Q.I. Hingora in *The Prophecies of the Holy Qur'an* and concurs with the number generally stated among Qur'anic scholars. They are found in the Qur'an as follows (a "Surah" is a chapter in the Qur'an):

- Surah 2:23-24; 3:10, 106, 107, 144; 5:70;
- Surah 8:7; 9:14; 15:9, 96; 24:55; 28:85;
- Surah 30:2-3; 41:42; 48:16-21, 27, 28;
- Surah 54:44-48; 56:1-56, and 110:1-2.

Some Muslims claim that the Qur'an in the above passages makes prophetic statements that have been fulfilled (FPs). Since this writing is not on the subject of Qur'anic prophecy, this treatment will be brief.

Most of the 22 claimed prophecies in the Qur'an concern the still future events of man (the antichrist, final judgment, etc.). Therefore, they cannot be claimed to be FPs; they do not fit the earlier definition of "*fulfilled prophecies.*" These future-state prophecies are found in: Surah 2:23-24; Surah 3:10, 106, 107, 144; Surah 8:7, Surah 9:14; Surah 28:85, Surah 48:16-21, 27, 28; and Surah 56:1-56.

This leaves us with the remaining eight passages: Surah 5:70; 15:9, 96; 24:55; 30:2-4; 41:42; 54:44-48; 110:1-2. They are as follows:

- Sura 5:70 – not one future tense verb used; it is in the past tense. Hence, not an FP.

- Sura 15:9 – this is only a promise to safeguard the Islamic message. Not an FP, it is also too general.

- Surah 15:96 – only a warning against adopting another god besides Allah. Not an FP.

- Surah 24:55 – only says Allah promises to bless those who believe, establishing the authority of their religion and giving them security and peace. This is so general and vague, it cannot be considered a fulfilled prophecy.

- Surah 41:42 – only promises that no falsehood will be in the Islamic message. Not an FP.

- Surah 54:44-48 – a threatened militant action by one group toward a group of unbelievers (possibly people of Quraish). This is not a prediction from Allah, but a threat by a group of people against another. Therefore, this is not an FP.

- Surah 110:1-2 – only promises help and victory from Allah. It is too general, as it does not name specific people or nations or time frames. Therefore, this is not an FP.

Lastly, this leaves only one Qur'anic possibility of a fulfilled prophecy in Surah 30:2-3. It reads,

> The Roman Empire has been defeated in a land close by: but they, (even) after (this) defeat of theirs, will soon be victorious within a few years.

The first part is past tense. So, the only future event predicted is that the Roman Empire (Byzantine Romans) would be victorious in a military battle within a few years. This is like predicting the Dallas Cowboys will win a football game in the next few years. The Romans were fighting several battles each year.

Second, this entire passage could have been written after the Roman victory. Muhammad was alive and still producing Qur'anic verses several years after the time of the Roman defeat, and quite possibly after the Roman victory as well. Thus, the time of writing cannot be determined. One historical account mentions a Roman victory in 624 AD; Mohammed would have had eight years to learn of that victory and pen the words in these verses. This does not fulfill the requirements of an FP.

In addition to the above references, a few Muslims sometimes reference Surah 4:120; 10:92; 16:8; 17:4-10; 17:105; 22:26-27; 30:42,; 41:21; 42:30; 54:1; 55:20, 21; 25:54; 81:2, 3, 4, 5, 6; 81:8- 111. However, none of these come close to meeting the requirements of an FP. The reader is encouraged to check them out online to verify they are not true FPs.

In summary, the Qur'an has no provable FPs. The suggested verses are not even close. This leaves only the Bible for consideration.

The Bible

Sixty-two of the 66 books of the Bible contain prophetic material. Of the 31,124 total verses, 8,352 are prophetic, which is 27% of the Bible. All of these prophetic passages total 1,817 total predictions with 737 separate matters predicted (John Weldon, "False Prophecy in the Watchtower Society," *John Ankerberg Show*, Sept. 2005; see E-Link Bibliography).

How many of the 1,817 total predictions fit the required definition for fulfilled prophecies (FPs)? Just like the Qur'an, the Bible has some prophecies concerning the future (the antichrist, the Second Coming of Christ, etc.); they cannot yet be claimed to be FPs. Also, like the Qur'an, the Bible does have some prophecies that are too general in nature (like "lawlessness shall increase" in the end times) to serve as an FP for our purposes here. Also, for now, we will not consider any New Testament (NT) passages indicating Old Testament (OT) prophecy fulfillment (unless verified by secular history), as the skeptic might contend, erroneously I might add, that we do not know if the NT is valid.

Using our definition, the exact number of FPs in the Bible will not be determined here. Jesus Christ alone fulfilled over 300 prophecies by his first coming, many of which would be considered FPs, if one trusts in the NT statements of their fulfillment (such as the Messiah was betrayed for 30 pieces of silver [Matthew 26:15] per the Old Testament prophecy in Zechariah 11:12-13).

The Bible clearly proclaims Jesus to be God, who took on human flesh; but if one were to assume he was merely a human being, most of the above-referenced 300 prophecies would be out of Jesus's control to self-fulfill (such as his genealogy, his place of birth, and many more).

If one does not consider any of the OT prophecies fulfilled in the NT (many of them through Jesus Christ), then we are limited to OT prophecy fulfillment via known secular, historical facts *outside* the Bible.

The FPs in the Bible are too numerous to discuss in this book. However, a few will be sampled here to prove the Bible does indeed contain FPs per secular history. Our discussion will deal with two areas:

- FPs *not* concerning Jesus Christ that are proven as fulfilled by history (this is where our main emphasis will be).

- Prophecies of the OT concerning Jesus Christ, proven by the NT and/or history. Again, the prophecies claimed to be fulfilled only by the NT will not be emphasized here and are not a part of this discussion, as a skeptic may try to contend, unjustly it might be added, the validity of the NT.

Fulfilled Prophecies (FPs) in the Bible Proven True by History Outside the Bible

Several FPs will be discussed here, although not in detail (since this is not a book wherein prophecy is a main emphasis). But enough information is presented to show them to be accurate. The reader is encouraged to research them further. Also, note that the Bible contains many more FPs than the mere sampling shown here.

For this discussion, we will consult the material compiled by mathematics professor Peter W. Stoner in his book *Science Speaks*, referenced earlier. Professor Peter W. Stoner, MS, was chairman of the departments of mathematics and astronomy at Pasadena City College until 1953; chairman of the science division, Westmont College, 1953-57; professor emeritus of science, Westmont College; professor emeritus of mathematics and astronomy, Pasadena City College.

Assisting Professor Stoner in authoring this book was Robert C. Newman, PhD in astrophysics, Cornell University, 1967; STM, Biblical School of Theology, 1972; associate professor of physics and mathematics, Shelton College, 1968-71.

Professor Stoner meticulously examined Bible prophecies concerning multiple cities and found a total of 47 FPs based on the record of secular history. He also added four more FPs concerning Jericho, which were fulfilled per I Kings in the OT.

He involved some 700 college students over a period of 10 years in estimating the odds of the prophecies being fulfilled by random chance/natural occurrences. The following procedures were used to ensure the accuracy of the proposed statistics or odds of the prophecies' being fulfilled by random or natural events:

- Students weighed all the factors;

- Students discussed each prophecy at length;

- Students examined the various circumstances to see if men had conspired together to self-fulfill any of the prophecies;

- The estimates of the odds of the prophecies being fulfilled by random chance were made conservative enough so all 700 college students agreed upon the odds;

- Professor Stoner double-checked the figures and made adjustments, in most cases making them even more conservative (more likely to be fulfilled by chance);

- Professor Stoner then had other skeptics/scientists provide estimates; and

- Lastly, he submitted the numbers to a committee of the American Scientific Affiliation.

To quote the forward of *Science Speaks* (also quoted earlier):

> The manuscript for *Science Speaks* has been carefully reviewed by a committee of the American Scientific Affiliation members and by the Executive Council of the same group and has been found, in general, to be dependable and accurate in regard to the scientific material presented. The mathematical analysis included is based upon principles of probability which are thoroughly sound, and Professor Stoner has applied these principles in a proper and convincing way.
>
> American Scientific Affiliation
> H. HAROLD HARTZLER, PhD
> Secretary-Treasurer
> Goshen College, Ind.

The details by Dr. Stoner of these 47 biblical FPs are contained in Appendix A of this writing. In summary, the chance of the fulfillment of all those prophecies by random chance has been calculated by the above conservative, methodical process at one chance in 5.76×10^{54}! This number does not include the four referenced Jericho prophecies (if these four are factored in, the odds would be in the neighborhood of 5.76×10^{59}). For example, the odds of guessing all 51 prophecies correctly would be similar to the following:

- Fill all the galaxies (estimate of 200,000,000,000) in the entire universe with dimes (i.e., 10^{60} dimes); mark one dime; mix it all up. Blindfold yourself and dive into the mass of dimes and come up with the right dime on the first try.

- The number of grains of sand on all of earth's beaches is about 10^{23}. Multiply all of those grains by one trillion, one trillion, one trillion times x 5.76 and mark one grain of sand; mix up all the grains of sand. Blindfold yourself and dive into the pile of sand and come up with the right grain of sand on the first try.

Based on the above evidence and the FPs detailed in Appendix A, it is very clear the Bible contains many proven FPs, and such prophecies can only logically come from a Divine source. This discovery, therefore, adds further support, in addition to the scientific evidence, that the God of the Bible is the true God we are searching for.

Jesus Christ and Prophecy

In the NT Jesus Christ fulfilled over 300 OT prophecies made about him and his first coming.

Up to this point, we have only looked at FPs, which require, among other things, proof from secular (non-biblical) history. These

OT prophecies fulfilled by Jesus Christ according to the NT are not included in the earlier FP category, but will be simply called NT-FPs.

The skeptic may say the writers of the NT merely created fictitious events/statements of Jesus to fulfill various OT prophecies. However, (i) this supposition conflicts with the available evidence; and (ii) no available evidence supports the fictitious events scenario.

First and foremost, all the apostolic writers of the NT gave up their lives for proclaiming the deity, resurrection, and other truths regarding Jesus Christ (except the Apostle John, who was dipped in hot oil per church history), including the ways he fulfilled OT prophecies of the coming Messiah. Men do not die for what they are not sure of.

Yes, men have often died for ideological positions and been wrong, but that is not what we are talking about with Jesus: we are talking about a physical, historical event (the resurrection), after which the disciples died for proclaiming that they had seen Christ alive three days after his death by crucifixion, claiming they touched him, talked with him, and ate food with him during a period of 40 days. (More on this in the chapter concerning the resurrection of Christ.)

Second, the apostles had nothing to gain by creating any so-called fictitious accounts of Jesus's fulfilling OT prophecies…the only physical outcome of preaching the risen Lord Jesus Christ was persecution, *not* money, power, and/or status of any kind.

Third, Jesus taught the high value of personal integrity and honesty ("Thou shalt not lie," etc.). If the writers of the NT fabricated events to fulfill OT prophecies, their behavior would have contradicted the well-known integrity and honesty of Jesus (and supposedly his followers).

Fourth, the Jewish NT writers of the first century considered the OT to be sacred, and thereby interpreted them very carefully.

Only Jesus fulfilled the over 300 OT prophecies concerning the Jewish Messiah's first coming. Due to this book's concise nature and the fact that prophecy is only one part of the evidence, the information below will examine only a few of the many prophecies Jesus fulfilled.

Sometimes Jewish prophecy had an immediate or near future

fulfillment and *also* a long-term fulfillment; for example, Isaiah 9:6 had a near future fulfillment, along with Matthew in the NT providing for the long-term fulfillment in the Messiah, Jesus.

Additionally, the following table contains what were known as *Messianic prophecies* in the OT by Jewish scholars before the advent of Jesus Christ. Messianic prophecies are those passages that are considered the foretelling of the Messiah's coming and other details about him. The OT was completed in the fifth century BC, and the Greek Septuagint of the OT was finished by the second century BC, both well before the events of the NT.

In studying the below table, ask yourself how many people in history could have or did fulfill the below 15 prophecies, let alone over 300 Messianic prophecies. Concerning the 15 prophecies, only one person in history fulfilled all of them: Jesus Christ! More on the boldfaced ones later.

No.	Prophesied Event about the Jewish Messiah	OT Ref. Prediction	NT Ref. Fulfillment
1	Timing of appearance (First)– Palm Sunday riding on a donkey *(see below comments)*	Daniel 9:25-26 **Zechariah 9:9***	Matthew 21:4-10
2	Lineage to be from King David	Jeremiah 23:5-6	Matthew 1 and Luke 3
3	Birth foretold, called "God"	Isaiah 9:6	Matthew 1:22-23
4	Messiah's mother a virgin	Isaiah 7:14	Matthew 1:22-23
5	Birthplace - Bethlehem	**Micah 5:2***	Matthew 2:1, 6
6	A messenger to prepare the way of Messiah (John the Baptist)	**Malachi 3:1***	Matthew 11:10; Mark 1:2; Luke 7:27

No.	Prophesied Event about the Jewish Messiah	OT Ref. Prediction	NT Ref. Fulfillment
7	Betrayed by a friend, with whom he also ate bread	Psalm 41:9; Zechariah 13:6*	Matthew 13:55; 26:25; 27:3; Mark 3:19; 14:10; Luke 6:16; 22:4; John 12:4; 13:2; 13:26-27 (bread ref.); 18:2
8	Betrayed for 30 pieces of silver	Zechariah 11:12*	Matthew 26:14–16
9	Betrayal money used to buy a potter's field	Zechariah 11:13*	Matthew 26:15; 27:3–10
10	Will remain silent in his defense against his accusers	Isaiah 53:7*	Matthew 27:12-14; Mark 15:3-5
11	To be killed/crucified	Daniel 9:25-26; Ps. 22:16*; Isaiah 53	Matt; Mark; Luke; John; Acts; Romans, etc.
12	Would die a sacrificial death for us	Daniel 9:26; Isaiah 53:8, 10-12	II Corinthians 5:21; etc.
13	Die with criminals; buried with wealthy (Joseph's tomb)	Isaiah 53:9	Matthew 27:57–60; Luke 23:33
14	Would be mocked, and people would gamble for his clothes	Ps. 22:1, 8, 18	Matthew 27:35
15	Remain dead for only 3 days – will rise again	Ps. 16:8-11; Isaiah 53:10	Matthew 28:6; Mark 16:6; Luke 24:1-6; John 20; I Corinthians 15:3-4; etc.

Prophecy Event #1: Timing of Messiah's Coming: The book of Daniel of the OT was written in the sixth century BC, during the Jewish captivity in Babylon.

During the 70-year Babylon captivity, Daniel predicted the timing of the coming Messiah at 483 years after a future order is given to rebuild Jerusalem, which was issued over 100 years later by the Persian

King Artaxerxes. The Media-Persian empire conquered the Babylonian empire.

Appendix B, "Daniel's Amazing Prophecy about the Coming of the Messiah," gives the details and timing of this prophecy. To make a long story short here, the Messiah had to proclaim himself, or he had to be proclaimed Messiah, by absolutely no later than 33 AD.

The above explanation at least means that the initial appearance of the Messiah could not occur after 33 AD. This is a very sobering thought to most Jews who are still anticipating the initial coming of the Messiah. Jews usually believe in only one coming of the Messiah; Christianity holds to two comings.

Prophecy Event #2: Jesus's Lineage (or Genealogical Address) to Be from King David: The OT explicitly says the coming Messiah would be from the line of Abraham and King David. In the NT, Matthew and Luke give in detail (though not intended to be comprehensive) the physical lineage of Christ from Adam through/from Abraham and through/from King David all the way down to Joseph and Mary. Joseph, a descendent of David through David's son Solomon, adopted Jesus (Jesus being conceived in the virgin Mary by God the Holy Spirit), providing Christ the legal right to be a descendant of David. Mary, also a descendant of David, provided the physical line of descent from David.

Even if Jesus Christ were a charlatan, liar, and deceiver who had a death wish to be excruciatingly killed via crucifixion with nothing to gain from it, he could have only manipulated 3 of the above 15 prophecies to enable them to be fulfilled. For example, unless Christ was God, he (i) could not have controlled his lineage, where and when and by whom he was born; (ii) could not have controlled the various details of his betrayal and his death; and (iii) certainly could not have physically raised himself from the dead (see the chapter on the resurrection for its historical evidence).

Eight of the above 15 prophecies are boldfaced and have an asterisk (*) by their OT reference. Using the meticulous method of statistical determination similar to that described earlier for the odds of biblical prophecies being fulfilled by chance by Dr. Stoner in his book

Science Speaks (in this case regarding Christ-related prophecies, over 600 [instead of 700] students from 13 classes), the odds of all eight of these prophecies being fulfilled by one man out of all the people who have lived on earth since these prophecies is 1 in 10^{28}.

If the preceding is not convincing enough, continue reading the following paragraphs; otherwise, you may skip to the conclusion of this chapter.

Apart from divine intervention, it would have required a miracle for these prophecies to be fulfilled. Dr. Stoner states:

> Let us try to visualize this chance. If you mark one of ten tickets, and place all of the tickets in a hat, and thoroughly stir them, and then ask a blindfolded man to draw one, his chance of getting the right ticket is one in ten. Suppose that we take 10^{17} silver dollars and lay them on the face of Texas. They will cover all of the state two feet deep. Now mark one of these silver dollars and stir the whole mass thoroughly, all over the state. Blindfold a man and tell him that he can travel as far as he wishes, but he must pick up one silver dollar and say that this is the right one. What chance would he have of getting the right one? Just the same chance that the prophets would have had of writing these eight prophecies and having them all come true in any one man, from their day to the present time, providing they wrote using their own wisdom. (*Science Speaks*, on-line edition)

Applying the same principles of probability, Professor Stoner calculated that the chance of one man's fulfilling 48 of the Messianic prophecies would be 1 in 10^{157} (assuming, for the moment, that the additional 40 prophecies were as difficult to fulfill as the first eight). This would be comparable to marking one of the 10^{78} protons/neutrons in the entire universe, then multiplying the 10^{78} by 6,500,000,000,000 times, and then having a blind person find the marked proton or neutron on the first try.

How about the odds of fulfilling all 300+ of the prophecies concerning the first advent of the Messiah? Well, we will not even go there. The point is made.

Conclusion

Using FPs as a determining factor, the Bible stands alone. And since only God can truly predict the future, the Bible's unique ability to have accurate FPs indicates the God of the Bible is the true God.

CHAPTER 15

MANUSCRIPT CONSIDERATIONS

In trying to decide if the biblical God is the true God as compared to other so-called gods, we need to examine the various religious books of the world to see what they teach on a variety of subjects (science, history, etc.), but especially on salvation.

We have already discussed how the Bible stands alone when it comes to scientific truths and fulfilled prophecies. This chapter will deal with the issue of the manuscript reliability of the Bible vs. other religious books, with an emphasis on the Qur'an for reasons previously mentioned.

Manuscript reliability evidence simply answers one question: does what we have today agree with what was originally written? If not, end of story. If so, then we can proceed to answer the next logical question: is what is written actually true? This latter question is one of many questions addressed in this writing.

If this topic were given a full treatment, it could take several books. What is presented below will not be comprehensive, but more of an overview. The reader is encouraged to study this area further, perhaps starting with some of the references given at the end of the book.

Of course, manuscript evidence itself does not solve our search for the one true God, but the importance of accurately transmitted information is significant.

Manuscript Evidence

The five issues that help to determine the reliability of manuscript copies made after the original work are organized in such a way for the reader to easily recall them. Remember the acronym **NOTES.**

- Number of Manuscripts: Generally, the more manuscript copies of an original work that exist, the better since the original words can be discerned with greater accuracy by cross-checking the various copies.

- Old – How old are the copies compared to the original? Generally, the closer the manuscript copies are to the original, the more reliable they tend to be.

- Time Span– The smaller the time difference between the events described and the writing thereof, the more accurate the accounts are likely to be.

- Eyewitnesses – The more eyewitness accounts included, the better—for obvious reasons.

- Supporting Information.

Apart from manuscripts of the Bible, ancient manuscripts of an original writing have the following typical characteristics:

- They number anywhere from 4 to 20 copies, a few a little higher.

- The earliest non-biblical manuscript copies are typically dated anywhere from 700-1500 years after the original work.

- Non-biblical ancient manuscripts are often written a very long time after the event (for example, the earliest manuscript about Alexander the Great is about 300 years after his death).

- Eyewitnesses are fairly rare.
- Supporting information is scarce.

The Bible: New Testament

The Bible has a preponderance of more manuscript evidence than any other writing of antiquity. If we were to throw out the Bible, we would have to eliminate everything we know of ancient history (approximately 1,000 AD and earlier for our purposes), as no other ancient documents or their early copies have anywhere near the Bible's manuscript evidence. For example:

- **Number of manuscripts** (partial or complete) - The New Testament (NT) has over 25,000 extant (existing) manuscript copies, with over 5,000 in Greek. Compare this to most early historical manuscripts, which have somewhere between 4 to 20 copies.

- **Old** – How old are the copies compared to the original? The earliest confirmed manuscript is within 25-35 years from the original; it is called the John Bodmer fragment of the Gospel of John. There is currently another earlier possibility under scrutiny, a part of Mark dated in the 60s; this manuscript is apparently not yet confirmed. Other manuscript copies appear in the middle of the second century (about 150 AD), and thereafter increase exponentially in number. This is unheard of in the area of manuscript evidence for other writings of antiquity.

- **Time Span** – except as noted below, the NT was likely written between 48/49 to 68/69 AD, possibly including John's Gospel and the Book of Revelation. Some date one or more, if not all, of John's five books from 85-95 AD. At least 22 NT books, if not all 27, were written within the lifetimes of most of the people who witnessed Jesus's earthly ministry. Again, this is unheard of in ancient manuscripts.

- **Eyewitnesses** – The NT was written by many eyewitnesses: Matthew, John, Peter, Paul, and Jesus's half-brothers, James and Jude. The Gospel of Mark was written by Mark, a protégé of Peter, with the Gospel of Luke written by Luke, a protégé of Paul. The above-mentioned books total 26 of the 27 NT books. For the twenty-seventh book, the book of Hebrews, the author is not definitively known (probably Barnabas, another eyewitness). Remember, all but one of the original apostles gave up their lives for proclaiming the resurrection of Jesus. This use of eyewitnesses is quite rare in ancient documents.

- **Supporting Information:** Much support could be offered here, but even if all the copies of NT books had been destroyed, we could accurately construct all but about eleven verses of the NT from the quotes of verses from the early church fathers prior to about 250 AD.

While brief, the above information confirms that the Bible's NT has astounding manuscript evidence authenticating what was originally written. Renowned biblical scholar Norman Geisler states the following concerning NT variant readings:

- First, NT textual authorities Westcott and Hort estimated that only about one-sixtieth rise above 'trivialities' and can be called 'substantial variations.' In short, the NT is 98.33 percent pure. Second, Greek expert Ezra Abbott said about 19/20 (95 percent) of the readings are 'various' rather than 'rival' readings, and about 19/20 (95 percent) of the rest make no appreciable difference in the sense of the passage. Thus, the text is 99.75 percent accurate. Third, noted NT Greek scholar A. T. Robertson said the real concern is with about a 'thousandth part of the entire text.' So, the reconstructed text of the New Testament is 99.9% free from real concern. (Norman Geisler, "A Note on the Percent of Accuracy of the New Testament Text" [article]; see E-Link Bibliography)

The variant readings usually involve only issues of grammar, spelling, scribal slips of the pen, etc., and in no case is any major teaching or doctrine affected. No other religious book of any religion can compare to the manuscript reliability of the NT.

The Bible: Old Testament

The Old Testament (OT) has been handed down with incredible accuracy. However, the manuscript scenario is a bit different from that of the NT.

The OT was written over a period extending from about 1446-1406 BC to the fifth century BC, and was predominantly written in Hebrew, with some Aramaic. However, some scholars claim the book of Job is the oldest book of the OT, perhaps originating during the patriarchal period. The Greek translation of the OT (called "The Septuagint") was completed in the third to second centuries BC.

Before the discovery of the Dead Sea Scrolls (DSS), the earliest *Hebrew* manuscript evidence dated to the tenth century (900s AD). When the DSS were discovered, over 300 Hebrew copies of OT books were included, dating from the third to the first centuries BC. All copies (parts, whole) of the OT books were included in the DSS, except for the book of Esther.

History shows that the Jewish transmission of the OT books was done by highly-qualified, specially-trained scribes to ensure accuracy.

When the DSS were discovered, the world then could compare the Hebrew documents from the third to first century BC to the later Hebrew manuscripts of the tenth century AD, a period of transmission of about 1100 years. The comparison showed that after 1100 years of transmission, the two sets of manuscripts were, for all intents and purposes, the same. For example, in the manuscript of Isaiah (second century BC, not the original writing of the eighth century BC), chapter 53, there are 153 words: of the 153 words, 152 are identical when compared to the tenth century AD manuscript of Isaiah. The one different word is a three-letter word for "light," and its presence or deletion does not significantly affect the meaning of the passage. In total, the two DSS Isaiah manuscripts were more than 95%

the same as current Hebrew texts. The five percent of variation consisted chiefly of obvious slips of the pen and variations in spelling.

Although the number of OT manuscripts are not as numerous as
the NT's, the transmission methodologies utilized ensured accuracy,
which in some ways explains the fewer number of manuscripts.

For example, in commenting on the Masoretic method (c. 500 –
950 AD) of copying manuscripts (the Masoretes were Jewish scholars
responsible for the standard Hebrew text today), Bible scholar Sir Frederic Kenyon states:

> The Masoretes undertook a number of calculations which
> do not enter into the ordinary sphere of textual criticism.
> They numbered the verses, words, and letters of every book.
> They calculated the middle word and the middle letter of
> each. They enumerated verses which contained all the let-
> ters of the alphabet, or a certain number of them. These
> trivialities, as we may rightly consider them, had yet the
> effect of securing minute attention to the precise transmis-
> sion of the text, and they are but an excessive manifestation
> of a respect for the sacred Scriptures which in itself deserves
> nothing but praise. The Masoretes were indeed anxious not
> one jot nor tittle, not one smallest letter nor one tiny part
> of a letter, of the Law should pass away or be lost (*Our Bible
> and the Ancient Manuscripts,* London, p. 38).

Scholar F.F. Bruce further states:

> They counted, for example, the number of times each letter
> of the alphabet occurs in each book (*The Books and Parch-
> ments: How We Got Our English Bible*, p. 117).

Using the English language for comparison, the number of times
the letter "a" appeared in the book of Isaiah would have been counted,
the same for "b" and so on through "z." The middle word and the
middle letter of each manuscript would have been identified; also the
verses, words, and letters of every book would have been counted. If

the resulting new copy differed from the prior copy (from which it was copied) by more than 3 differences (based on the above methodology), the new copy was destroyed. When a successful new copy was accomplished, the old copy was either thrown out or delegated for use in schooling, etc.

Prior to the Masoretic scribes, the Jewish Talmudists (c. 100 AD to 500 AD) had a very rigid process for copying OT books. Samuel Davidson describes the process (numbers added by Bible Scholar Norman Geisler; below quote from Josh McDowell, *The New Evidence that Demands a Verdict*, 1999, p. 74):

> [1] A synagogue roll must be written on the skins of clean animals, [2] prepared for the particular use of the synagogue by a Jew. [3] These must be fastened together with strings taken from clean animals. [4] Every skin must contain a certain number of columns, equal throughout the entire codex. [5] The length of each column must not extend over less than 48 or more than 60 lines, and the breadth must consist of thirty letters. [6] The whole copy must be first-lined; and if three words be written without a line, it is worthless. [7] The ink should be black, neither red, green, nor any other colour, and be prepared according to a definite recipe. [8] An authentic copy must be the exemplar, from which the transcriber ought not in the least deviate. [9] No word or letter, not even a yod, must be written from memory, the scribe not having looked at the codex before him. [10] Between every consonant the space of a hair or thread must intervene. [11] between every new parashah or section, the breadth of nine consonants; [12] between every book, three lines. [13] The fifth book of Moses must terminate exactly with a line but the rest need not do so. [14] Besides this, the copyist must sit in full Jewish dress, [15] wash his whole body, [16] not begin to write the name of God with a pen newly dipped in ink, [17] and should a king address him while writing that name, he must take no notice of him (Samuel Davidson, *The Hebrew*

Text of the Old Testament. London: 1856. Quoted in Norman L. Geisler and William E. Nix, *General Introduction to the Bible*. Chicago: Moody Press, p. 89).

Copies not adhering to the above principles were buried or burned or banished to the schools to be used as reading books. Once certified, the new manuscript was considered just as valid as the prior copy, which was destroyed when any age-related issues occurred to the manuscript itself.

The Zugoth were assigned to the OT transmission from the second to first centuries BC. The Tannaim ("repeaters" or "teachers") were active until 200 AD. The Sopherim were Jewish scholars and custodians of the OT text between the fifth and third centuries BC.

The above does not present all the relevant information on the transmission of the OT, but presents enough information to prove the incredibly accurate transmission of the OT through the centuries.

Qur'an's Manuscript History

Muhammad claimed to receive revelations from Allah through the angel Gabriel. These revelations took place over a period of 22-23 years and were given in discrete surahs (or chapters), which eventually became the Qur'an. Muhammad himself did not write any of them down, but memorized passages and preached them. Those around him committed parts to memory; other parts were written down on parchment, stone, palm leaves, and the shoulder blades of camels according to Islamic sources.

During Muhammad's sessions with the supposed angel Gabriel, Muhammad would sometimes go into convulsions, roar like a camel, and foam at the mouth.

According to Ahmad ibn Hanbal, "He [Muhammad] became distressed, foaming at the mouth and closing his eyes. At times he snorted like a young camel" (Ahmad b. Hanbal I, 34, 464, vi.163). Some have surmised that Muhammad was epileptic; that is one possible conclusion.

According to 'Amr Ibn Sharhabil, Muhammad mentioned to his

wife, Khadija, that he feared he was possessed by demons and wondered whether others considered him possessed [i.e. evil spirits] (source: *pfanoter* 1910:345).

The reported physical symptoms of Muhammad when he saw the spirit were not made by strangers or non-Muslims, but by people very close and committed to him, including Aisha, his wife.

However, his prior wife Kadija convinced him that what he was experiencing was not evil, but from God. To make a long story short, on one occasion she asked Muhammad if he saw the supposed angel, to which he responded, "Yes." She asked two more times, and he said, "Yes" both additional times. She then, according to a number of (but not all) Islamic sources, exposed one of her breasts and then asked Muhammad if the angel was still there. Muhammad said, "No." She then assured him it was not an evil spirit.

It is interesting to note that per Muhammad's so-called revelations, which ended up being the Qur'an, Gabriel claimed there was no Son of God (Surah 17:111) and that Jesus Christ did not die on the cross (Surah 4:157). These and other Qur'anic verses contradict biblical statements, including the Bible's statement of Gabriel visiting Mary and telling her she would bear the Son of God (Luke 1:35). Other Qur'an and Bible contradictions exist, but suffice it to say that both could not have come from the same source, as discussed earlier.

In Islamic history, Caliph Abu Bakr, the first leader of the Muslim community after Muhammad's death in 632, ordered the scribe Zaid to collect all Qur'anic material and for the material to be put into one volume.

However, during the following 20 years, different versions existed. So in about 650 AD, under the third Caliph Uthman ibn Affan, *the scribe Zaid located all the various versions still existing, determined which material was correct, and then burned the rest.* This final written version was then copied and distributed to the main cities under Muslim rule and is believed by Muslims today to be the exact revelations that were delivered to Muhammad.

The development phases of the Qur'anic material of most concern are two areas:

- The recording method by various unknown people on things like parchment, stone, palm leaves and the shoulder blades of camels was seemingly a very unregulated process prone to errors. We do not know who these people were, and therefore we do not know their qualifications, etc.

- The process used by Zaid and Caliph Uthman ibn Affan to determine which of the existing material should be destroyed and what material should constitute the genuine version is unknown. Apparently, after this it appears the transmission of the Qur'an remained stabilized.

The above information on the Qur'an's transmission is per well-recognized Islamic historical documents. In addition to the above two potential issues is the fact Muhammad did not write down any of the revelations (encompassing the entire Qur'an), but only memorized them. Others, as noted, wrote down his verbal representations.

Final Comparison

The Bible was penned by 40 different authors with many different backgrounds (from leaders, prophets, kings, fishermen, etc.) from about 1446 BC to the first century AD, producing 66 books. However, as stated earlier, some scholars claim the book of Job is the oldest book of the OT, perhaps originating during the patriarchal period. The Qur'an came from one supposed source, Muhammad, over a 22-to-23-year period, and then made use of two additional sources (Zaid and Caliph Uthman ibn Affan). Acting as collectors and editors, these additional sources determined, by unknown methods, what material of the multiple sources should constitute a final singular version.

In the case of the Bible, all the authors agree with one another on multiple topics, with a total of over 25,000 manuscripts (partial and whole manuscripts) for the NT alone. There is proven manuscript accuracy (accuracy of the copies compared to the originals) for both the OT and NT, and the numerous manuscripts can be used to cross-check the others for accuracy.

The Qur'an cannot take advantage of this valuable process since the Qur'an has one original, official copy (which does not now exist, only copies thereof). The Qur'an was derived from various versions, collected and edited by two men by an unknown process, with the remaining material being burned.

The situation with the Bible is comparable to a college class of 100 students who each copy verbatim a 10-page document handed out in class. When all 100 papers are collected, the results are open for all in the class to see. Assume that the original ten-page document that was handed out is no longer available and only the 100 copied versions remain. If it is shown that the written accounts agree with one another perfectly except for one added word, and of the 100 written accounts only one has the extra word, the obvious conclusion, without any other relevant data, is that the 99 accounts are correct and the one different one is in error. The over 25,000 manuscripts of the NT can be cross-checked in this fashion.

Using the same scenario with the Qur'an, however, only one student collects all 100 copies, keeps them to himself, decides along with one other person which set of words is correct by an unknown methodology, and then burns the remaining material before making the result public.

Question: If one assumes no divine influence, which process would you trust more? Conversely, assuming divine influence on the process, which writing (Bible vs. Qur'an) shows itself to be more divinely inspired based on the scientific and prophetical evidence presented thus far?

CHAPTER 16

CHARACTER OF ISLAM'S ALLAH AND MUHAMMAD

In nearing our final determination of selecting either Islam's Allah or the Bible's God (Jehovah or Yahweh) as the true God, we must examine their respective natures; i.e., what kind of God is each one?

This chapter examines the characters of Mohammad (Islam's founder) and Islam's God, Allah. The next chapter looks at the character of Jesus Christ (Christianity's founder, who also claimed to be Creator God) and the Bible's God.

In theory, the true God we seek could be an evil, morally reprehensible God. If God were evil, he hypothetically could still be the true God of the universe. Of course, this author does not believe such is the case. Quite the contrary.

Also, we must recognize that a prophet of God could communicate various truths about the true God yet have character flaws (such as David's adulterous affair with Bathsheba in the Bible's Old Testament [OT]). However, presently we are comparing the founder of Islam and the basis for Christianity (Jesus Christ). Therefore, a character analysis of each is warranted.

The author has no desire to misrepresent anything about Islam, especially about Muhammad. The intent here is to simply let the historical facts speak for themselves.

The reader should realize that in the Qur'an if a verse contradicts a previously given Qur'anic verse (earlier in time), the second one takes precedence. This process is called *abrogation* in Islam. Allah has the right to contradict himself.

For example, the Qur'anic verses advocating killing nonbelievers supersede the earlier verses which advocate more peaceful actions, if meant in the same way. The Qur'an is not arranged in chronological or topical order; the surahs (chapters) are arranged only in terms of length (longest first). To determine the proper context of a Qur'anic text, one often has to consult one or more of the Islamic *hadiths*, written over 100 years after Muhammad's death, which recount the life and sayings of Muhammad. These hadiths are second only to the Quran in Islamic authority and truth. And some hadiths are more respected than others.

In examining the character of Muhammad and Allah, the researcher would, of course, find positive attributes. However, because of the length and purpose of our discussion, only two areas will be discussed: (i) Islamic violence and (ii) women. In spite of whatever positive characteristics Muhammad and Allah may have per the Qur'an and Islam, we have to ask ourselves what Muhammad and Allah were like overall *according to Islamic sources*. Do these two areas reflect a loving and moral God and his prophet? Or…

Muhammad/Allah and Islamic Violence

Before Medina, when living in Mecca, Muhammad had little political power, and the Qur'anic verses written during this time reflect a nonviolent approach. Only after moving to Medina did Muhammad gain significant political and military influence; at this point, the verses in the Qur'an take on a more violent tone.

For example, Surah 2:256 says there is to be no compulsion (force) in religion. This was written by Muhammad in the years before his move to Medina. The more violent verses (some given below) were written after he moved to Medina and had gained political and military power. Since these verses were written after the passages promoting peace, the violent verses take precedence whenever the two passages conflict in intended meaning/context, according to the Islamic principle of abrogation.

The verses written after moving to Medina often advocated violence, sometimes intended for the specific situation for which the passage was written and/or sometimes as a general principle for the future. Even Muslim imams (spiritual leaders) disagree about whether certain verses establish a general principle for the future or not. At least some of the passages are plainly intended for all times. Some of the violent passages are Surah 2:216-217; 4:89, 101; 8:12, 60; 9:5, 29, 111; 33:57; 47:4, etc.). Surah 9 was the last Surah penned by Muhammad. Listed below are a few examples of these violent passages (some versions of the Qur'an have inserted bracketed words to clarify the meaning):

- Surah 4:89 - But if they turn away, then seize them and kill them wherever you find them and take not from among them any ally or helper.

- Surah 9:5 - And when the sacred months have passed, then kill the polytheists wherever you find them and capture them and besiege them and sit in wait for them at every place of ambush. But if they should repent, establish prayer, and give zakah, let them [go] on their way. Indeed, Allah is Forgiving and Merciful.

- Surah 9:29-31 - Fight those who do not believe in Allah or in the Last Day and who do not consider unlawful what Allah and His Messenger have made unlawful and who do not adopt the religion of truth from those who were given the Scripture - [fight] until they give the jizyah willingly while they are humbled. The Jews say, 'Ezra is the Son of God'; the Christians say, 'The Messiah is the Son of God.'…God assail them! How they are perverted! They have taken their rabbis and their monks as Lords apart from God [Allah].

- Surah 9:11 - Indeed, Allah has purchased from the believers their lives and their properties [in exchange] for that they will have Paradise. They fight in the cause of Allah, so they kill and are killed.

- Surah 47:4 - So when you meet those who disbelieve [in battle], strike [their] necks until, when you have inflicted slaughter upon them, then secure their bonds…He could have taken vengeance upon them [Himself], but [He ordered armed struggle] to test some of you by means of others. And those who are killed in the cause of Allah – never will He waste their deeds.

The below analysis does not intend to disparage Muhammad's character or offend Muslims, but only to show what authoritative Islamic sources have to say about Muhammad and specifically about his and Islam's violent past. The facts of Islamic history speak for themselves.

I freely admit that I am not an expert on the violent aspects of Muhammad's life and the Qur'anic verses on violence. Therefore, an analysis of each of the purported acts of violence concerning Muhammad will not be given; it is not the purpose of this book.

Sometimes even Muslim scholars disagree on the subject of violence. A definite part of the problem is that some Islamic imams (spiritual leaders in Islam) will make statements on these verses, but upon an in-depth examination of the subject, *using original, authoritative Islamic sources,* a different conclusion seems obvious. Sometimes imams may even advocate ignoring some of the original Islamic sources, perhaps because the violence aspect is too uncomfortable or not politically expedient.

Therefore, to facilitate the understanding of the subject and to avoid the possibility of erroneously using sources out of context (which some researchers have done), this treatment will use the observations of a former Muslim, Nabeel Asif Qureshi (1983–2017). Nabeel was a well-known international writer and speaker on Islam and its violent origins. As a Muslim, he had specialized in Islamic apologetics (defending Islam) until later in his collegiate years. Upon more closely examining the claims of Islam and Christianity, he converted to Christianity. Holding four master's degrees and a doctorate, Nabeel spoke at over

100 universities, authored three books (including *Seeking Allah, Finding Jesus: A Devout Muslim Encounters Christianity*) and various articles in well-known publications and conducted debates with Islamic apologists.

For those reading this text in an electronic format, the underlined words in the material from Nabeel are links to supporting information. In the case of Islamic sources, they are links to the original Islamic documentation in both English and Arabic. Those reading the hard copy of my book should use the link to the *Huffington Post* article given in the E-Link Bibliography; the reader can then click on the underlined areas to go to the original Islamic documentation.

The referenced article from the *Huffington Post* is quoted in full. Except for the title, all boldfacing in the text is my emphasis:

Do the Roots of Jihad Lie in the Qur'an?
by Nabeel Qureshi
04/04/2016 05:06 pm ET **Updated** Apr 05, 2017

Perhaps the most exciting outcome of my op-ed in USA Today are the responses and open discussion of the Qur'an's teachings in popular news sources, including TIME Magazine, the Huffington Post, and a Patheos blog. Such public dialogue and discussion is the key to moving forward and addressing the roots of jihad.

In my article I propose that, 'when everyday Muslims investigate the Qur'an and hadith (or sayings of the Muhammad) for themselves, **bypassing centuries of tradition and their imams' interpretations**, they are confronted with the reality of violent jihad in the very foundations of their faith.' Nonetheless, I suggest that the vast majority of Muslims are peaceful and innocent and should be received with friendship and love.

That is a very short digest of my recent book, *Answering Jihad: A Better Way Forward*. In the opening chapter of that

book, I describe why it took me years to come to this conclusion: I had always been taught Islam was a religion of
peace and that Muhammad was a kind, peaceful man, in
fact the most perfect who ever lived. It took years of studying the [Islamic] sources to move away from the interpretations that the imams in my denomination had taught
me. Incidentally, those are the same imams who taught all
three of the respondents above, as I grew up in the same
sect of Islam that they are a part of. How is it that people
can come to such differing conclusions about the person
of Muhammad?

The answer has to do with the incredible number of traditions of Muhammad's life. Although the Qur'an only
mentions Muhammad by name four times, the body of
literature known as hadith contain hundreds of thousands
of accounts and anecdotes. These are not full narratives of
Muhammad's life, but discrete stories of specific events or
sayings. Islamic tradition does also record narrative biographies of the life of Muhammad, and those are called sirah,
but they hold a lesser place in the eyes of most Muslims.

Here is my point: when a Muslim gets his information
about Muhammad directly from these sources, **rather than
from imams or traditions that selectively filter them**, they
have no alternative but to conclude that the life of Muhammad, and therefore the context of the Qur'an, culminates
in violence.

Consider two well-known hadiths from the anthologies of
Sahih Bukhari and Sahih Muslim, considered to be the two
most authentic collections of hadith. In one, Muhammad
says, 'I will expel all the Jews and Christians from the Arabian peninsula and not leave any but Muslim.' In another,
he says, 'I have been ordered to fight against the people
until they testify that none has the right to be worshipped
but Allah and that Muhammad is Allah's Messenger…

then they save their lives and property from me.' These authentic hadiths are illuminating when trying to understand the Qur'an's commands to kill polytheists (9.5) and fight Jews and Christians (9.29-30). Muhammad was fighting people for their beliefs, not for their actions, with the intent to expel or convert. Only by going against the grain of Islamic tradition, deeming these traditions to be unreliable, can an investigator avoid the violence inherent in the origins of Islam.

When I was a Muslim, I tried my best to do exactly that, individually dismissing account after account of Muhammad's violence. **But after at least a hundred such accounts,** I realized they were ubiquitous. Considering just one aspect of his life in tradition, his conduct with enemies, we find that Muhammad would invoke curses upon them, encourage his men to compose insults and abusive poetry, on one occasion asking Allah to fill peoples' homes with flames simply because they delayed the Muslims in their daily prayers.

At other times Muhammad sent assassins to kill his enemies in their sleep, and even to deceive and abuse trust in order to assassinate. He punished some enemies by cutting off their hands and feet, branding their eyes with heated iron, and causing them to lick the dust until they died.

He led battles against unarmed cities. He allowed even women and children to be exposed to danger during nighttime raids. On more than one occasion Muhammad decimated tribes by killing all their men and teenage boys while distributing their women and children as slaves. This is the man that the Qur'an tells all Muslims to emulate (33.21).

When I asked various imams to explain these traditions, they could do so only **by ignoring or dismissing** all these traditions that record the historical context of the Qur'an, even though they come from the most authentic collection in Islamic tradition, Sahih Bukhari.

Similarly, while still a Muslim, I asked my peace-loving imams to explain the ancient biographies of Muhammad. In the earliest such biography, Ibn Ishaq's *Sirat Rasul Allah* we find that chapter 9 of the Qur'an is the last major chapter of the Qur'an to be composed, and its most expansively violent chapter. The biography gives the context of the Qur'anic verse that says 'Slay the infidels wherever you find them' on pages 617-619. There it makes clear that not just the one tribe of polytheists who broke a treaty, but all polytheists would have to leave Arabia or be slaughtered. Those who had broken the treaty and shown hostility with Muslims 'should be killed for it,' those who had a general truce with Muslims would be given four months, and those who had a treaty with Muslims for a set term would be allowed to complete their term, but after that they were at risk of being slain by the command of the Qur'an. This is not a bizarre or idiosyncratic interpretation, but the standard interpretation of classical Islam and many Muslim scholars today. It is the interpretation provided by a popular Pakistani commentator today, Taqi Usmani, which can be downloaded for free on the Qur'an Explorer app.

A few pages later, this earliest biography of Muhammad's life explains why Muslims are told to 'Fight the People of the Scripture (Jews and Christians)… until they pay the ransom tax and feel subdued.' The answer is given in the previous verse: the polytheists, now being expelled or slaughtered, would no longer be able to bring their trade to Mecca, and the Muslims were afraid of losing this income.

The biography says that Jews and Christians would be made to pay the Muslims money, 'as a compensation for what you (the Muslims) fear to lose by the closing of the markets.' (620) The justification for fighting the Jews and

Christians is given in the next verse, 9.30: 'The Jews say Ezra is the Son of God and the Christians say the Messiah is the Son of God… May Allah destroy them!' Once again, this is the clear reading of the words in the Qur'an, the biography supports it, classical Muslim scholars advocated it, and respected Muslim scholars today agree.

In fact, this interpretation is the only one that explains why Muslims had the impetus to fight one third of the known world immediately after Muhammad died. His final teachings, recorded in the Qur'an and hadith, led them to conquest from the shores of the Atlantic to the valleys of India, at times slaughtering even undefended cities, such as in the conquest of Nikiu, which occurred during the reign of Umar ibn al-Khattab, a man most Muslims think was divinely guided.

Once again, **my imams dismissed the historical records and traditions, advising me to ignore them**. Since these are the very sources that tell us about Muhammad, I cannot selectively ignore the portions I find problematic. When others do, though, my argument in the USA today article still stands: people have to filter the traditions to produce a peaceful Islam. When everyday Muslims investigate the Qur'an and hadith for themselves, **without their imams filtering the traditions**, they are confronted with the reality of violent jihad in the very foundations of their faith.

I am thankful that the respondents have opened the door for discussion, because that is the best way to finding a solution to the problem of radical Islam. In that spirit I invite all three of them to public dialogue, so that together we can find the best way of Answering Jihad." *[end of citation]*

The invasion of Banu Qurayza took place in the Dhul Qa'dah during February and March of 627 AD. After the defeat of the Muslim's adversaries, a political ruling was given wherein 600-900 Jews should be beheaded. Muhammad approved of the ruling. He apparently did not issue the ruling, nor did he conduct any of the beheadings, but the fact he approved of the beheadings is revealing enough. Relevant Islamic sources include:

- Rahman al-Mubarakpuri, Saifur *(2005) The Sealed Nectar,* Darussalam Publications, 201–205 (online*).*

- Ibn Kathir, Saed Abdul-Rahman (2009), *Tafsir Ibn Kathir Juz'21,* MSA Publication Limited, 213 (online).

- Al Tabari (1997), *Volume 8, Victory of Islam,* translated by Michael Fishbein, State University of New York Press, 35–36.

- *Sunan Abu Dawud 14:2665;*

- *Sunan Abu Dawood, 38:4390;*

- Sahih al-Bukhari, 4:52:280

For another source concerning the violence of Muhammad see: https://wikiislam.net/wiki/List_of_Killings_Ordered_or_ Supported_ by_Muhammad. Although I have not verified these references for accuracy, and sometimes Wiki can contain errors, they at least appear to me to be fairly well-documented from original Muslim sources. Regardless, it definitely deserves a careful examination.

The topic of Muhammad and related violence warrants further discussion, such as the multiple military raids of Muhammad against caravans, etc. However, the above examples are enough to prove the point: Muhammad was an extremely violent individual. Per Islamic and non-Islamic sources, Islam was largely spread by the sword, by a preponderance of violence. Compare this to early Christianity, where its adherents loved their opponents and were killed *by* the sword.

Muhammad and Women

Although the number may vary, Islamic sources typically state that Muhammad had 11 official wives (some were the result of political alliances):

Khadija-Shahih Bukhari (Muhammad's first wife to whom he remained married and apparently faithful to for 25 years until her death); later polygamous marriages with Aisha-Shahih Bukhari; Hafsa bint 'Umar-Shahih Bukhari; Sauda bint Zam'a-Shahih Bukhari; Um Salama-Sahih Muslim; Hadrat Maimuna-Sahih Muslim; Zainab bint Jahsh-Shahih Bukhari; Safiya bint Huyay-Shahih Bukhari; Ar-Rubai bint Muauwidh-Shahih Bukhari; Um Habiba-Shahih Bukhari; Juwayriya-Sahih Muslim.

When Muhammad was 54 years old (after Khadija's death), he married a 6-year-old girl, Aisha, and consummated the marriage when she was age 9 (Note: not all Muslim scholars agree on the given ages, but *the majority of the traditional Islam sources and hadiths claim the above-stated ages*). For example, the below Islamic source states regarding Aisha and her age (boldfacing is this author's emphasis):

> And this has to do both with unambiguous nature of the sources describing this aspect of the Prophet's life, and their credibility: Muhammad's marriage contract to 'Āisha bint Abī Bakr (d. 58 AH/678 CE) when she was six years old, and her joining his household and the consummation of the marriage when she was nine....When we look at prophetic traditions, **there are several** *hadīth* reports (which I label the 'Āisha-age traditions) which go back to 'Āisha with almost the same wording:
>
> تزوجني رسول الله صلى الله عليه وسلم لست سنين وبنى بي وأنا بنت تسع سنين
>
> Translation: *The Messenger of Allah married me when I was six years old and consummated the marriage with me when I was nine years old.* (These words can be found in the *hadīth* collections of al-Bukhārī, Muslim, Ahmad, and al-Nisā'ī. See: Muhammad al-Shawkānī, *Nayl al-Awtār* (Egypt: Dār al-Hadīth, 1993), 6:224-225. Ibn Hajar al-'Asqalānī, *Fathal-Bārī Sharh Sahīh al-Bukhārī* (Beirut:

Dār al-Maʿrifah, 1379 AH, 7:224-225). (Arnold Yasin Mol. Article "Aisha (ra): The Case for an Older Age in Sunni Hadith Scholarship." *Irving, TX: Yaqeen Institute for Islamic Research*, Oct. 3, 2018; see E-Link Bibliography).

Arnold Yasin goes on to show the reliability of the above sources. However, 1300 years later, due to a presentation of a series of complex date analyses outside the scope of this writing, he claims these authoritative Islamic sources are wrong on the 6- and 9-year-old age claims. Interesting.

Another source, concerning the practice of "thighing" (touching of a male's penis on/between thighs of a young girl or boy), a more current Islamic Fatwa (a legal pronouncement in Islam issued by a religious law specialist on a specific issue) can be found at the following source: Bharata Bharati, "Thighing – Muslim Scholars" *(article)*, 10/11/2011; see E-Link Bibliography). In part it reads as follows:

> **Islam Fatwa Number 41409** dated 7-5-1421 or August 8, 2000:
>
> The permanent committee for scientific research and religious sanctions [in Saudi Arabia] are:
>
> • Abdel Aziz ben Abdullah ben Mohammed Aal Sheikh, Chairman
>
> • Bakr ben Abdullah Abu Zeid, Member
>
> • Saleh ben Fozan Al Fozan, Member
>
> …The committee, after studying the [a previously stated] request, has ruled the following:
>
> '…As for the thighing of the messenger of God [Muhammad] to his fiancée Ayesha [Aisha], **she was six years old** and he could not engage in sexual intercourse with her because of her young age, therefore he used to place his

penis between her thighs and rub it lightly. In addition, the messenger of God had full control of his penis in contrary [sic] to the believers.'

The full context of the above is in response to a request to clarify if it was all right to perform "thighing" on boys, with the response being that it was not.

Allah, Muhammad, and the Qur'an state it is all right for soldiers, whether married or not, to have sex with captured, consenting slave girls (the Qur'an elsewhere requires that the female must be consenting). Qur'an, Sura 23:5-6, says:

> And they who guard their private parts. Except from their wives or those their right hands possess, for indeed, they will not be blamed -

In a commentary on the above Qur'anic passage, Sayyid Abul A'La Maududi states:

> [5] [Most certainly true believers] . . . guard their private parts scrupulously, [6] except with regard to their wives and those who are legally in their possession, for in that case they shall not be blameworthy. (Sayyid Abul A'La Maududi, *The Meaning of the Qur'an*, Vol. 3, p. 237.)

The key words are "those who are legally in their possession." Sayyid Abul A'la Maududi (d. 9/22/79) was a highly respected commentator on the Qur'an, and he interprets the plain meaning of the clause, saying that sex with [consenting] slave-girls is lawful. Maududi writes:

> Two categories of women have been excluded from the general command of guarding the private parts: (a) wives, (b) women who are legally in one's possession, i.e. slave-girls. Thus the verse clearly lays down the law that one is allowed to have sexual relations with one's slave-girl as with one's wife, the basis being possession and not marriage. If marriage had been the condition, the slave-girl also would

have been included among the wives, and there was no need to mention them separately. (***Ibid.*** p. 241, note 7.)

So adultery and fornication in the stated context is an accepted practice by Allah and Muhammad. Allah in the Qur'an approved of polygamy, another form of adultery. Quite a contrast to one of the Ten Commandments in the Bible, which states, *"Thou shalt not commit adultery"* (Exodus 20:14), as well as other commands (I Corinthians 6:18-20, etc.), which state that one should not engage in pre-marital sex. Although polygamy was practiced by some in the Old Testament, it was forbidden by God (Deuteronomy 17:17, etc.).

Conclusion

It should be added that Muhammad never claimed to be sinless and never laid claim to performing any miracles.

Much more could be discussed in relation to the character of Muhammad and Allah, and not all would be negative. Remember, all of the Qur'an supposedly comes from Allah; therefore, his commands reflect on him as well as on Muhammad.

CHAPTER 17

CHARACTER OF BIBLE'S GOD/JESUS CHRIST AND HIS IDENTITY

This chapter will briefly examine the characteristics of the Bible's God (Yahweh) and Jesus Christ, providing a stark contrast to the nature of Allah and Muhammad, as shown in the previous chapter.

Since Jesus Christ claimed to be the one true God (Yahweh) of the Bible in the New Testament (NT), talking about God is equal to talking about Jesus Christ and vice versa. **In Appendix C, the biblical claims, and accompanying details, for Christ being God are listed** (the Father, Jesus, and the disciples claimed that Christ was God). Just a few examples here:

- Hebrews 1:8 – the Father calls the Son "God": *"But about the Son he* [the Father] *says, 'Your throne, O God, will last for ever and ever."*

- John 1:1 – *"In the beginning was the Word* [Christ – see v.14], *and the Word was with God, and the Word was God."*

- John 8:58 – Christ claims to be the "I AM" (*ego eimi* in Greek) of Exodus 3:14 of the Old Testament (OT), a term used by God in reference only to himself.

- Matthew 14:33; Matthew 28:9; John 9:38; Hebrews 1:6 – Christ accepts worship due only to God.

- Mark 2:5-12; Luke 5:20-26 – Christ forgives sins against God, which only God can do.

- Revelation 1:8, 11, 17 – Christ is said to be "the first and the last," a term used by God of himself in Isaiah 44:6; 48:12.

The next chapter will show the historicity of Christ's physical resurrection, thereby proving historically his deity.

Bible's God/Jesus Christ

Since Jesus Christ is identified in the Bible as the Creator God, he therefore would possess all of God's moral and ethical characteristics and vice versa.

God is the Creator of the universe. He accepts worship, is holy/sinless, forgives sins against himself, judges sin, has all power (omnipotent) and authority, and is ever-present (omnipresent), and is all-knowing (omniscient). The Bible is clear that only God has these characteristics. Jesus Christ claimed the same things about himself (**see Appendix C**). Christ has all authority and power, which only God has (Matthew 28:18; Ephesians 1:20-21; Colossians 1:16).

The Bible is emphatic that God is a truly loving God. In fact, I John 4:8 says "God is love" (note it does **not** say "love is God"). John 3:16 states, *"For God so loved the world that he gave his one and only Son, that whoever believes in him shall not perish but have eternal life."* Both the OT and NT are filled with numerous passages concerning how much God loves, further distinguishing the Bible's God from the Qur'an's Allah.

Claims by Jesus Christ, God the Father, and others in the NT that Christ is God leave us with only three possibilities:

1. Jesus is telling the truth that he is God, or

2. Jesus is a lunatic, deluded, or

3. Jesus is the biggest liar and hypocrite in history.

This has often been called the *Lord, Liar, or Lunatic* choices regarding Jesus Christ.

Some people reply with, "Jesus was a good man and moral teacher but was *only* a human being, not God." This option is not open to us since anyone who claims he is Creator and God is either an honest truth-teller, a raving lunatic, or a grandiose liar. If one refuses to believe Christ's claims to deity, that person has, by logical implication, concluded that Christ is a lunatic or a liar.

Some may say Jesus never claimed to be God. This is an incorrect claim (refer to Appendix C). According to church history, all of Jesus's original apostles died for proclaiming Christ's deity and his physical resurrection, except for John who died of old age after facing torture.

The God Who Also Became Man

Before his incarnation in Mary, Jesus was eternally God. When he took on human flesh, took on humanity, he was still fully God but also fully human from that point and thereafter. Jesus is both fully God and man.

> [1]*In the beginning was the Word* [Jesus Christ] *and the Word was with God, and the Word was God.* [2]*He was with God in the beginning.* [3]*Through him all things were made; without him nothing was made that has been made.* [14]*The Word became flesh and made his dwelling among us. We have seen his glory, the glory of the one and only Son, who came from the Father, full of grace and truth* (John 1:1-3, 14).

In addition to the biblical passages showing Christ's deity (referenced in Appendix C), the Bible shows his humanity as well. In addition to John chapter 1 above, we find passages like this:

> *For there is one God and one **mediator** between God and mankind, the man Christ Jesus* (1 Timothy 2:5).

Now some groups (such as Jehovah's Witnesses) try to take the "humanity-describing" passages of Christ and claim Jesus Christ was not God. In so doing, they are ignoring all the passages stating Christ is indeed Creator God (Appendix C). In addition, they incorrectly interpret certain passages.

For example, in John 14:28 Christ says, *"the Father is greater than I."* Their argument is that nothing is greater than God, so since Christ said the Father is greater than he is, he (Jesus) cannot be God. The Greek word for "greater" in this passage is *meizon*. It is a comparison of "function," not of "the value or quality of personhood or being." In Philippians 2:6-9, it is clear that when Christ took on humanity (became a man, born of the virgin Mary), he voluntarily lowered himself (on a temporary basis) to a subservient role or function to that of the Father to carry out his earthly ministry. The president of the United States has a greater function (*meizon*) than I do, but our innate value as individuals is equal.

One more example of a sometimes-misinterpreted passage is Colossians 1:15-19, where it says the following:

> [15] *The Son is the image of the invisible God, the firstborn over all creation.* [16] *For in him all things were created: things in heaven and on earth, visible and invisible, whether thrones or powers or rulers or authorities; all things have been created through him and for him.* [17] *He is before all things, and in him all things hold together.* [18] *And he is the head of the body, the church; he is the beginning and the firstborn from among the dead, so that in everything he might have the supremacy.* [19] *For God was pleased to have all his fullness dwell in him.*

Jehovah's Witnesses like to contend that verse 15 teaches that Christ is not God, claiming that he supposedly had a beginning point of existence. They point to the phrasing that says Christ is the "firstborn of all creation" (they use the word "of" rather than "over").

The full context of the above passage shows clearly that Christ is Creator (verses 16-19). Verse 17 even says that everything in the cosmos is held together by Christ. Also, the Greek word for "firstborn" is *prototokos*, which can either mean "to be the firstborn" with chronological aspects OR "to have sovereignty or priority over" **without** any chronological inferences. The latter is clearly meant here since Christ is described as the Creator and is said to have supremacy. That is why the NIV translation, along with others, uses the word "over" as the clearer translation. Elsewhere in Jewish literature, the term *prototokos* is used in reference to God!

Other examples and their explanations could be referenced, such as Christ calling the Father his God, etc., but such references are due to Christ's taking on humanity, becoming a man. All such examples must be viewed alongside the passages that identify Christ as God.

More on Christ's Moral Character

In his earthly ministry, Jesus did not commit murder or violence. On two occasions Jesus overturned the tables of the money changers in the Temple for their greed and unrighteousness (one could say "they had it coming").

Jesus also did not advocate sexual immorality, quite the opposite. Christ never married, and he advocated monogamy: Deuteronomy 17:17 and Christ's reference to the beginning with Adam and Eve when a man shall leave his mother and father and take himself a (singular) wife (Matthew 19:5; Mark 10:7).

Jesus claimed in John 8:46 to be sinless; no one else has ever made that claim.

Per the NT, Christ performed many miracles, including raising people from the dead four times, healing physical ailments like blindness, inability to walk, etc., and even controlling the weather (Mark 4:39).

As previously discussed, Jesus claimed to be the biblical God in the flesh, a claim no one else has ever made.

While truth is certainly not determined by what most people think it might be, the following is worthy of consideration: when people are asked who the most righteous or best person who ever lived was or which single individual has had the most positive impact on the world, the answer, on a worldwide basis, is invariably Jesus Christ – if they know about him.

Jesus, more than anyone else, gave the most sublime spiritual insights and truths. No one else has come close. As Christian scholar and apologist Josh McDowell has said regarding Christ's ethical/moral/ spiritual character, etc.: "If Jesus were not God, then he deserved an Oscar."

Fill in the following blank: "If God did take on human flesh and appear to humanity, the person most likely to have been that individual was _____."

God's/Jesus's Love

Through the centuries man has often abused God's/Jesus's name and character for their own selfish ambitions. However, we should look to the Bible for an accurate characterization of God/Jesus.

In I John 4:16 the Bible says, *"And so we know and rely on the love God has for us. God is love."* The words *God is love* illustrate how loving his character is. John 3:16 states, *"For God so loved the world that he gave his one and only Son, that whoever believes on him shall not perish but have eternal life."* And, of course, there is the famous love of God illustrated in the prodigal son parable of Luke 15:11-32.

Entire books have been written on the loving character of God/ Jesus. However, I will list just a few passages (of hundreds) to illustrate the point, first from the NT and then the OT:

> Jesus said, *"As the Father has loved me, so have I loved you. Now remain in my love"* (John 15:9).

> But God demonstrates his own love for us in this: While we were still sinners, Christ died for us (Romans 5:8).

> Greater love has no one than this: to lay down one's life for one's friends (John 15:13).

> [9] This is how God showed his love among us: He sent his one and only Son into the world that we might live through him. [10] This is love: not that we loved God, but that he loved us and sent his Son as an atoning sacrifice for our sins. [11] Dear friends, since God so loved us, we also ought to love one another (I John 4:9-11).

³⁸For I am convinced that neither death nor life, neither angels nor demons, neither the present nor the future, nor any powers, ³⁹neither height nor depth, nor anything else in all creation, will be able to separate us from the love of God that is in Christ Jesus our Lord (Romans 8:38-39)

But because of his great love for us, God, who is rich in mercy, ⁵made us alive with Christ… (Ephesians 2:4-5).

Give thanks to the God of heaven. His love endures forever (Psalm 136:26)

But you, Lord, are a compassionate and gracious God, slow to anger, abounding in love and faithfulness (Psalm 86:15).

He will take great delight in you; in his love he will no longer rebuke you, but will rejoice over you with singing (Zephaniah 3:17b).

"Though the mountains be shaken and the hills be removed, yet my unfailing love for you will not be shaken nor my covenant of peace be removed," says the Lord, who has compassion on you (Isaiah 54:10).

"For I know the plans I have for you," declares the L ORD, *"plans to prosper you and not to harm you, plans to give you hope and a future"* (Jeremiah 29:11).

Jesus vs. Muhammad

Although many more examples could be provided in this area, the information given thus far should enable the reader to view an accurate comparison of Jesus and Muhammad, making the case that Jesus Christ/God of the Bible, rather than Allah/Muhammad, offers the best evidence for the true God we are seeking.

What About the Bible's God and Violence in the OT?

Violence in relation to Muhammad and Allah was discussed in the previous chapter, so it is only appropriate to raise the issue in relation to the Bible's God, especially in the OT concerning his (i) direction of the Israelites to conquer the land of Canaan, and (ii) disciplining of Israel's disobedience.

First, regarding Israel's conquering of the Canaanites, let me recommend the excellent book *Is God a Moral Monster?* by Paul Copan. It provides extensive research and valuable insights into the "Israel's conquering of Canaan" scenario.

Since God is holy and just, he cannot tolerate sin, especially unchecked, wanton sin. (See chapter 20 on the topic of salvation for a fuller explanation of the relationship of God's holiness to our sin.)

According to the OT, God was punishing Canaan for its extreme depravity; Canaan was beyond "saving" or redemption. It was, in essence, a culture filled with a runaway spiritual cancer that needed to be eliminated. The Canaan societies had become so degenerate that God could not let them go on any longer. Also, if left unchecked, their horrific immorality and practices would have continued to spread, like a cancer.

Examples of their depravity included the sacrificing of infants in fire to one of their false gods, Moloch; occultic practices wherein interaction with demonic forces was not uncommon; various expressions of commonplace sexual immorality; religious prostitution; widespread, if not pandemic-level, sexually transmitted diseases within the culture; rampant murder; and the list could go on and on.

Some 400 years previous to the Israelite invasion of Canaan, God had told Abraham that the Amorites' (one of the Canaanite cultures) evil had not yet reached intolerable levels. Consequently, God was not swift to condemn those he deemed wicked (Genesis 15:16). God gave them a fair chance.

So, as in the case of a human consumed with cancer the loving thing is to remove the cancer in order to save the person's body, the spiritual/moral cancer of the Canaanites needed to be removed for the benefit of humanity. It had reached that point. God used the Israelites as the means of performing the needed operation. It was a one-time operation (over several years), performed on one specific culture (or set of cultures in the area), not to be repeated. However, the Israelites failed to complete the task, due to their disobedience to God.

When the OT used phrases such as "Israel wiped out every living thing," etc. in reference to some of the Canaanite cultures, such wording was not necessarily literal, as in "every single living individual." These phrases were sometimes used as idiomatic expressions to describe the thorough defeat of their foes. This is illustrated more than once when the OT says a certain group of people was wiped out; then we find later on the mention of those same people as still being around. Thus, we can see that such expressions were at times used to express a thorough routing or defeat of the enemy. These types of expressions were commonly used to describe the defeat of governmental centers or towns, not necessarily the surrounding suburbs. Even today we use such expressions in a way that is not literal, like the "Rams [football team] totally destroyed [or wiped out] the Eagles."

Regarding God's periodic discipline of Israel via the invasions by foreign military powers (such as the Assyrians, Babylonians, etc.), such drastic measures were needed to stop the evil contamination and rebellion against God in Israelite society. Israel had even adopted some of the detestable practices of the Canaanite cultures around them (such as worshipping their false gods, sacrificing their infants in fire to the false god Moloch, etc.). Israel needed to be disciplined/punished so it would correct/stop its destructive, reprehensible behavior in the future. Re-establishing a healthy relationship with God was for their benefit.

The God of the OT was not different from the NT's depiction of a loving God. The OT simply, at times, shows the justice aspect of God's character, along with many stories and passages concerning his tender love, patience, and care of humanity. Just as it would be unjust to characterize human parents as unloving when they discipline their children, likewise it would be inaccurate to characterize God in the OT as unloving for his acts of discipline.

CHAPTER 18

EVIDENCE FOR CHRIST'S RESURRECTION

"...I say unequivocally the evidence for the Resurrection of Jesus Christ is so overwhelming that it compels acceptance by proof which leaves absolutely no room for doubt."
(Lawyer, former atheist, Sir Lionel Luckhoo)

All the evidence examined thus far shows the God of the Bible to be the God we are searching for: scientific and prophetic evidence, supporting manuscript evidence, and moral/ethical factors. We have found our true God! (Appendix C offers additional overwhelming evidence from the Bible that Jesus Christ is that one true God.)

Although not required to show the God of the Bible to be the reasonable, logical choice as the true God, one critical supporting piece of evidence remains to be examined: the physical death and resurrection of Jesus Christ. Is it fact or fable? What does the evidence say?

> *If Christ did raise himself from the dead, it truly demonstrates that he is God (the one true God of the Bible), and your personal salvation and quality of life depends on it! Only God could raise himself from the dead.*

"The reason my Father loves me is that I lay down my life – only to take it up again. No one takes it [Christ's life] *from me, but I lay it down of my own accord. I have authority to lay it down and I have authority to take it up again"* (John 10:17-18). (Note: The Father and Holy Spirit [see next chapter on the Trinity] are also involved in the resurrection; see Romans 6:4; Romans 8:11; Acts 2:32).

Christ predicted his death/resurrection: See Matthew 12:39-40; Matthew 16:21; Matthew 27:62-64, etc.

The New Testament (NT) asserts Christ's death (via crucifixion) many times: read the last parts of each of the four NT Gospels (Matthew, Mark, Luke, John); Acts 2:23, 2:36, 4:10; I Corinthians 1:23-24; 2:2; Galatians 3:1; Philippians 2:8; etc.

Jesus raised four other people from the dead per the NT, and only one person has ever raised himself from the dead in the history of humanity, and that is Jesus Christ.

All other religious/spiritual figures of the past remain buried, except for Jesus Christ. Except for Jesus Christ, the very few who claimed to be "god" were quite evil and/or often insane.

Now we will look at the evidence for the resurrection. Some people are inclined to think that since the alleged event happened about 2,000 years ago, the evidence must be lacking or at least is sketchy. This is simply not true; actually, the historical evidence is quite convincing, even compelling.

Many books have been written concerning the evidence of the resurrection. This treatise contains only one short chapter that touches on some of the highlights. (Refer to the Bibliography and Recommended Sources for additional information.)

Skeptics Turning Believers

Before turning to the evidence itself, which has turned numerous skeptics into believers, let us consider a few examples.

Simon Greenleaf is recognized historically as one of America's top lawyers – ever. He was the co-founder of Harvard Law School. He wrote *A Treatise on the Law of Evidence* (1842), which is still considered the greatest single authority on evidence in the entire literature of legal procedure. He wrote the rules of evidence for the US legal system. He was an atheist Jew until he examined the historicity of Christ's resurrection. After examining the evidence, he became a Christian.

Lionel Luckhoo, recorded in the *Guinness Book of World Records* as the *World's Most Successful Advocate* with 245 consecutive murder acquittals and twice knighted by Queen Elizabeth, was an atheist most of his life. However, after examining the historical evidence regarding the resurrection, he became a Christian and made the statement quoted at beginning of this chapter.

> "...I say unequivocally the evidence for the Resurrection of Jesus Christ is so overwhelming that it compels acceptance by proof which leaves absolutely no room for doubt."
> (Sir Lionel Luckhoo, *The Question Answered: Did Jesus Rise from the Dead?*, back page).

Josh McDowell, one of Christianity's leading apologists for the past 50 years, was challenged as a college student to examine the resurrection. He was definitely anti-Christian at that time. Taking up the challenge, he suspended his college training in an attempt to disprove the resurrection. He spent two years, 900 hours of research, involving some of the great libraries of the world. He became a Christian as a result of the evidence. (Refer to the list of his books in the Bibliography and Recommended References.)

Lee Strobel, also a leading Christian apologist, was once an atheist. After obtaining a master of studies in law from Yale Law School, he worked as an award-winning journalist for 13 years. When his wife became a Christian, his life was thrown into turmoil, and he reluctantly examined the evidence for the life and resurrection of Christ, trying to disprove the whole thing. However, he ultimately became a Christian because of the evidence for Christ's resurrection; he could not refute it, in spite of all his legal background and expertise. (Refer to his books and material in Recommended References.)

Lord Lyndhurst, attorney general for Great Britain and three times high chancellor of England, in his private papers wrote: "I know pretty well what evidence is; and I tell you, such evidence as for the Resurrection has never broken down yet."

What exactly did these highly qualified men, as well as other intelligent men and women, find? Let us look at a summary of some of the evidence. The world's leading authority on the resurrection today is probably Gary Habermas. As of this writing, he is in the middle of producing a 3,000-page/10-volume work documenting the evidence for the resurrection. (See the Bibliography and Recommended References at the end for some of his existing material.)

Finally, there is the witness of the NT writers; initially they were all skeptical of Christ's resurrection. They changed their minds upon Christ showing of himself. All of the apostles, except for John who was tortured, lost their lives for proclaiming the deity and resurrection of Jesus Christ. The NT books are based on eyewitness testimony. We have already noted in an earlier chapter the amazing accuracy of the NT manuscripts. These books fully document the crucifixion (death) and resurrection of Jesus Christ, and are history's closest, oldest, and best documentation of the event.

> [1]*Many have undertaken to draw up an account of the things that have been fulfilled among us,* [2]*just as they were handed down to us by those who from the first were eyewitnesses and servants of the word.* [3]*With this in mind, since I myself have carefully investigated everything from the beginning, I too decided to write an orderly account for you, most excellent Theophilus,* [4]*so that you may know the certainty of the things you have been taught* (Luke 1:1-4).

> [1]*That which was from the beginning, which we have heard, which we have seen with our eyes, which we have looked at and our hands have touched – this we proclaim concerning the Word of life.* [2]*The life appeared; we have seen it and testify to it, and we proclaim to you the eternal life, which was with the Father and has appeared to us* (I John 1:1-2).

> *We did not follow cleverly devised stories when we told you*

about the coming of our Lord Jesus Christ in power, but we were eyewitnesses of his majesty (II Peter 1:16).

Did Jesus Christ Ever Exist?

The beginning point is to ask, "Was there ever a person in history named Jesus Christ of Nazareth in the first century?" If there was not, then a resurrection obviously would not be possible.

No serious historian today really questions the existence of Jesus Christ as a historical person. At least seventeen first century sources outside of the Bible and early church fathers include Christ as being a real person of history, and several even mention his crucifixion. Ten of these sources are shown below:

Author (all AD)	Document	Nature of Reference/ Quote
Cornelius Tacitus (55-120); Greatest Roman Historian	Annals 15.44	Refers to Christ, plus his crucifixion under Pontius Pilatus (Pilate)
Suetonius Roman (2nd C); Roman Historian; Chief Secretary to Emperor Hadrian	Claudius 25	Refers to Jewish disruptions in Rome (AD 49) due to Christ
Flavius Josephus (37/38 – 97)	Antiquities (circa 95) 200:9	Refers to James, "the brother of Jesus who was called the Christ"
Flavius Josephus (37/38 – 97)	Antiquities 18:3	Parts are debated, but that Christ is referenced as a real person is not.
Pliny the Younger; Roman Author, Governor	Letters, V. II, X:96 (circa 112)	States Christians worship Christ as deity
Jewish Oral Traditions (Compiled by 135, Revelation 200)	The Babylonian Talmud, V.III, Sanhedrin 43a	From portion of 70 – 200, "On the eve of the Passover Yeshu [Jesus] was hanged" [i.e., crucified; Galatians 3:13 equates hanging w/crucifixion]

Author (all AD)	Document	Nature of Reference/ Quote
Lucian (Greek Satirist), 2nd C.	The Death of Peregrine, 11-13	"The Christians... worship a man to this day...who introduced their novel rites, and was crucified..."
Phlegon (b. 80); Freedman of Emperor Hadrian as Quoted by Origen (Early Church Father in 4th C)	Quoting Phlegon's Work, Chronicles, Origen in Contra Celsum XIV in the Anti-Nicene Fathers	"Now Phlegon, in the thirteenth or fourteenth book...of his Chronicles, not only ascribed to Jesus a knowledge of future events...but also testified that the result corresponded to His predictions."
Mara Bar-Serapion (a Syrian, between 1st – 3rd C)	Letter from Mara to his Son Serapion, British Museum, Syriac Manuscript, Additional	"What advantage did the Jews gain from executing their wise King? [only Jesus could fit this] It was just after that their kingdom was abolished..." (i.e., 70 AD, fall of Jerusalem)

Justin Martyr (an early church father), around 150 AD in his *First Apology, XXXV, to the Emperor Tiberius*, stated,

> And the expression, 'They pierced my hands and my feet,' was used in reference to the nails of the cross which were fixed in His hands and feet. And after He was crucified, they cast lots upon His vesture, and they that crucified Him parted it among them. And that these things did happen you can ascertain in the 'Acts of Pontius Pilate.'

A person needs to ask, "Why would Justin write to the *Roman emperor* and tell him to reference a nonexistent document in support of his (Justin's) argument?" Simply put, he wouldn't. Hence, the document must have existed.

Further, Justin Martyr, again to the Emperor, in regard to Christ performing miracles stated,

And that He [Christ] did those things, you can learn from the 'Acts of Pontius Pilate' (*First Apology*, XLVIII).

Jesus's Burial – Friday Afternoon

Jesus was wrapped in cloth strips according to Jewish custom (John 19:39). Between each strip a glue-like substance of myrrh and aloes was applied (John 19:39 says about 75 lbs. worth). This resulted in a hard casing around the body.

Christ's body was then placed into a rock tomb belonging to Joseph of Arimathea. According to archaeology, these kinds of tombs would have a 1.5 – 2-ton stone rolled in front of the only entrance/exit (Matthew 27:60; Mark 15:46). A few men could put the stone into place, but it took up to twenty men to remove it.

When the tomb was still open, the stone was put at the top of a V-shaped groove in front of the tomb. A wedge was put under the stone. To close the tomb, the wedge was removed, making it a not-too-difficult task to row the stone downhill into the bottom part of the V-shaped groove. Removing the same stone would require moving the stone uphill (up the V-shaped groove), a very difficult task that could take up to twenty men to remove it.

Matthew 27:65 records that the Jewish leaders convinced Pilate to agree to post a Roman guard at the tomb to prevent anyone from attempting to steal Christ's body. The tomb was sealed with a Roman seal, and Jewish Pharisees asked Pilate for the Roman guards, after telling him that Christ, when he was alive, had predicted his resurrection. They were afraid the disciples would steal the body and then claim a resurrection.

From Roman military history, we know that this Roman unit of men was a group of 4 – 16 highly trained and feared individuals. They were sort of the first century's equivalent to a special forces unit in terms of their abilities to fulfill their mission.

Although some may say the Jewish Temple police were the ones used as guards, we will see it was indeed a guard of Roman soldiers. (More on this aspect later when we examine an erroneous theory that Jesus's disciples stole the body while all the guards fell asleep at their posts.)

Sunday Morning: Empty Tomb

The Bible is clear about the reason for the empty tomb: Christ had risen bodily from the dead. The resurrection!

Can the empty tomb be proved historically? This is relatively easy. If the tomb were not empty but still had Christ's body, Christ's opponents (the Jewish ruling religious leaders and the Romans) would have simply gone to the tomb and dragged the body out to show everyone and, in so doing, would have squashed Christianity instantly. The enemies of Christianity would have loved that. This one fact, that no body was shown, demonstrates that there was no body to reveal.

In addition, the following two secular Jewish sources attest to the empty tomb and the lack of a body:

- In a sixth century Jewish document from the Jewish community, the Jewish Toledoth *Yeshu* describes Christ as a disrespectful deceiver, etc., and it also said,

    » Diligent search was made, and he [Jesus] was not found in the grave where he had been buried.

- Justin Martyr, around 165 AD, in his *Dialogue with Trypho*, at the beginning of chapter 108, records a Jewish community letter about the empty tomb:

    » [A] godless and lawless heresy had sprung from one Jesus, a Galilean deceiver, whom we crucified, but his disciples stole him by night from the tomb, where he was laid…

> We are left with an empty tomb; this is abundantly clear. The real issue is, how did the tomb become empty three days later?

Theoretical Explanations for the Empty Tomb

The table on the next page shows seven theories that have been proposed over the centuries in efforts to explain away the resurrection. It shows how the seven erroneous theories attempting to explain away the resurrection cannot adequately dismiss most of the twelve stated historical facts agreed upon by virtually all critics. Only the resurrection is able to account for all of them. The others, in theory, might explain up to four of the twelve agreed-upon historical facts.

The table is credited to Gary Habermas, referenced earlier. Gary's research is based on reviews of over 1400 scholarly treatments of Christ's death, burial, and resurrection published since 1975 in English, German, and French. The table shows 11 historical facts all critics (skeptic or not) agree on, with 75% agreeing on No. 4 (already discussed – the empty tomb).

A total of 18 historical facts could be listed on which the majority of critics (pro and con) agree. More than 18 facts could be listed upon which the pro and critics would agree.

It has often been said, "Once you eliminate the impossible, whatever remains, no matter how improbable, must be the truth" (*Sherlock Homes*, Arthur Conan Doyle). In this case, however, it can be claimed that the divine miracle of the resurrection is not improbable when all things are considered; instead, it is the only viable answer.

HISTORICITY OF JESUS CHRIST'S RESURRECTION									
HISTORICAL FACTS			**ERRONEOUS THEORIES**						
Almost Every Critic of Jesus's Resurrection Agrees on 11 of the below 12 Historical Facts, and 75% agree on Point No. 4 (which has already been discussed)		RESURRECTION (only explanation meeting all agreed- upon historical facts)	Trying to Explain Away the Resurrection ("x" means the theory in question could possibly meet the historical fact)						
			Did not Die	Wrong Tomb	False Legend	Body Stolen	Hallucinations	Used a Twin	Rose a Spirit*
			A	B	C	D	E	F	G
1	Jesus died by crucifixion	X		X		X	X	X	X
2	Jesus was buried	X	?	X		X	X	X	X
3	Disciples lost hope, were in despair	X	X	X		X	X	X	X
4	Tomb was empty	X	X	X		X			
5	Disciples believed he was risen	X							
6	Disciples changed to bold proclaimers	X							
7	Resurrection is the basis of early Church	X							
8	Message proclaimed amidst eyewitnesses	X							
9	Resurrection caused birth of Church	X							
10	Sunday became new main day of worship**	X							
11	James converted from skepticism	X							
12	Paul converted from skepticism	X							

*"Rose a Spirit" erroneously assumes the spirit died and then was re-created.

**Would require something *very drastic* for orthodox Jews to switch Sabbaths.

Did Jesus Christ Actually Die by Crucifixion?

There cannot be a resurrection if there was no death. Therefore, the historicity of Christ's execution/death on the cross needs to be examined next.

Previously, we have seen that three secular sources attested to Christ's death by crucifixion, including the Roman senator and historian Tacitus. If you were crucified, you died. One of the above sources actually stated that Christ was "executed."

Not one viable historical reference denies the crucifixion and death by crucifixion of Christ. Further, not even Jesus's opponents (such as the Jewish Pharisees and Romans) tried to claim he did not die.

Matthew 27:26, Mark 15:15, and John 19:1 record that before being crucified, Christ was subjected to the Roman flagrum or whipping. This was typical Roman practice. The whip had leather strings with hard balls of lead and sharp pieces of metal at the ends.

This Roman whipping was so severe that sometimes people died from it before they were crucified. The whip would dig into the victim's back, and then the Roman doing the whipping would pull down on the whip, further tearing into the victim's back. The victim's inner organs were often exposed due to the tearing away of the flesh and muscles.

The act of crucifixion was/is probably the worst execution method ever devised. If the person did not die due to the wounds, he would die of suffocation on the cross. A person hanging on the cross would occasionally push himself up to obtain a breath of air and then have to lower himself (due to lack of strength) back to the lower, hanging position where he could not breathe. Eventually, the crucified victim did not have enough strength to push himself up again to get a new breath of air, which resulted in suffocation.

It did not require rocket science to tell when a person was not breathing. In fact, if the death process needed to be sped up, the Roman soldiers would break the legs of crucifixion victims so the ones being crucified could not raise themselves up any more to take a breath; suffocation resulted.

In John 19:34, the Apostle John records that a Roman soldier thrust a spear into Christ's side, which resulted in blood and water coming out. The Apostle John may have understood this to be a sign of death, but he probably did not understand the medical reason for it, which was that the spear pierced Jesus's pericardium (the sac surrounding the heart). The release of blood and water was a definite sign of death.

Typically, three Roman coroners would check a crucified body to be sure the person was dead before disposing of the body. The Romans were experts in death. Most likely Christ was so examined, especially considering the importance of his death to the Romans and Jewish leaders.

Lastly, Christ's body was carried off by Joseph of Arimathea and Nicodemus (John 19:39), prepared for burial, and placed in Joseph's tomb (Matthew 27: 57-61; Mark 15:42-47; Luke 23:50-55; John 19:38-42). These two men were well-known and well-respected Jewish leaders: Joseph was a voting member of the Jewish Sanhedrin and, per Luke 23:50, a good and upright man; and Nicodemus was a Pharisee (John 3:1). When preparing Christ's body for burial, they would have easily known if he was still breathing. Obviously, they would not have buried him if he was.

The above information shows that Christ died by crucifixion. With that being said, one could imagine the pitiful shape Christ would have been in had he not died. Such a condition certainly would not have inspired his followers to risk their lives and change the world.

The Wrong Tomb Theory

A now defunct theory postulated that those who went to the burial place of Jesus ended up at the wrong tomb. This is nonsensical; it would mean that Joseph of Arimathea (the tomb's owner), Nicodemus (who helped bury Jesus), the women who went with Joseph to bury Jesus, the Romans, the Pharisees, and Jesus's apostles and disciples all went to the wrong tomb. This is a stretch beyond all believability.

In addition, this theory does not account for all the appearances of Christ afterwards. All the evidence mitigates against the wrong tomb theory; it would require more faith to believe such a theory than to claim the tomb was empty.

Lastly, even the Jewish leaders and Romans did not try to promote the outlandish idea of a wrong tomb. A variation of the wrong tomb theory is that Jesus's body was put into another unknown tomb by others. This theory totally contradicts the NT record, there is no evidence for it, and it is negated by arguments against the *disciples stole the body theory* (given below). It is not a theory even the liberal critics seriously try to offer. In addition, remember that two highly respected men of the community (Joseph and Nicodemus) buried him, so they knew where Christ's body was; recall that Joseph's own tomb was used.

The "Legend Theory": Was the Resurrection Only a Legend Later Created by the Early Church?

This outdated "Legend Theory" does not potentially explain any of the known historical facts.

The best scholarly views of when the crucifixion occurred are either 30 or 33 AD (see Appendix B). Except for the Gospel of John and I, II, and III John and the book of Revelation, the NT books were written from about 48/49 to 64/68 AD (Matthew: 50s –60s; Mark: 50s–60s; Luke: 60; I Corinthians: 55; Galatians: 48-49; all of Paul's epistles: from 48 to 64/68 AD. John's Gospel and Revelation were possibly written by 68/69 AD, but most say they, along with I, II, and III John, by 95 AD.

Typically, legendary tales take two to three hundred years to develop, but certainly longer than the 16-to-38-year span between when the Gospels and Epistles were written compared to the actual event. Therefore, these books were written within the lifetimes of people who were alive during the event(s) claimed. False legends can easily be refuted by living eyewitnesses. For example, if someone today tried to claim President John F. Kennedy was stabbed to death in a restaurant (instead of being shot when in his motorcade), can you image how many people who were alive in 1963 (almost 60 years ago) would come forward and object to the false story, even without the recordings of modern media.

In addition, NT books have resurrection creeds imbedded in their texts that can be traced to even earlier periods than the written dates of the NT books – even to the early to middle 30s. For example, the Apostle Paul says:

> [3] *For what I received I passed on to you as of first importance: that Christ died for our sins according to the Scriptures,* [4] *that he was buried, that he was raised on the third day according to the Scriptures,* [5] *and that he appeared to Cephas, and then to the Twelve.* [6] *After that, he appeared to more than five hundred of the brothers and sisters at the same time, most of whom are still living, though some have fallen asleep.* [7] *Then he appeared to James, then to all the apostles,* [8] *and last of all he appeared to me* (I Corinthians 15:3-8).

Due to stylistic and vocabulary characteristics, this creed, a stylized hymn, is thought by most scholars to have originated as far back as the resurrection itself. Conservative and liberal scholars generally accept the date of Paul's conversion within a few years of the crucifixion, perhaps only 1-2 years. Additionally, since this creed existed at the time of Paul's visit to Peter and James during 34-36 AD (when he discussed the gospel with Peter and James), the creed had to originate even before.

It is interesting to note in this passage that Paul is essentially saying, "If you don't believe I saw the risen Lord, check it out with any of the over 500 people who saw the risen Christ at one time."

Atheist writer, Bart Ehrman states:

> Historians, of course, have no difficulty whatsoever speaking about the belief in Jesus' resurrection, since this is a matter of public record. For it is a historical fact that some of Jesus' followers came to believe that he had been raised from the dead soon after his execution. (*Jesus: An Apocalyptic Prophet of the New Millennium*, p. 231)

Scholar Gerald O'Collins states that the sermon content in the book of Acts (by Luke):

Incorporates resurrection formulae which stem from the thirties. (*Interpreting Jesus*, pp. 109-110)

Scholar John Drane adds:

> The earliest evidence we have for the resurrection almost certainly goes back to the time immediately after the resurrection event is alleged to have taken place. This is the evidence contained in the earlier sermons in the Acts of the Apostles. (*Introducing the New Testament*, p. 99)

According to Gary Habermas, almost all the critical scholars (liberal or conservative) agree the resurrection story goes back to just after the crucifixion, and early Christians *believed* they had experiences of the risen Lord Jesus Christ. Habermas includes scholars who deny the literal physical resurrection of Jesus.

In light of the above, the *legend theory* has been discarded. The next theory is:

Did Jesus's Apostles Steal the Body of Jesus and Then Proclaim He Had Risen?

This "Disciples Stole Jesus's Body" is the oldest theory. In fact, Matthew himself brings this theory up in Matthew 28:11-15, wherein he states the Jewish authorities bribed the Roman guard protecting Jesus's tomb to spread the rumor the body of Jesus had been stolen by his disciples while they (the guards) were asleep (the Greek word *koustodia* is used to refer to the "guard," a term used to reference the Roman guards).

A theory to explain something is certainly lacking credibility when the theory itself contains a glaring inconsistency in logic. In this case, how could the Roman guard have known who stole the body if they were asleep when it happened?

Referenced earlier, but it bears repeating, Justin Martyr, around 165 AD, in his *Dialogue with Trypho* at the beginning of chapter 108, records a Jewish community letter about the empty tomb and the theory of the disciples stealing the body:

> [A] godless and lawless heresy had sprung from one Jesus,
> a Galilean deceiver, whom we crucified, but his disciples
> stole him by night from the tomb, where he was laid.

Notice the Pharisees did not claim that Christ was still alive after his crucifixion nor that everyone went to the wrong tomb (both untenable theories discussed earlier). They fabricated a lie that the disciples stole the body while the Roman guard was asleep. This explanation was their best attempt to explain away the empty tomb. Can you imagine in a court of law today a person claiming his TV set was stolen by his neighbor while the accuser was sleeping the entire time on a nearby sofa. The judge would ask the accuser if he had any corroborating evidence. If the person said no, he would be laughed out of court – since he was in effect unconscious (sleeping) when the theft occurred.

From Josh and Sean McDowell's book, *Evidence of the Resurrection, What It Means for Your Relationship with God* (pp. 123-126), the following quote discusses at length the situation regarding the Roman guard (note: the superscripts imbedded in the quote are bibliographical references in that book to various authoritative works on the statement/task discussed):

> The Jewish officials panicked because thousands were turn-
> ing to Christ. To avoid a political problem, it was to the
> advantage of both the Romans and Jews to make sure Jesus
> was put away for good. So after the crucifixion, the chief
> priests and Pharisees said to Pilate:

> "Sir, we remember what that deceiver once said while he
> was still alive: 'After three days I will rise from the dead.'
> So we request that you seal the tomb until the third day.
> This will prevent his disciples from coming and stealing
> his body and then telling everyone he was raised from the
> dead! If that happens, we'll be worse off than we were at
> first." Pilate replied, "Take guards and secure it the best you
> can." So they sealed the tomb and posted guards to protect
> it (Matthew 27:63-66) [the NASB version reads 'they set

a seal on the stone,' which is a more literal rendition than 'they sealed the tomb'].

Some people argue that Pilate was actually saying, "Look, you have your Temple police. You take them and go make the tomb secure."

If it was the Temple police that guarded Christ's tomb, that unit would not have been slouches at their job. Temple guards were responsible for protecting the courts and gates of the Temple. A unit consisted of 10 Levites who were placed on duty at strategic locations about the Temple. There were 27 such units, or a total of 270 men on duty.

The guardsmen were thoroughly trained, and the military discipline of the guard was excellent. In fact, at night, if the captain approached a guard member who was asleep, he was beaten and burned with his own clothes.[16] A member of the guard also was forbidden to sit down or to lean against anything while on duty.

We are convinced, however, that it was the Roman guard who was ordered to secure the tomb of Christ. A. T. Robertson, noted Greek scholar, says that Pilate's response to the Jews' request is phrased in the present imperative and can refer only to a Roman guard, not the Temple police. According to him, Pilate literally said, "Have a guard."

Robertson adds that the Latin form *koustodia*, the term Pilate used in this passage to designate the guard he authorized, occurs as far back as the Oxyrhynchus papyrus (AD 22). This term is always used only in reference to the Roman guard.[18] Pilate wanted to prevent any tampering with Jesus' tomb, so he was very likely to want his own soldiers guarding the tomb.

The great New Testament scholar Raymond Brown offers five reasons why the guard was Roman:

1. The apocryphal Gospel of Peter clearly understands Pilate to offer Roman soldiers to protect the tomb.

2. If the Jewish leaders had wanted to use their own Temple police, why would they request Pilate's help at all?

3. Matthew's use of *koustodia* matches the picture of a Roman prefect assigning Roman troops.

4. Matthew refers to the guards as 'soldiers,' the plural of *stratiotes*. Twenty-two of twenty-six uses of *stratiotes* in the New Testament refer to Roman soldiers. In another three references (Acts 12:4, 6, 18), *stratiotes* refers to the soldiers of King Herod Agrippa I. Never in the New Testament does the term refer to the Temple police.

5. If the guards were Jewish, why would they be responsible to the governor of Rome for failing to fulfill their duties, as Matthew 28:14 implies?[19]

Also worth noting is that John reports the involvement of a Roman cohort in the arrest of Jesus (see 18:12). This clearly indicates that the Roman authorities were deeply concerned with the fate of Jesus. As John Wenham has observed, "It is a great mistake to underestimate the anxiety which the following of Jesus caused the authorities."[20] The arrest of Jesus by a Roman cohort also gives precedence for the reporting of Roman troops to Jewish authorities in specially assigned instances.

As Dr. Brown notes above, if the priests had wanted to post Temple police at the tomb, they would not have needed the orders of the governor to do it. Their request indicates that they were seeking assignment to them of a unit of Roman soldiers. That this was indeed the case is affirmed by the fact that the Roman soldiers later came to the chief priests for protection because they knew that they would have influence over Pilate: "If the governor hears about it, we'll stand up for you so you won't get in trouble" (Matthew 28:14).

At this point a critic might say, "See, the guards came to the high priest. That shows that they were the Temple guard." The context is clear, however, that they came to the high priest because he had influence with the Roman authority, and appealing to him was the only possible way to save their necks from Roman reprisal for their failure. What was their failure? They were ordered to protect the tomb of Jesus to keep his body from being stolen, and the body was missing. They reported to the high priest that they saw an angel as bright as lightning come down from heaven and move the stone before they fainted dead away in terror. The high priest could not allow such a story to get out, so he bribed the guards into reporting that the disciples of Jesus stole his body while they were sleeping (see Matthew 28:11-15). Such a bribe would have been nonsensical if these guards had been the Temple police. Since the high priest was their supervisor, a simple order would have sufficed. Instead, the priest gave the guards money and assured them that he would intervene to save their lives when the news reached Pilate. *[end of citation]*

Matthew 27:66 says the guard sealed the tomb. This is a reference to the use of the Roman seal, not the putting of the huge stone in front of the tomb (that was done earlier). The seal used had leather strings with sealing clay at both ends, which were stamped with the Roman seal. According to scholar A.T. Robertson, this seal was only put on in the presence of the Roman guard (not the Temple police). To break the seal meant death.

The Roman penalty for a Roman guard unit to fall asleep at their posts was death. No wonder the Pharisees said they would protect them from Pilate if necessary. According to Roman military history, members of the Roman guard would take shifts sleeping while the majority would stay awake.

In addition, could you image Jesus's disciples, who were scared out of their wits that they might be found by the authorities at this point, physically taking on the Roman guard? Or could you imagine the disciples rolling a 1.5 – 2-ton stone out of its place in front of the tomb without waking any of the guards? Of course, this would never happen.

This theory grows worse by accusing the disciples of a cover-up involving lying, deceit, etc. Such behavior would have totally contradicted their ethic of honesty and morality and risked their eternal destinies according to Jewish law.

Lastly, this theory cannot explain why the disciples all gave up their lives for proclaiming the resurrection. If they knew it was a cover-up, a lie, they would not have given up their lives for propagating it, receiving only persecution and death in return.

Some in the past have given up their lives for ideological/spiritual ideas, which, although false, they believed to be true. However, that is different than the scenario with Jesus's followers. Their claims involved physical events (seeing Jesus, eating with him, touching him, etc.) that they would have known to be true. Conversely, if it had not happened, they would not have given up their lives for a false claim of resurrection.

> The disciples claimed to have seen the risen Christ, to have eaten with him, to have touched him for up to forty days after the resurrection. If all this was false, they knew it; therefore, they would not have died for proclaiming the resurrection as true while knowing it was false. But since they gave up their lives for the resurrection and for the reports of their repeated interactions with Christ afterward, it had to be true.

The stolen body theory dies as a result of its internal and external problems with logic and evidence.

Were All the Appearances of Christ to His Followers Only Hallucinations?

The favorite explanation today, of the seven proposed theories to explain away the resurrection, appears to be that people must have experienced hallucinations of Christ when they thought they saw him.

Today many skeptics are *not* promoting any of the other possible explanations for the resurrection, considering the many pitfalls, inconsistencies, and lack of historical evidence for these theories. To explain away the multiple sightings and the abrupt change in the history of mankind as a result, they suggest that when Christ's followers saw him, they only *thought* they saw him; in other words, they must have experienced hallucinations.

To again quote from the atheist writer, Bart Ehrman, he states:

> Historians, of course, have no difficulty whatsoever speaking about the belief in Jesus' resurrection, since this is a matter of public record. For it is a historical fact that some of Jesus' followers **came to believe** that he had been raised from the dead soon after his execution. (*Jesus: An Apocalyptic Prophet of the New Millennium,* p. 231) (bold-faced emphasis is mine)

Notice the words "came to believe." The translation of Ehrman's words was "hallucinations," or "they thought they saw him but really did not."

Regardless, the question we must answer is: "Are hallucinations adequate to explain away what people saw when they saw the risen Christ?" The definitive answer is no.

Hallucinations are the result of the subjective mind's anticipations, such as seeing a mirage of water in a desert when one is desperate for water. However, the case with Christ's followers is this: Jews in this period of history did not believe in a physical resurrection of the dead until the end of time (the end of the world as we know it). They in no way were hoping for a resurrection in the middle of time. It was outside their worldview. Plus, if the NT accounts are to be considered, Christ's followers were depressed, frightened, and initially did not believe the initial reporting of sightings of Jesus. Theirs was not an anticipation of a risen Jesus. This mindset goes against the mechanisms of hallucinations.

Second, hallucinations are very individualistic; they vary from individual to individual. Hallucinations are not shared experiences, and they typically only occur to one individual at a time in a given timeframe.

In the case of Jesus, different people from different locales, under different emotional states, over a period of forty days, all saw the same thing: the risen Lord. In fact, over 500 people at one time saw him according to Paul in I Corinthians 15. All of these characteristics defy the behavior of hallucinations. Further, people touched him, ate with him, and conversed with him. Hallucinations after Jesus's death do not fit the scenarios of Jesus and his followers; they never have, never will.

Was It a Twin or a Double of Jesus Who Died on the Cross While the Real One Stayed Alive?

Islam, for example, has tried to say that the real Jesus was never crucified; rather, it was either a twin or a double.

This idea is so unrealistic it has never gained much traction over the centuries. First, what would have been the incentive for the twin or double to act in Jesus's place to be tortured and crucified? There would have been no incentive, except the incentive *not to* do it. Second, according to all we know of Jesus's family, there was no twin. To find a physical duplicate outside of the family and get him to volunteer for such an excruciating task is unrealistic.

Another problem with this suggestion would be the moral character of Jesus himself: it would mean he was involved in the wrongful death of another person in order to fool the entire world and history into believing the biggest lie ever fostered upon humanity. This would not fit Jesus's moral character, nor his teachings for which he lived and died.

Finally, the disciples and Jesus's family would have been aware of this bait-and-switch scheme, thereby involving them in the greatest deception of all time. Such behavior on their part would have involved another set of issues and problems, including their risking their eternal destinies as Jewish adherents. And, as stated before, they would not have given up their mortal lives for a lie they had supposedly propagated and for which there was no motive.

Lastly, what would be the feasibility of a reverse switch: i.e., if the real Jesus died on the cross and a duplicate or twin was substituted as the risen Jesus? What would have been the incentive on the part of the living, fake Jesus and his followers? According to church history, proclaiming the resurrection only got all of Jesus's apostles killed (except one, John, who was tortured). Realistically, at least a few, if not all of them, would have divulged the plot in order to save their lives. There was no incentive, monetary or political, to propagate such a scenario. And it is totally unrealistic to think there could have been a situation where only the fake Jesus knew about the ruse. His apostles would have caught on, not to mention his family. Again, for devout Jews to propagate such a lie would have risked their eternal destiny.

Jesus Raised Only as a Spirit?

This theory is primarily advocated by Jehovah's Witnesses, who do not believe in the physical resurrection of Christ. I Peter 3:18 is taken out of context, where it says: *"He* [Christ] *was put to death in the body but made alive in the Spirit."* Jehovah's Witnesses, while ignoring all the other biblical passages concerning Christ's physical resurrection, contend "made alive in the Spirit" means only a spiritual resurrection.

First, the Jews never believed in a mere spiritual resurrection. They only believed in a physical one at the end of time, as previously stated. The Bible teaches that upon physical death, the spirit goes either to God or is separated from God, for eternity. Since the spirit of a person continues to exist, a spiritual resurrection does not make any sense. The Jehovah's Witnesses incorrectly believe the spirit ceases to exist upon physical death and is recreated at the end of time.

The Bible disagrees with this theory on many levels. First, when the women visited the empty tomb on Sunday morning, the angels they encountered said:

> [6]*He is not here; he has risen, just as he said. Come and see the place where he lay.* [7]*Then go quickly and tell his disciples: 'He has risen from the dead'* (Matthew 28:6-7). (Also see Mark 16:4-7; Luke 24:1-7.)

In the above accounts, the angels point to the lack of a physical body in the empty tomb to prove a physical resurrection. The lack of a body would prove nothing in terms of a mere spirit being recreated.

In all four Gospels, Jesus shows his resurrected body is a physical one. For example:

> [39]*"Look at my hands and my feet. It is I myself! Touch me and see; a ghost does not have flesh and bones, as you see I have."* [40]*When he had said this, he showed them his hands and feet.* [41]*And while they still did not believe it because of joy and amazement, he asked them, "Do you have anything here to eat?"* [42]*They gave him a piece of broiled fish,* [43]*and he took it and ate it in their presence* (Luke 24:39-43).

> *Then he said to Thomas, "Put your finger here; see my hands. Reach out your hand and put it into my side. Stop doubting and believe"* (John 20:27).

Conclusion

As stated at the beginning of this chapter, the evidence presented in this book is not all of the evidence available; it represents the mere highlights. However, such evidence is convincing and compelling. It has withstood the closest scrutiny by many highly intelligent individuals over the centuries.

We can truly concur with the Christians in the first century, who often greeted one another with the words, "He has risen!" The response would be, **"He has risen indeed!"**

CHAPTER 19

IS THE TRUE
GOD TRIUNE?

So far we have identified, based on a preponderance of evidence, who the one true God is and that he came as Jesus Christ. The final question to be asked here is: Is God triune? Meaning, is the one uncreated God a singular (Judaism) or triune (Christianity) being? "Triune" (i.e., the Trinity) means that the one God is composed of three personages, Father/Son/Holy Spirit, who each are equally and fully the same one true God.

The Bible explicitly claims there is only one true God: see Isaiah, chapters 43-45; Deuteronomy 4:6, 39; Joel 2:27; I Corinthians 8:4-6, James 2:19, etc.

Orthodox Judaism contends the God (Yahweh) of the Old Testament (OT) is a singular unity, whereas Christianity purports Yahweh of the OT and New Testament (NT) to be a composite unity (the Trinity). Which is he?

After looking at the Trinity from a biblical perspective, a look at the Trinity from a scientific perspective will be offered: how is it possible that God can be three in one?

Biblical Evidence of the Trinity

The Bible claims there is only one true God; however, Scripture also states that the Father is God, Jesus is God, and the Holy Spirit is God (see Appendices C, D, and E). Further, the Bible clearly shows each one to be a person. Therefore, based on biblical logic, the one God must be a composite unity of the persons of the Father and Son and Holy Spirit, yet while separate persons, each is fully the same true God. (Refer to Appendix E on the Trinity for the biblical references and logic).

Beginning in Genesis, we have indications that God is a composite unity. Genesis 1:26-27 states (underlining is my emphasis):

> [26] *Then God said, 'Let us make mankind in our image, in our likeness,' …* [27] *So God created mankind in his own image, in the image of God he created them; male and female he created them.*

First the Hebrew word for God is *Elohim*, which has a plural ending, literally meaning "gods." However, when used to refer to the one true God of Israel, *Elohim* is always used with a singular verb (although it may seem to be bad grammar, it is an excellent way, grammatically, to show a plurality within the one God). An alternate explanation offered by some is that the plurality aspect of *Elohim* is an indication of God's glory and majesty. Perhaps it is both.

More notably, in Genesis 1:26 God is referred to as "us" or in the plural; then in the next verse he is referred to in the singular "his." The "us" cannot refer to the angelic hosts being involved in creation since Malachi 2:10 and other verses say only God created us. A similar plural usage of "us," along with the singular usage of "the Lord," is used of God when he visited the Tower of Babel (Genesis 11:7-8).

A foundational confession in Judaism is located in Deuteronomy of the OT:

> *Hear, O Israel: The LORD* [*Yahweh* in Hebrew] *our God, the LORD is one* [*echad* in Hebrew] (Deuteronomy 6:4).

If God were a singular unity, as orthodox Judaism claims, the Hebrew word for a singular unity, *yachid*, would have been used for the word *one* in Deuteronomy 6:4. However, as shown, the Hebrew word *echad* is used, which means a composite unity (think of one clump of grapes).

In Isaiah, God has to be a composite unity for the following passage to make any sense:

> ¹²*I am he; I am the first and I am the last.* ¹³*My own hand laid the foundations of the earth, and my right hand spread out the heavens; …*¹⁶*Come near me and listen to this: "From the first announcement I have not spoken in secret; at the time it happens, I am there." And now the Sovereign LORD [YAHWEH] has sent me, endowed with his Spirit.* ¹⁷*This is what the LORD [YAHWEH] says—your Redeemer, the Holy One of Israel: "I am the LORD [YAHWEH] your God, …* (Isaiah 48:12-13, 16-17).

As previously stated, *Yahweh* is the Hebrew name for the one true God of the Bible. Yahweh is the one talking in the above passage, and he refers to himself as the Creator; in addition, only Yahweh (God) in the Bible is referred to as "the first and the last." Then Yahweh (who has been doing all the speaking thus far as the first and the last) says the Sovereign Lord (or Yahweh) has sent him (Yahweh). Further, it says he is endowed with his Spirit (i.e., the Holy Spirit). If God is *not* a composite unity, we have some problems here. But rest assured, God and Isaiah are not going to contradict themselves within a span of a few words. Give them more credit than that.

In the OT, the Holy Spirit (God's Spirit, the Spirit of God, the Spirit, etc.) is referenced a number of times. Even God's Son is referenced in Psalm 2:10-12. (Refer to Appendix D for biblical verses regarding the Holy Spirit as a person and as God.)

Although there are other OT passages that describe the one God as a composite unity while clearly stating that there is only one true God, the above OT verses make the point sufficiently.

In the NT the Trinity is further clarified, not by the usage of that actual word, but by referring to the Father, the Son, and the Holy Spirit and their personages and deity. As in the OT, the NT clearly proclaims there is only one true God. At the same time, the NT proclaims the persons of the Father, the Son, and the Holy Spirit to each be the same one true God. (Refer to Appendix E for these biblical references.)

Although the word *Trinity* is not found in the Bible, it is a term expressing the Bible's description of God.

Could it be that the Bible simply contradicts itself? The biblical writers, most of them Jews, were ardent monotheists. There is no way any of them would have claimed a plurality of gods. As stated, both the OT and NT are filled with the proclamation: *There is only one true God.* And then in the next breath we have the writers showing a composite unity: and/or the Father is God, and/or the Son is God, and/or the Holy Spirit is God. It would stretch the limits of believability to think the writers of Scripture, let alone God who inspired them, would have made such obvious, blatant errors, saying there is one God and then saying there are three. The clear conclusion is that the persons of the Father, Son, and Holy Spirit are all the one same God.

The belief called "modalism" contends that the Father and Son and Holy Spirit are only three different *ways* or *modes* in which God presents himself and are not three distinct persons. See Appendices C, D, and E, showing the Father, Son, and Holy Spirit are each distinct personages and are the same true God. In the NT, for example, we see the members of the Godhead communicating to one another...impossible if they are all the same person (and a schizophrenic God is simply not in the cards).

Scientific Perspective on the Trinity

The reader may be asking, "How in the world can God be a three-in-one being? Isn't that contradictory within itself?"

If we have a God who is limited to the three dimensions of space (height, width, and depth), the Trinity would be a contradiction. However, God is not limited by the three spatial dimensions, just as he is not limited to one dimension of time (as discussed previously).

Mathematically, four dimensions can be demonstrated, which means one can draw four straight lines that are 90 degrees or perpendicular to each of the others. It is easy to draw three lines that are perpendicular to each other in our three-dimensional space reality. However, try to draw a fourth straight line perpendicular to each of the previous three; you can't do it in three-dimensional space. However, mathematically it can be done in four-dimensional space. Mathematically in four dimensions one can turn a basketball inside out without popping it! Do not even try to understand that one.

Can you understand a four-dimensional reality? Stop trying; you can't. We are limited to three-dimensional thinking.

An example can prove helpful. Let us assume there is a two-dimensional world of width and depth, but no height. In this reality we have two people, Mr. and Mrs. Flat (this analogy is owed to astrophysicist Dr. Hugh Ross of *Reasons to Believe*). Mr. and Mrs. Flat have no perception, and can have no perception, of a third dimension of height.

In Mr. and Mrs. Flat's two-dimensional reality, what would they perceive if I, a three-dimensional creature, were to stick my five fingers into their two-dimensional space? They would see five separate circles (a thin slice of each finger and thumb); they would not perceive any height. If you tried to explain to them that these five circles were really part of a singular three-dimensional hand, they would think you were nuts.

Now back to our reality. Just as in the case of Mr. and Mrs. Flat's two-dimensional reality, where adding a third dimension made no sense to them, likewise we, with our three-dimensionally-limited minds, cannot understand a fourth dimension, a fifth, a sixth, and so on.

We can see the big difference that adding one dimension makes, whether it be from two to three or three to four. Imagine the possibilities if we exceeded ten dimensions? According to the field of astrophysics and string theory, the big bang initially included ten dimensions (nine spatial and one of time) but then quickly (within a ten millionth of a trillionth of a trillionth of a trillionth of a second) changed to a universe with three spatial dimensions, with the curling up of the extra six spatial dimensions so we don't experience them.

The point of the above discussion is that God is beyond all dimensional limitations, regardless of whether there are four, five, ten, or whatever. In God's reality, it can be argued that a Trinity presents no logical problems whatsoever.

In closing, it might be further pointed out that we human beings cannot even fully understand ourselves! How much more impossible it is for three-dimensionally-limited creatures (us) to understand an infinite God.

Two Last Considerations

God is complete within himself. He does not need us or anything/anyone else. The Bible tells us in I John 4:8 that *"God is love"* (note that this passage does *not* say "love is God"). Therefore, as a complete being, God would have to have the capacity to love.

Love always needs two or more personalities to exist; it is an outward expression/action. For example, if in all the universe there was only one human being, that person could not love since he or she would be the solitary intelligent being in the universe (leaving God out of the discussion for just a moment). Nor could this person experience love since that would require at least a second personality to give love.

Therefore, if God were only one person, he would have been incapable of giving or receiving love before he created anything. God would have been incomplete without love, and if he were only a singular being (one God, one person), love could not have existed in that singularity; therefore, love would not be part of his character. However, being a composite unity, as discussed, God the Father could love God the Son, God the Son could love the Father, the Son could love the Holy Spirit, and so on. God was, and is, complete within himself.

Consequently, it can be argued that a non-trinitarian (or in theory a "non-binitarian") God would, in reality, be incomplete. However, since the Bible clearly claims God is self-sufficient, perfect, without need, and has *always* been loving, then he would have to be a composite unity like biblical Christianity proclaims.

Lastly, if humanity were to create a god, it would not have come up with something like the Trinity. Rather, a god would have been created that was understandable to the finite human mind. So the fact that finite humans cannot fully comprehend the one, true infinite God should not be of any surprise.

SECTION III

FINDING TRUE FULFILLMENT

CHAPTER 20

DEFEATING DEATH, FEAR, AND UNCERTAINTY

Introduction

Up to this point, the evidence presented overwhelmingly points to:

- A Creator God
- The Bible's God as the true God
- Jesus Christ as the biblical God
- The biblical God as a triune God.

However, we are not done yet. Now that we have established the identity of the one true God, we need to discuss how we relate to the true God. How do we get "right" with Him? How are we saved? Do we need to be saved? What does it mean to be "saved"? How do we invite God and his presence into our individual lives? And do we even need him? Such are the subjects of this and the next chapter.

This chapter will examine the logic, the "how to" of the Bible's salvation through Jesus Christ and his death/resurrection. It will examine why such a means of salvation is the only logical, feasible way of defeating death, inheriting eternal life in heaven and on the new earth, and having a personal relationship with God himself. We will discuss the way to heal our broken relationship with God. The following chapter will look at the results of such a salvation: fulfillment and true purpose. In other words, we will learn where the rubber meets the road in finding true fulfillment, peace, hope, and love. Together these two chapters will show how to defeat death, fear, and uncertainty.

Not "Churchianity"!

Before proceeding, one thing needs to be made very clear: biblical salvation is not found by going to church. Going to church does not save a person any more than going into a garage makes one a car!

Attending a biblically-based, Christ-centered church is a good thing; however, some churches over the years have deviated from God's wishes and God's message. Biblical salvation is found in a personal relationship with Christ—not in a certain church.

Have the Right God

Obviously human beings cannot possess spiritual salvation of their souls with a false, nonexistent god; they need the one true God. Finding the true God is what the first 19 chapters of this book have been about: showing that the Bible's God is the true God, that he came as Jesus Christ, and that only biblical Christianity teaches this. All other religions teach contrary gods and ways of salvation, and anything contrary to truth cannot be true.

As pointed out earlier, this logical conclusion is not a mere matter of semantics, of calling the one true God by different names; it is a crucial matter of core identity. The other gods of other religions do indeed refer to so-called gods who are different, contrary things or beings when compared to the personal, biblical God.

The above statement may sound judgmental or narrow-minded, but it is no more narrow-minded than to insist that two plus two always equals four and only four. Anything contrary to truth is wrong by definition, regardless of the subject matter. Jesus said:

> *I am the way and the truth and the life. No one comes to the Father except through me* (John 14:6).

> One cannot get to God but through God himself, and
> Jesus is this one true God. Therefore, Jesus was right when
> he said he was the only way, the truth, and the life.

The book of Acts in the New Testament (NT) says there is no salvation outside of Jesus Christ:

> *Salvation is found in no one else, for there is no other name*
> [Jesus Christ] *under heaven given to mankind by which we*
> *must be saved* (Acts 4:12).

Various religious systems apart from biblical Christianity may use the name Jesus Christ, but they change his identity. For example, Jehovah's Witnesses teach Jesus Christ is only a created being, the archangel Michael. Mormons, as previously discussed, teach he is one of trillions of gods and goddesses in the cosmos and is not the one true Creator God of all the cosmos. Jesus said:

> *For many will come in my name, claiming, 'I am the Messiah,'*
> *and will deceive many* (Matthew 24:5). (Also see Mark 13:6
> and Luke 21:8.)
>
> *For if someone comes to you and preaches a Jesus other than the*
> *Jesus we preached....* (II Corinthians 11:4).

God's Love

The subject of God's love was shown from the Bible in chapter 17 under the subsection entitled "God's/Jesus's Love." When talking about eternal matters, salvation, heaven and hell, keep in mind that God is a truly incredible, loving God, as we saw in chapter 17. However, he is also a just God who must therefore punish sin. More on his love and justice later.

Definition of Salvation

The biblical term salvation means to be in a right relationship with

God, to be fully forgiven of all sin in our lives and therefore to be seen by God as righteous (right standing with God). This is also referred to as justification in the Bible. Salvation also means to have a personal relationship/friendship with the God of the universe, with whom we experience an eternal, growing relationship of love, power, meaning, and fulfillment. Salvation, or the lack of it, includes both our present existence on earth and where we will spend eternity: heaven or hell.

Unforgiven sin separates us from God, so we need to have our sins forgiven.

This brings us to define what sin is…

Definition of Sin

> God's laws are not just a list of do's and don'ts. God is not that petty. His laws (such as the Ten Commandments) reflect who God is; they reflect his holy character and therefore reflect on what reality should be. Anything less is "broken."

On a human level of looking at things, you may be a very good and moral person. However, according to biblical Scripture, we are not just guilty of a sin now and then, but we are in a state of ongoing sin.

What Exactly Is "Sin"?

Sin is the breaking of God's laws and rejecting God's authority in our lives. The core of sin is pride, as we want to run our own lives and thereby rebel against God, which is actually spiritual high treason. Very serious. Pride is saying that we want to be the god of our own lives. This Satanic delusion is what tripped up Adam and Eve.

Sin is not simply the BIG sins we first think of…murder, adultery, robbery, etc. According to the Bible, sin is anything less than obeying God's perfect laws perfectly. Every day we all repeatedly sin.

All Have Sinned

At the core of our being, we know how imperfect we are. The Bible says:

- *for all have sinned and fall short of the glory of God* (Romans 3:23).

- *[10]There is no one righteous, not even one; [11]there is no one who understands; there is no one who seeks God. [12]All have turned away, they have together become worthless; there is no one who does good, not even one* (Romans 3:10-12).

- *If we claim to be without sin, we deceive ourselves and the truth is not in us* (I John 1:8).

To help illustrate the problem of sin, consider the following:

- How **often** do we fail to meet the greatest two commandments of God? Jesus said:

  [37]"Love the Lord your God with all your heart and with all your soul and with all your mind.' [39]And 'Love your neighbor as yourself'" (Matthew 22:37, 39).

- How often are we less than patient, not honest, selfish, less than kind, etc. in either our thoughts and/or actions?

Jesus helps illustrate the prevalence of sin in our daily lives:

[27]"You have heard that it was said, 'You shall not commit adultery.' [28]But I tell you that anyone who looks at a woman lustfully has already committed adultery with her in his heart" (Matthew 5:27-28).

(Note: "lustfully" here does not mean normal physical

attraction to the opposite sex, but to want or think of someone sexually with whom you are not married.)

Every person after the age of puberty who ever lived is guilty (many times) of that one. Again, not to belabor the point, but everyone has lied at some point. We have all been unkind, impatient, etc. with people on numerous occasions. These are sins of commission. This means we are all adulterous, dishonest, unkind, lying, and impatient individuals— many times over. And we have not even mentioned the sins of omission, such as not helping the poor more, not being more patient, kind, etc.

Further, as if the above picture is not bad enough, James says:

> For whoever keeps the whole law and yet stumbles at just one point is guilty of breaking all of it (James 2:10).

What James is saying, in part, is that even IF a person were to keep the whole law except for one time, the end result is the same as multiple sins: separation from God. Sin, or spiritual cancer if you will, is still cancer; whether it be one cell or many, it needs to be removed. Spiritual cancer, sin, also needs to be addressed, or it will kill you and me.

Of course, none of us, except for Jesus, can keep all of God's laws. Compared to Jesus Christ, we fall very short. And that's the point. God, as Jesus, showed us how our lives should be lived to truly experience the abundant life we were meant to have.

Nature of God and Sin

The Bible says many times that God is righteous, just, and holy. Just a sample:

> And the heavens proclaim his righteousness, for he is a God of justice (Psalm 50:6).

> For the LORD is a God of justice (Isaiah 30:18).

> Exalt the LORD our God...for the LORD our God is holy (Psalm 99:9).

God is totally holy and sinless. Just as a person cannot truly go against his or her nature, God cannot go against his. He cannot be something other than what he is! Being holy means that he cannot tolerate sin, lest he become unholy.

An illustration will help. Let us say a mother has a little boy who is stealing things at the store. She makes it clear to him that stealing is wrong, but he continues to steal. She does nothing to properly discipline him or punish the sin, if you will. Her lack of action against the sin would mean she is, in effect, condoning/tolerating the boy's sin of stealing. Further, the boy's life would soon be out of control. To be truly caring, she would take the time and energy to discipline him and hopefully change his behavior for his future welfare.

Now let us consider God and human beings. God has given us his laws (do not lie, cheat, or steal; love your neighbor as yourself, etc.), yet human beings continue to violate God's laws. Now if God did nothing in response to our breaking of his laws, he would, just like the mother, be in effect condoning/tolerating our lawlessness. If such were the case, he would no longer be holy and perfect. Therefore, God must punish sin due to his very nature/character and to maintain "divine" justice. So what are the consequences of unforgiven sin?

Consequences of Sin

The Bible says the wages (results) of sin (or spiritual treason against God) is death:

> *For the wages of sin is death, but the gift of God is eternal life in Christ Jesus our Lord* (Romans 6:23).

Sin separates us from God in this lifetime and, in a far more profound way, for all eternity unless something is done to correct the sin problem before we physically die. Compare this to a husband who habitually commits adultery. As long as he continues to do so, his relationship with his wife is broken, a natural result of his actions.

The nature of sin is to be in a state of rebellion against God. When we take authority over our lives, it might rightly be described as spiritual adultery against God. Therefore, it separates us from intimacy with God. God, in effect, says, "If not my will, your will be done." God does not force himself on anyone; he respects our God-given free will too much. If we walk away, he lets us.

In this lifetime, being separated from an intimate relationship with God has all sorts of negative consequences (fear, anger, insecurity, etc.). Plus, those who are separated from God lack the power and love of God in their lives.

If a person continues in a state of unforgiven sin until physical death, the person will experience complete spiritual death for eternity. Spiritual death means eternal separation from God and all he has to give (including all the positive aspects of life, such as love, hope, comfort, peace, purpose, etc. which are innate to God's nature). Without God and all of the good gifts he offers, hell is the only alternative. Such a state is the only possible one for a person who has permanently rebelled against God, with hell as the ultimate consequence of their decision. We have no concept of how bad hell really is.

The Bible's hell (Sheol in OT/Hades in NT) is connected to the Greek word Gehenna, which comes from the Hebrew *ge-Hinnom* (literally valley of Hinnom). The valley of the sons of Hinnom in the OT was the place where children were sacrificed in fire to the false god Moloch. Gehenna also referred to a garbage dump outside of the walls of Jerusalem, where fires were always kept burning to consume waste and garbage, keeping down the stench, and it was the location where bodies of executed criminals were dumped. I, and others, believe that the biblical "fire" descriptions of the real hell are metaphorical (hence, not a literal fire), a horrible place like the cursed valley of Hinnom. People are not tortured in hell (God does not torture), but hell is a place of great personal torment.

God will not force a person into an eternal existence with him (God) against their will. Again God says, "If not my will, your will be done." Unforgiven sin cannot exist in heaven and the new earth as described in the Bible. Therefore, people with unforgiven sin choose hell by rejecting God, and thus God sentences them there. It is analogous to a criminal's being justly sentenced to prison for a crime…it is really not the judge who initiates the sending of the criminal to prison; it is the criminal who chooses his fate by committing the crime.

One Type of Salvation Works; One Type Does Not

Salvation, in a spiritual sense, is to be in right relationship with God, so the most important question is simply: How does one get into a right relationship with God?

First, you need the right God; we have covered the details of this search and the reasons for choosing the triune God of the Bible.

Second, salvation involves the forgiveness of one's sins, wherein a person is no longer in a state of rebellion against God, but is in a harmonious relationship with him with their sins forgiven.

In theory, there are two basic, but mutually exclusive, types of salvation or getting right with God. By the law of non-contradiction, if one is true, the other must be false.

The first theoretical type of salvation is what is called "salvation by works." This type of salvation teaches that a person can get right with God by being good enough or by doing enough good works or deeds. Typically, people who hold to this paradigm feel that if their good works outweigh their bad deeds, they can get right with God. In this view of salvation, God will supposedly accept a person if they are good enough. The works required, and/or their degree, differ from one religious system to another, but the concept basically boils down to you having to be good enough to be saved. Bottom line, it teaches that a person somehow atones for his own sins by being good enough (whatever that may mean).

Most people tend to believe this type of idea. ALL religions of the world, except one (see below), teach some form of salvation by works. For example, reincarnation is basically a system of salvation by works.

The second type of salvation is not by works; it is through faith in Jesus Christ as God and Savior. This means:

- being sorry for one's sins and repenting of them (at its core, this is not merely an emotional response, but a sincere regret over one's sins and of being in a state of sin/ rebellion).

- depending on/trusting in Christ's death on the cross and resurrection as the means by which Christ paid the penalty for one's sins.

By doing the above, the person hands the lordship (or control) of his or her life over to Jesus Christ (God).

The above explanation is called "salvation by faith in Jesus Christ," as defined only in the Bible. Salvation is a free gift (it is not earned); it is a gift of God through Jesus Christ and his atonement for our sins and his resurrection.

So which type of salvation is valid: the one by works or the one by faith in Jesus Christ as God and Savior? And why? One is salvation by humanity's ability, and the other is by God's ability. There are no other alternatives.

Illogic of Salvation by Works

Salvation by works is a failed paradigm. It is humanity's attempt to reach God by its own good deeds/works. Can enough good works result in God's forgiveness of our sins? Can good works atone (make up) for our sins?

The answer is a resounding "No!" For example, in day-to-day human relationships, a wrongdoer can only "atone" or make things right for their wrong by truly apologizing to the wronged party.

Let us say Person A hits Person B in the face. This act obviously damages the relationship. Now let us say Person A then goes off and does a series of good works/deeds, whether they be helping charities, individual people, etc. Do such good deeds heal the broken relationship Person A has with Person B? Obviously not. How can that relationship be healed? Healing can only come when Person A goes to Person B with **true** remorse, asking for forgiveness (and hopefully Person B forgives Person A). Forgiveness is a free gift or transaction.

All religions (except biblical Christianity) teach salvation by works and are therefore teaching that people heal their damaged relationships with God by performing enough good deeds. This makes no more sense than it did in the scenario above with Persons A and B.

Further, it does not matter how many good things a person may have done, they are still guilty of many sins. If a person commits a murder but was perfect in every other way (an impossibility), a judge in court would not say something like: "Oh, okay, you can go." The crime of murder still has to be dealt with by appropriate punishment in order for justice to be fulfilled, regardless of how "good" that person may have been otherwise.

The Bible makes it clear that no one is saved by good works/deeds. The Bible uses the phrase "works of the law" or "the law" (in reference to salvation) to refer to good works/deeds done in an effort to be saved by a person's own efforts (salvation by works). Listed below are just a few of the many verses that could be listed:

> *Therefore no one will be declared righteous in God's sight by the works of the law; rather, through the law* [in our efforts to be good enough] *we become conscious of our sin* (Romans 3:20).

> *Know that a person is not justified by the works of the law, but by faith in Jesus Christ. So we, too, have put our faith in Christ Jesus that we may be justified by faith in Christ and not by the works of the law, because by the works of the law no one will be justified* (Galatians 2:16).

> *I do not set aside the grace of God, for if righteousness could be gained through the law, Christ died for nothing!* (Galatians 2:21).

> *Clearly no one who relies on the law is justified before God, because "the righteous will live by faith"* (Galatians 3:11).

> *You who are trying to be justified by the law have been alienated from Christ; you have fallen away from grace* (Galatians 5:4).

> [8] *For it is by grace you have been saved, through faith – and this is not from yourselves, it is the gift of God –* [9] *not by works, so that no one can boast* (Ephesians 2:8-9).

Logic of Salvation NOT by Works but through Faith in Jesus Christ

We have already described the Bible's salvation by faith in Jesus Christ and what it means. The Bible alone teaches that good works result from true salvation, but do not contribute toward it. A dog barks because it is already a dog, not to become a dog. We do good works (out of love and appreciation) because we are already saved, not to become saved.

The Bible teaches that the only way to heal the damaged relationship is to go back to God (Jesus Christ) and ask for forgiveness. It is the only means of salvation that makes any logical sense, just as in the case of Persons A and B.

The reader may be asking, "Okay, that makes sense, but why 'insert' Jesus Christ into one's salvation? Why not just go directly to God and ask for forgiveness?" The answer is simple but two-fold: (1) One must go to the true God, and Jesus Christ is the one true God; (2) Notice the following illustration and analysis.

At the end of World War II, if Hitler would have survived the war and simply said he was sorry for all of the atrocities he had committed, would it have been right to let him off the hook and not impose any penalties? Would justice have been served by letting Hitler go free without any consequences?

The obvious answer is no. You would probably add, "It would have been a travesty of justice; justice would not have been served." And you would be right. The Bible and logic agree.

Now let us switch to a person's damaged/broken relationship with God, caused by the person's numerous crimes of sin (a sin is a crime against God). Would justice be served if a person were to simply go to God and ask for forgiveness? Where are the consequences of justice?

Breaking God's Laws (Just as in Civil/Criminal Laws) Demands Justice

Even more so, when a person breaks God's laws, divine justice requires punishment against the crimes of sin. It is the very fabric or logic of justice. This now brings us to the necessity/logic of Jesus's blood atonement and subsequent resurrection.

> Jesus Christ satisfied God's justice for our sins. Jesus paid
> the penalty/consequences of our sins by dying on the cross.
> Through Jesus's death on the cross, he satisfied God's jus-
> tice/penalty against our sins. And it is Jesus's resurrection
> that proves he is God, his atonement for sin is valid, and
> he has power over sin and death. The Apostle Paul states
> in I Corinthians 15:14 & 17: "And if Christ has not been
> raised, our preaching is useless and so is your faith...And
> if Christ has not been raised, your faith is futile; you are
> still in your sins."

An analogy is useful for clarification at this point. In a courtroom
the judge pronounces a fine of $1,000,000 against the guilty person.
After that, the defendant and the judge have a private talk wherein the
defendant expresses that he is sorry for his crime and accepts respon-
sibility to pay the fine. However, the defendant confesses that even if
he worked for the rest of his life, the fine owed could not be paid for.
The judge then takes off his robe and pays the fine for the guilty person.
Civil justice has been met.

Similarly, God (Jesus Christ) has pronounced the penalty for our
sins. He then stepped down from the heavenly realm and paid the penalty of our sins by dying on the cross. Only after Jesus's death and resurrection could a person freely and sincerely ask for forgiveness of all
their sins; with Jesus's sacrifice, the penalty of one's sins was taken care
of, and justice was served.

When a person follows the below instructions on how to be saved,
they are covered in the righteousness of Christ, meaning God the
Father sees that person as "clothed with" Christ's righteousness, not
their own unrighteousness. In effect, Christ takes our sins, and we get
his righteousness. The Bible describes this as involving (but not limited to) a legal transaction, a transaction wherein we receive Christ and
his righteousness in exchange for giving or surrendering to him our
unrighteousness.

The Bible's Salvation by Faith in Jesus Christ

In the Bible, a person is saved from their sins when he or she:

- Confesses to God they are a sinner
- Are sorry for their sins; repents
- Asks Jesus for forgiveness of all their sins (including future sin, since God is not bound by time)
- Depends on Christ and his atonement/death on the cross and resurrection as the means by which their sins are paid for and forgiven.

In doing the above, a person surrenders their life to Christ, making him the Lord of their life.

Here are but a few of the many biblical verses concerning the above (words in brackets are this author's):

- Confession:

    If we confess our sins, he is faithful and just and will forgive us our sins and purify us from all unrighteousness (I John 1:9). (Also see Romans 10:9 below.)

    And without faith it is impossible to please God, because anyone who comes to him must believe that he exists and that he rewards those who earnestly seek him. (Hebrews 11:6).

- Justified, forgiven, and saved through Christ's atonement on the cross:

    And the blood of Jesus, his Son [his atonement on the cross paying for our sins], *purifies us from all sin* (I John 1:7).

Since we have now been justified by his blood [Christ's death atonement on the cross], *how much more shall we be saved from God's wrath* [against sin] *through him!* (Romans 5:9).

In him we have redemption through his blood [Christ's death atonement on the cross], *the forgiveness of sins, in accordance with the riches of God's grace* (Ephesians 1:7).

- Belief (faith), confession, and salvation through faith in Christ:

    If you declare with your mouth, "Jesus is Lord," and believe in your heart that God raised him from the dead, you will be saved (Romans 10:9).

    [15] That everyone who believes may have eternal life in him. [16] For God so loved the world that he gave his one and only Son, that whoever believes in him shall not perish but have eternal life (John 3:15-16).

    [11] And this is the testimony: God has given us eternal life, and this life is in his Son. [12] Whoever has the Son has life; whoever does not have the Son of God does not have life. [13] I write these things to you who believe in the name of the Son of God so that you may know that you have eternal life (I John 5:11-13).

    Jesus said: Very truly I tell you, the one who believes [on me] *has eternal life* (John 6:47).

- Salvation is through faith in Christ not by good deeds:

    Know that a person is not justified by the works of the law, but by faith in Jesus Christ. So we, too, have put our faith in Christ Jesus that we may be justified by faith in Christ and not by the works of the law, because by the works of the law no one will be justified (Galatians 2:16).

[8] *For it is by grace you have been saved, through faith—and this is not from yourselves, it is the gift of God—* [9] *not by works, so that no one can boast* (Ephesians 2:8-9).

Surrendering one's life to Christ is sort of like a marriage, albeit a spiritual one. Once saved (becoming a Christian) one has been made right in God's sight (received Christ's righteousness as explained). However, on a day-to-day existence, Christians are far from being perfect; they still are suffering from the effects of sin. They are forgiven sinners. But they are being transformed. God accepts us in Christ where we are, but he does not leave us there.

Salvation is a free gift and an event in a person's life, but one's transformation (called sanctification in the Bible) is a lifelong process with the leadership and help of God the Holy Spirit. More on that in the next chapter.

Is *Cheap* Grace Being Advocated Here?

Some people, after reading the above explanation might misinterpret part of what is being said and claim, "You mean all I have to do is say I am sorry and then I can go on and do whatever I want to do?"

No! Definitely not.

The Bible is clear. We are saved by God's grace and through faith in Jesus Christ; salvation is **not** earned. The biblical term grace means "unmerited or undeserved love." However, the Bible is also clear that when people truly surrender/devote their life to Christ, their life will be changed.

For example, if a person claimed he stuck his finger into a live electrical wall socket and there was no reaction, it can be concluded he lied about sticking his finger into that socket. In other words, if a person sticks his finger into a socket, there will be a physical reaction. Cause and effect.

Similarly, if a person plugs (surrenders) his life into Christ, the ultimate power and love of the universe, then his life will show a reaction. This is simply cause and effect. Salvation causes or produces a changed life, not the other way around. Again, a dog barks because it is already a dog, not to become a dog. If one has genuinely been saved, then the natural result is a changed life. ***Salvation by faith alone saves, but saving faith is never alone.*** Jesus said:

> *You will know them by their fruits. Grapes are not gathered from thorn bushes nor figs from thistles, are they?* (Matthew 7:16 NASB).

Various people mature spiritually at different rates and in different ways after devoting their lives to Christ. Sometimes they go into spiritual batting slumps for a time. But in an overall sense, their lives will be changed. They will not become sinless in their everyday lives, but overall they should be getting better at sinning less. The Apostle John wrote:

> *⁵But you know that he appeared so that he might take away our sins. And in him is no sin. ⁶No one who lives in him keeps on sinning. No one who continues to sin has either seen him or known him* (I John 3:5-6).

John is using the above wall socket logic. Plug your life into Christ, and you will react or change. The Greek words for "keeps" and "continues to sin" here mean an unrepentant, habitual lifestyle of sin, where the person also does not think it is wrong to sin and has no problem with sinning. While a Christian, a follower of Christ, will have issues and struggles against sin, he knows the sin is wrong and will endeavor, with God's help, to improve by sinning less. And they are not in a lifestyle of sin, where it is a normal mode of existence for them. Even the Apostle Paul struggled with his sinful nature and knew that only by God's Holy Spirit's power could he overcome it:

> *¹⁸For I know that good itself does not dwell in me, that is, in my sinful nature. For I have the desire to do what is good, but I cannot carry it out. ¹⁹For I do not do the good I want to do, but the evil I do not want to do—this I keep on doing* (Romans 7:18-19).

Lastly, regarding the charge of cheap grace, salvation cost Jesus plenty as he hung on the cross, taking the sins of the entire world on himself. We have no real concept of how horrible that was – physically, and most of all, spiritually.

How about Those Who Have Never Heard about Christ?

One may ask, "What about those people who have never heard about Jesus Christ and his atonement/resurrection?" This would include people both before and after Christ and his crucifixion, atonement, and resurrection.

First and foremost, remember that God is a just and loving God, not willing that any should perish. Out of love, God (Jesus Christ) died on a cross for our sins:

> *The Lord is not slow in keeping his promise, as some understand slowness. Instead he is patient with you, not wanting anyone to perish, but everyone to come to repentance* (II Peter 3:9).

Concerning people who have never heard, much has been written over the years, so this book does not pretend to offer new insights on this issue. However, the following three scenarios are the most likely possibilities in this author's opinion:

First possible scenario: this is where one assumes that someone does not necessarily have to hear (or read) the full gospel to be saved. (*Romans 1:18-23 has potential relevancy here.*) This first scenario could apply to people both before Christ's death on the cross and after.

Here God would judge such a person based on their reaction to the amount of light God had given them. If they rejected such limited truth, they would stand condemned, but if they accepted what knowledge they had received from God, they would be saved, but only *because Jesus Christ paid the penalty for their crimes of sin on the cross,* even though they were not aware of his historical/spiritual act of atonement and resurrection. So their salvation would ultimately be only through Christ and his redemptive act of dying on the cross and resurrection.

Please note that the above-referenced "limited truth" cannot refer to any of the other religions of the world, such as Hinduism, Islam, etc., as such religions clearly contradict the full light of the gospel of Jesus Christ, as has been discussed at length in this book. God does not contradict himself.

Second possible scenario: If one assumes a person must hear (or read) and accept the *full* gospel message…then it can be argued God would make sure the person hears the full gospel by some means during their normal course of life, or in the closing moments before death by special revelation from God to that person. (*Romans 10:14 might apply here.*) Remember, God loves the person, wants him or her to be saved, and will do whatever is necessary to achieve that (short of violating the person's free will).

Third possible scenario: If one assumes a person must hear and accept the full gospel message by hearing God *only* through a human source or by the reading of the Gospel, then God will simply arrange things so such a person will have that happen if God knows in his foresight that the person would accept the gospel of Christ. Again, *Romans 10:14 has potential applicability here.* In this scenario, a person may wonder about all the people who did not hear before their death. My response is that they are the ones God knew beforehand who would not accept the gospel if they indeed did hear it.

A Brief Word on Old Testament Sacrifices

From the beginning (after Adam and Eve's sin) the necessity of blood atonement for the remission of sins is contained in the Bible. In fact, Hebrews 9:22 states:

> *Without the shedding of blood, there is no forgiveness.*

God instituted in the OT, the sacrificial system of killing a spotless lamb, shedding its blood on an altar for the forgiveness of sins (after the sacrifice, the lamb was used as food, its skin for clothes, etc.).

In the NT, it is made clear that the shedding of a lamb's blood never really took away sins (Hebrews 10:4). It was only a sort of prototype sacrifice, pointing toward/leading up to the only true sacrifice that could indeed take away sin…the sacrifice of the perfect Lamb of God, Jesus Christ. John the Baptist proclaimed upon seeing Jesus,

> *Look, the Lamb of God, who takes away the sin of the world!* (John 1:29).

It was Christ's later sacrifice that God would retroactively credit to the person in the OT times who expressed his or her true repentance through the animal sacrifices (they were acting based on the light they received from God).

The blood atonement of innocent lambs was a very ugly ritual. It was a horrible, bloody mess. It was indeed a vivid reminder of the horribleness of one's sins, of how disgusting they are to God. Imagine God (Jesus) dying on the cross, shedding his blood. Crucifixion is probably the worst means of death ever devised.

CHAPTER 21

YOUR FULFILLMENT, MEANING, AND PURPOSE

The purpose of this book is ultimately established in the previous chapter and this one: it is to introduce people to Jesus Christ as God, Savior, and best friend so they can have a spiritually rewarding relationship with him. Jesus said the following:

> *I am the way and the truth and the life. No one comes to the Father except through me* (John 14:6).

> *³² Then you will know the truth, and the truth will set you free." ³⁶ So if the Son sets you free, you will be free indeed* (John 8:32, 36).

> *I have come that they may have life, and have it to the full* (John 10:10b).

> *I have told you this so that my joy may be in you and that your joy may be complete* (John 15:11).

Jesus also stated:

> *Whoever comes to me I will never drive away* (John 6:34b).

Indeed, Jesus will accept anyone who wants to make him their Lord and God of their life. He even accepted the thief on the cross next to him when he asked Jesus for forgiveness. Jesus promises freedom (spiritual and emotional), a fulfilling life, and joy. This does not mean life will be problem-free; more on that later.

Remember the popular saying about Jesus mentioned earlier: "*He will accept you where you are, but he will not leave you there.*"

Up to this point, we have used evidence and logic in our search for the one true God and to show that he came as Jesus Christ, that salvation is through him and his death on the cross and resurrection. The last chapter described how a person may come to Christ for salvation and eternal life. This chapter will discuss one's life as the result of coming to Christ. How does accepting Christ as God and Savior affect everyday life? And what does a person do after becoming saved through Christ?

At the beginning of this chapter, you read the Scripture where Jesus promised an abundant or fulfilling life, true freedom, and joy that can only come from a personal relationship with him. Whereas the last chapter discussed the *how* of getting that personal relationship, this chapter will discuss the *what* of that relationship. What does God/Jesus promise in that personal relationship when he becomes Lord of our lives? And what does he expect of us? What does a life in Christ look like?

In attempting to answer these questions, authors have over the years written thousands of books on living a truly fulfilled life in Christ. This chapter will not add anything new per se, but will hopefully discuss a few helpful aspects.

We human beings need and crave relationships. We were created to be in relationships. When we lack relationships or have damaged ones, things are just not right, to say the least. Our life becomes out of balance. We desire to be right with people. Even more so, we desire and need to be right with God (whether we recognize the telltale symptoms or not), and until we are, life is just not the way God intended it to be and how we truly wish it were.

As critically important as salvation through Christ is, it is only the beginning of our walk with the Lord. Just as a human marriage is the start of something wonderful (or at least should be), Jesus desires to cultivate an eternal relationship, starting now, with each one of us, transforming us more and more into the image of Christ as we were created to be. And when we become more of what we were intended to be, the happier we will become.

Imagine becoming more and more like Jesus Christ in our character as we grow in spiritual maturity. What does this mean? In becoming more like Christ, the result is, but is not limited to, having more of his love, joy, peace, forbearance, kindness, goodness, faithfulness, gentleness, and self-control (Galatians 5:22). It is often noted that the longer two people are married, the more alike they become. The same logic applies in our spiritual marriage to Christ (we become more like him, not the other way around). Paul the Apostle states:

> *The mind governed by the flesh is death, but the mind governed by the Spirit is life and peace* (Romans 8:6).

> *Do not conform to the pattern of this world, but be transformed by the renewing of your mind. Then you will be able to test and approve what God's will is—his good, pleasing and perfect will* (Romans 12:2).

> *And we all, who with unveiled faces contemplate the Lord's glory, are being transformed into his image with ever-increasing glory, which comes from the Lord, who is the Spirit* (II Corinthians 3:18).

> *It is for freedom that Christ has set us free* (Galatians 5:1a).

> *And have put on the new self, which is being renewed in knowledge in the image of its Creator* (Colossians 3:10).

All of the above means our life in Christ can be more meaningful (fulfilling God's purpose for one's life), more joyful, more fulfilled, more peaceful, less stressful, less worried, less conflicted, and on and on…the way God intended our life to be. Lest it not be clear, the above is meant to apply to one's "internal" life and being, helping us to know how to relate to or cope with what life brings. It does not mean the Christian life is devoid of external circumstances that may, at times, present persecution and other trials (the early followers of Christ experienced a lot of that).

Make no mistake, surrendering one's life to Christ does not mean one becomes a "clone" Christian or some kind of spiritual robot. Quite the contrary. Christ created us as unique individuals, and he wants each of us to fully realize that individuality and uniqueness; only then will we realize our full purpose for existence.

We are Secure in Christ.

When we enter a relationship with Christ, it is like a marriage, albeit a spiritual one, as mentioned previously. Scripture is clear that the relationship is a "forever" arrangement; God will not let us go (John 6:37; John 10:27-29; Romans 8:38-39; etc.). In a human marriage when we relate to our spouse in a wrong way (i.e., an unkind word or attitude, etc.), it does not destroy the marriage, but it might "cloud up the lines of communication" between the couple. The offending party needs to apologize to maximize the relationship. It is basically the same with our relationship with Christ. When we sin, it does not destroy our salvation! But we need to repent and apologize to him to maximize the relationship.

Does Life in Christ Mean No More Problems?

After reading the above, a person may ask, "If I give my life to Christ, does that mean my problems will be over?"

The simple answer is no. Heaven knows, all of us have seen Christians who still have problems. I never met one who didn't, and this author has certainly had his share.

Recall the incident when the apostles were in a fishing boat on the Sea of Galilee during a violent storm (Mark 4:37-38) and their boat was filling with water. Jesus was also in the boat; however, he was asleep. The apostles were scared to death, thinking they were within the jaws of death, but Christ continued to sleep peacefully in the boat.

Finally, they woke Christ up and said, "Teacher, do you not care that we are perishing?" This is the account where Christ then commanded the wind and seas to calm down, and they did, bringing peace. Jesus's response to their fear was, "Why are you so afraid? Do you still have no faith?"

I don't know about you, but if I had been in that boat, I would have empathized with the apostles…unfortunately. Some people might comically respond, "I think they needed a bigger boat!" In reality, what they needed was a *bigger view* of Jesus! They needed to realize exactly *who was in the boat with them.*

Similarly, in the trials and tribulations we all face, God has reassured us of his unfailing presence with us:

> *Be strong and courageous. Do not be afraid or terrified because of them, for the* LORD *your God goes with you; he will never leave you nor forsake you* (Deuteronomy 31:6). (Also see Deuteronomy 31:8.)

The context of the above verse is a time when the Israelites were about to go into the Promised Land to fight the Canaanites. Battles were ahead, but God promised to be with them.

Similarly, in the various battles of life, big or small, Jesus will be with us, and he will help us weather those storms. Sometimes, he may actually deliver us from experiencing them altogether. At other times, he may permit them and use them to help us grow, while all the while holding our hand, although it may not always seem that he is.

If God permits trouble in our lives, he works it out for our good, as much as we do not like trouble or want it (after all, who wants pain?).

> *And we know that in all things God works for the good of those who love him, who have been called according to his purpose* (Romans 8:28).

It is a sad commentary on our spiritual immaturity, but sometimes growing through pain is the only way we will learn and spiritually grow. Christian author and theologian C.S. Lewis described pain as the megaphone of God. For younger readers, a megaphone was a cone-shaped device used to increase volume by yelling into it or to increase hearing by putting it to your ear.

Personally, I have grown the most in my spiritual life during times of pain and trials. Paul the apostle, no stranger to various trials and pain (tortured, whipped, stoned [by rocks], shipwrecked twice, etc.), said:

> [3] *Not only so, but we also glory in our sufferings, because we know that suffering produces perseverance;* [4] *perseverance, character; and character, hope.* [5] *And hope does not put us to shame, because God's love has been poured out into our hearts through the Holy Spirit, who has been given to us* (Romans 5:3-5).

Christians can rest assured during the rough times of their life that if God permits pain and suffering, they are for a good reason: the spiritual benefits and growth outweigh the pain and suffering. We may come to know the reason(s), or sometimes we may not. But just as I, a loving parent, would not intentionally let my son undergo needless pain, neither will our loving heavenly Father, with his infinite power, knowledge, and foresight, allow needless pain in our life.

> [8] *For everyone who asks receives; the one who seeks finds; and to the one who knocks, the door will be opened.* [9] *Which of you, if your son asks for bread, will give him a stone?* (Matthew 7:8-9).

As followers of Jesus, it is sometimes easy to fall into the temptation of limiting or questioning God in rough times. We need to remember that our God is good, righteous, loving, and all powerful:

> [5] *Trust in the* LORD *with all your heart and lean not on your own understanding;* [6] *in all your ways submit to him, and he will make your paths straight* (Proverbs 3:5-6).

> *And the peace of God, which transcends all understanding, will guard your hearts and your minds in Christ Jesus.* (Philippians 4:7)

As the heavens are higher than the earth, so are my ways higher than your ways and my thoughts than your thoughts (Isaiah 55:9).

When Christians truly know and trust in the Lord to take care of them, the levels of worry and fear can be minimized, if not eliminated, in times of trouble. We are not the victims of mindless forces at work but are under the constant care of the Father. This is even true when we cause our own problems by our own stupidity, short-sightedness, etc. Sometimes God lets us experience the natural consequences of our own immaturity, thereby resulting in growth and learning from our mistakes. By knowing and trusting in the Lord to take care of them, Christians can find their levels of peace, comfort, and joy to be correspondingly maximized.

Does this author fully trust in the Lord in all situations? Unfortunately, no. I am still under construction. Often my emotions need to catch up to my intellectual acknowledgments. I know for a fact that Jesus is my Lord, God, Savior, and best friend, and he is capable of anything; I have no doubts there. However, in the day-to-day applications of living out my faith, I often fail, especially in my emotions, like any other fallen individual during times of trouble. I become like the disciples in the boat during the storm instead of being calm, fully trusting in the Lord. I am imperfect, but with God's help, I try to do better over time. In other words, over time I should grow more mature in my spiritual walk.

The Bible is clear that if you try to live the Christian faith in your *own strength,* you will fail and be miserable. That is why the Holy Spirit is there to help lead, guide, and provide us with his power to live the abundant life.

*The L**ORD** is with me; he is my helper. I look in triumph on my enemies* (Psalm 118:7).

And I will ask the Father, and he will give you another advocate [the Holy Spirit] *to help you and be with you forever—* (John 14:16).

You who are my Comforter in sorrow, my heart is faint within me. (Jeremiah 8:18).

Good relationships require time and effort. Although our salvation is a gift of grace by God through Jesus Christ and his atonement and resurrection, we must allow God to work in and through us if we are to mature in our relationship with him. This is not some laborious task of performing to get God's attention or approval, but is just like any other relationship, which requires quality time and communication. At http://christianbook.com one can find many book and DVD sources on living a fruitful Christian life, dealing with life's problems, and other areas of needed growth.

The best way to enhance our relationship with the Lord is through prayer (a two-way communication between God and us) and spending time in his Word, the Bible (God communicating to us). The Bible can be many things to a Christian, one of which is a user's manual on how to best live life!

There is no secret formula on how to pray. What God wants most in prayer is for a person to be open and honest, qualities important for any relationship. In addition to expressing our needs and problems, one critical element of prayer is to let God express himself to us; we need to listen! Although the following is not a formula, the acronym "ACTS" is a helpful prayer aid:

> A: "Adoration:" Start by worshipping God, adoring him, appreciating him. This helps us to spiritually focus in our prayers, getting rid of extraneous thoughts.

> C: "Confession:" If there are some sin(s) you need to specifically confess and ask for forgiveness, do so; get "sin" out of the way.

> T: "Thanksgiving:" Express thanksgiving for God and what he has done in your life and for what he will be doing.

> S: "Supplication:" Make known requests and needs for yourself and others; thank him for what he will do.

Another aspect to growth in the Christian life is for a person to have fellowship with other Christians:

> *Not giving up meeting together, as some are in the habit of doing, but encouraging one another* (Hebrews 10:25a).

Being part of a regular fellowship of believers in a good, Bible-believing church is crucial. We do not go to church to be saved, but because we are already saved. Associating with other people who are following Christ helps us avoid the effects of bad company. "*Bad company corrupts good character*" (I Corinthians 15:33b). But the opposite is also true: Good company encourages us and prompts proper actions. Associating with fellow believers in Christ provides an excellent climate wherein they can love, help, and encourage us and vice versa. Also, there is much to learn from other believers who are more mature in the faith than we might be (such as leaders, pastors, and other believers). Young believers can teach older believers some things, too. People need other people! God uses people to help others.

Yes, unfortunately there are some less than ideal churches out there, and even some bad ones. That is not the fault of Christ and his church but the result of the shortcomings of flawed human beings who are not doing what Jesus wants them to do.

However, there are a lot of very good Christian churches! Be sure the church you are considering teaches that the Bible is the inerrant Word of God, is biblically based, and has a loving congregation of people guided by the Comforter and Helper, the Holy Spirit.

Can a person find the perfect church? If you do, it will not remain that way if you (or I) join it! The church is a collection of forgiven, imperfect people who are under spiritual construction. Humans make mistakes. But in the church, God wants us to grow in spiritual maturity in a bond of love, peace, and patience. Don't miss out!

APPENDICES

BIBLE'S FULFILLED PROPHECIES

In accordance with chapter 14, starting on the next page in this appendix is a table of Bible-fulfilled prophecies (FPs), prophecies which have been fulfilled in history. The following list concerns multiple cities, totaling 51 individual prophecies.

All of the following prophecies were written before the Greek Septuagint of the Old Testament was completed in the third to second centuries BC (since they are in the Greek Old Testament). All were fulfilled in history after the writing of the Greek Septuagint. In fact, only nine of them were fulfilled before the completion of the earthly ministry of Jesus Christ in the first century AD.

Refer to chapter 14 for the details of how the odds were meticulously calculated for the prophecies' being fulfilled by random events (rather than by Divine foreknowledge); the methodology used involved 700 students over 10 years.

The odds of all these prophecies' having been fulfilled by random chance (lucky guesses) have been calculated to be 1 out of 5.76×10^{59} (for explanation, see chapter 14). The size of this number clearly shows these prophecies were NOT fulfilled by luck, but by the only other alternative: divine inspiration from the true God.

The information content in Appendix A is from Peter W. Stoner's *Science Speaks*, as referenced in chapter 14. The organization of the information is this author's.

SOME EXAMPLES OF FULFILLED PROPHECIES IN THE BIBLE
Copies of all the below prophecies are in the Greek Septuagint of the Old Testament, written between 250 – 150 BC. The originally written dates of the prophecies are indicated below.

Prophecy Description *Numbers in brackets, e.g., [1 in 3], are the odds of that prophecy coming true by natural events.*	Comments/Fulfillment *Except as noted for Tyre and Jericho,* **all the below prophecies were fulfilled** *after the time of Christ.*

City of Tyre Destruction (Ezekiel 26:3-5, 7, 12, 14, 16): Originally Written 590 BC	
Passage predicts the following: 1. Nebuchadnezzar shall take the city of Tyre. [1 in 3] 2. Other nations are to participate in the fulfillment of the prophecy. [1 in 5] 3. The city is to be made flat like the top of a rock. [1 in 500] 4. It is to become a place for spreading of nets. [1 in 10] 5. Its stones and timber are to be laid in the sea. [1 in 10] 6. Other cities are to fear greatly at the fall of Tyre. [1 in 5] 7. The old city of Tyre shall never be rebuilt. [1 in 20]	No. 1 fulfilled in 573 BC when mainland portion of city taken by Nebuchadnezzar, who failed to take the nearby island portion of the city. Nos. 2, 3, and 5 fulfilled in 332 BC when Alexander the Great, with others, scrapped the old ruins of mainland Tyre and put the debris into the sea, building a causeway of land (land bridge) to the island part of Tyre, before taking it. *Never in history has this happened elsewhere to a city.* Nos. 4, 6, and 7: Fulfilled subsequent to 332 BC until today. *Most major cities are either rebuilt or remain a "heap" or mound of dirt.*
Calculated Odds of Happening by Random Chance: *1 in 3 x 5 x 500 x 10 x 10 x 5 x 20 = 1 in 75,000,000*	

SOME EXAMPLES OF FULFILLED PROPHECIES IN THE BIBLE	
Copies of all the below prophecies are in the Greek Septuagint of the Old Testament, written between 250 – 150 BC. The originally written dates of the prophecies are indicated below.	
Prophecy Description *Numbers in brackets, e.g., [1 in 3], are the odds of that prophecy coming true by natural events.*	**Comments/Fulfillment** *Except as noted for Tyre and Jericho, all the below prophecies were fulfilled after the time of Christ.*

Jerusalem Enlarged (Jeremiah 31:38-40): Originally Written 600 BC	
The passage reads: *"The days are coming," declares the* LORD, *"when this city will be rebuilt for me from the Tower of Hananel to the Corner Gate. The measuring line will stretch from there straight to the hill of Gareb and then turn to Goah. The whole valley where dead bodies and ashes are thrown, and all the terraces out to the Kidron Valley on the east as far as the corner of the Horse Gate, will be holy to the* LORD. *The city will never again be uprooted or demolished."* - Jeremiah 31:38-40.	Old City of Jerusalem had six corners from which growth could have occurred, plus the various sides. History has born out Jerusalem's growth in the locations and sequence stated in Jeremiah, totaling nine prophecies.
Odds of Above Happening by Random Chance: 1 in 8 x 10^{10}	

City of Jericho (Joshua 6:26): Originally Written in 1451 BC	
Passage predicts the following: 1. Jericho shall be rebuilt. [1 in 2] 2. It shall be rebuilt by one man. [1 in 10] 3. The builder's oldest son shall die when the work on the city starts. [1 in 100] 4. The builder's youngest son will die as the gates are being hung. [1 in 100]	According to I Kings, all four parts were fulfilled. The book of I Kings was written about 1000 BC.
Odds of Above Happening by Random Chance: 1 in 2 x 10 x 100 x 100 = 1 in 200,000	

SOME EXAMPLES OF FULFILLED PROPHECIES IN THE BIBLE	
Copies of all the below prophecies are in the Greek Septuagint of the Old Testament, written between 250 – 150 BC. The originally written dates of the prophecies are indicated below.	
Prophecy Description *Numbers in brackets, e.g., [1 in 3], are the odds of that prophecy coming true by natural events.*	**Comments/Fulfillment** *Except as noted for Tyre and Jericho, all the below prophecies were fulfilled after the time of Christ.*

Moab and Ammon (Ezekiel 25:3-4, 9-10; Jeremiah 48:47; and Jeremiah 49:6): Originally Written 590, 600, and 600 BC, respectively	
Passage predicts the following: 1. Moab and Ammon shall be taken by men of the east, and they shall eat the fruits of the land. [1 in 5] 2. Men from east will build palaces in Ammon. [1 in 10] 3. The Moabites and Ammonites will eventually be returned and given their land again. [1 in 20]	Arabs repeatedly raided these two countries, taking their fruits. Arab-built palaces are still in use. The land is now being protected by the British against raids, the land is again being tilled, and cities are rapidly growing.
Odds of Above Happening by Random Chance: 1 in 5 x 10 x 20 = 1 in 1,000	

SOME EXAMPLES OF FULFILLED PROPHECIES IN THE BIBLE
Copies of all the below prophecies are in the Greek Septuagint of the Old Testament, written between 250 – 150 BC. The originally written dates of the prophecies are indicated below.

Prophecy Description *Numbers in brackets, e.g., [1 in 3], are the odds of that prophecy coming true by natural events.*	Comments/Fulfillment *Except as noted for Tyre and Jericho, all the below prophecies were fulfilled after the time of Christ.*

Babylon (Isaiah 13:19-21): Originally Written 712 BC

| Passage predicts the following:

1. Babylon shall be destroyed. [1 in 10]

2. It shall never be re-inhabited. [1 in 100]

3. The Arabs shall not pitch their tents there. [1 in 200]

4. There shall be no sheepfolds there. [1 in 5]

5. Wild beasts shall occupy the ruins. [1 in 5]

6. The stones shall not be taken away for other buildings. [1 in 100]

7. Men shall not pass by the ruins. [1 in 10] | Babylon, perhaps the greatest city of all times, conquered in 538 BC (for example, walls were 90 feet thick and 300 feet high, with even higher towers, 14-mile-long walls on each side, a river flowing through it and enough crop land within its walls to survive sieges).

Arabs are superstitious about Babylon: will not pitch tents there, but will in nearby areas; will not stay overnight. It is uninhabited by humans; jackals and wild beasts live in the ruins. There are no sheepfolds, and the rocks that were imported to Babylon at great cost have never been moved. |

Odds of Above Happening by Random Chance: *1 in 10 x 100 x 200 x 5 x 5 x 100 x 10 = 1 in 5,000,000,000*

SOME EXAMPLES OF FULFILLED PROPHECIES IN THE BIBLE

Copies of all the below prophecies are in the Greek Septuagint of the Old Testament, written between 250 – 150 BC. The originally written dates of the prophecies are indicated below.

Prophecy Description *Numbers in brackets, e.g., [1 in 3], are the odds of that prophecy coming true by natural events.*	Comments/Fulfillment *Except as noted for Tyre and Jericho,* **all the below prophecies were fulfilled after the time of Christ.**

Palestine (Leviticus 26:31-33; Ezekiel 36:33-35): Originally Written sometime during 1446-1406 BC, and in 587 BC, respectively

Passage predicts the following:	Fulfillment started with Roman destruction of Jerusalem in 70 AD and was completed in succeeding years.
1. The cities of Palestine [Israel's territory] shall become waste. [1 in 10]	
2. The sanctuaries shall become desolate. [1 in 2]	Visitors to Palestine before 1900 reported that very little of the land was tilled, that the great mass of it was total desolation.
3. The land shall become desolate. [1 in 10]	
4. Enemies shall inhabit the land. [1 in 2]	Palestine became the stronghold of the Muslims
5. The Jews shall be scattered. [1 in 5]	Under prior persecutions, Jews largely stayed together as a people, but after the Roman destruction, they were scattered into many nations.
6. A sword shall go out after the Jews. [1 in 10]	
7. The Jews shall return to Palestine; the cities shall be rebuilt, and its land shall be tilled. [1 in 10]	Never has there ever been such a persecuted race as the Jews. The Jews did return to Palestine (Israel), mainly with Israel's becoming a nation in 1948 and afterwards.

Odds of Above Happening by Random Chance:
1 in 10 x 2 x 10 x 2 x 5 x 10 x 10 = 1 in 200,000

SOME EXAMPLES OF FULFILLED PROPHECIES IN THE BIBLE
Copies of all the below prophecies are in the Greek Septuagint of the Old Testament, written between 250 – 150 BC. The originally written dates of the prophecies are indicated below.

Prophecy Description *Numbers in brackets, e.g., [1 in 3], are the odds of that prophecy coming true by natural events.*	Comments/Fulfillment *Except as noted for Tyre and Jericho, all the below prophecies were fulfilled after the time of Christ.*

Zion (Micah 3:12): Originally Written 750 BC	
The passage reads: *Zion will be plowed like a field* - Micah 3:12. [1 in 100]	Parts of Jerusalem have often been destroyed and rebuilt. In 1543 AD when walls of Jerusalem were rebuilt by Sultan Suleiman, that part known as Zion, the City of David, was left outside the walls. That area is plowed for grain and other crops and is the only part of the old city that was ever plowed.
Odds of Above Happening by Random Chance: 1 in 100	

SOME EXAMPLES OF FULFILLED PROPHECIES IN THE BIBLE	
Copies of all the below prophecies are in the Greek Septuagint of the Old Testament, written between 250 – 150 BC. The originally written dates of the prophecies are indicated below.	
Prophecy Description *Numbers in brackets, e.g., [1 in 3], are the odds of that prophecy coming true by natural events.*	**Comments/Fulfillment** *Except as noted for Tyre and Jericho,* **all the below prophecies were fulfilled after the time of Christ.**

Gaza and Ashkelon (Zephaniah 2:4, 6; Amos 1:8): Originally Written 630 BC and 787 BC	
Passage predicts the following: 1. The Philistines shall perish. [1 in 5] 2. Gaza shall become bald. [1 in 100] 3. Ashkelon shall become desolate. [1 in 5] 4. The vicinity of Ashkelon shall become the dwelling place of shepherds with their sheep. [1 in 5]	At time of the prophecy, Philistines were most powerful race in the country. Have ceased to exist. New research found original location of Gaza – buried under sand dunes. Ashkelon was a prosperous city even in time of Christ, destroyed in 1270 AD, never rebuilt, and has become a grazing place for sheep flocks.
Odds of Above Happening by Random Chance: 1 in 5 x 100 x 5 x 5 = 1 in 12,500	

SOME EXAMPLES OF FULFILLED PROPHECIES IN THE BIBLE
Copies of all the below prophecies are in the Greek Septuagint of the Old Testament, written between 250 – 150 BC. The originally written dates of the prophecies are indicated below.

Prophecy Description *Numbers in brackets, e.g., [1 in 3], are the odds of that prophecy coming true by natural events.*	Comments/Fulfillment *Except as noted for Tyre and Jericho, all the below prophecies were fulfilled after the time of Christ.*

Samaria (Micah 1:6,): Originally Written 750 BC	
Passage predicts the following:	Was still a major city at time of Christ.
1. Samaria shall be destroyed. [1 in 4]	Became a heap of stones and ruins.
2. It shall become as a heap of the field. [1 in 5]	Later was cleared.
3. Vineyards are to occupy its site. [1 in 100]	Foundation stones taken to the edge of the hill and rolled down into the adjacent valley.
4. Its stones shall be poured down the sides of the hill on which it stands. [1 in 10]	Now covered with gardens and vineyards.
5. Its foundation is to be dug up. [1 in 2]	
Odds of Above Happening by Random Chance: 1 in 4 x 5 x 100 x 10 x 2 = 1 in 40,000	

SOME EXAMPLES OF FULFILLED PROPHECIES IN THE BIBLE	
Copies of all the below prophecies are in the Greek Septuagint of the Old Testament, written between 250 – 150 BC. The originally written dates of the prophecies are indicated below.	
Prophecy Description *Numbers in brackets, e.g., [1 in 3], are the odds of that prophecy coming true by natural events.*	**Comments/Fulfillment** *Except as noted for Tyre and Jericho, all the below prophecies were fulfilled after the time of Christ.*

Edom (Jeremiah 49:16-18): Originally Written 600 BC	
Passage predicts the following: 1. Edom shall be conquered. [**1 in 10**] 2. Edom shall be desolate. [**1 in 10**] 3. Edom shall not be reinhabited. [**1 in 100**]	When prophesy originally written, Edom was a very prosperous country. Its soil was among richest in the world. On many major trade routes. Its capital, Petros, hewn out of solid rock, had perhaps best natural defenses of any city in the world. Remained prosperous long after Christ. Taken by Muhammadans in 636 AD. Since then has lain desolate, with practically no people or animals.
Odds of Above Happening by Random Chance: 1 in 10 x 10 x 100 = 1 in 10,000	

SOME EXAMPLES OF FULFILLED PROPHECIES IN THE BIBLE

Copies of all the below prophecies are in the Greek Septuagint of the Old Testament, written between 250 – 150 BC. The originally written dates of the prophecies are indicated below.

Prophecy Description	Comments/Fulfillment
Numbers in brackets, e.g., [1 in 3], are the odds of that prophecy coming true by natural events.	*Except as noted for Tyre and Jericho, all the below prophecies were fulfilled after the time of Christ.*

The Golden Gate (Ezekiel 44:1-3): Originally Written 574 BC	
The passage reads:	Gate in use at time of Christ.
Then the man brought me back to the outer gate of the sanctuary, the one facing east, and it was shut. The Lord said to me, "This gate is to remain shut. It must not be opened; no one may enter through it. It is to remain shut because the LORD, the God of Israel, has entered through it. The prince himself is the only one who may sit inside the gateway to eat in the presence of the LORD. He is to enter by way of the portico of the gateway and go out the same way."- Ezekiel 44:1-3. [1 in 1,000]	In 1543 Sultan Suleiman ordered gate closed, but instead of building the wall across where the gate had been, he restored the gate with its arches and ornaments and then walled its opening up. Has never been opened since (looks like it is ready for Christ's entry).
Odds of Above Happening by Random Chance: 1 in 1,000	

FINAL RESULTS ON NEXT PAGE

FINAL RESULTS OF
ABOVE FULFILLED PROPHECIES

> ### THE ODDS OF ALL OF THE ABOVE BEING
> ### FULFILLED BY CHANCE IS 1 IN 5.76 X 10^{59}
> (or about 1 in 5.76 x 10^{54} if the Jericho prophecies not considered)
>
> 1 in 5.76 x 10^{59} is comparable to:
>
> * Filling all the galaxies in the entire universe with dimes; mark one dime; mix them all up. Blindfold yourself, dive into the mass of dimes, and get the right one on the first try.
>
> * The number of grains of sand on all of earth's beaches is about 10^{23}. Multiply all that by one trillion, one trillion, one trillion times x 5.76 and mark one grain of sand; mix them all up. Blindfold yourself, dive into the mass of dimes, and get the right one on the first try.

DANIEL'S AMAZING PROPHECY ABOUT THE COMING OF THE MESSIAH

Daniel 9:25-26—²⁵ *"Know and understand this: From the time the word goes out to restore and rebuild Jerusalem until <u>the Anointed One</u>, the ruler, <u>comes</u>, there will be seven 'sevens,' and sixty-two 'sevens.' It will be rebuilt with streets and a trench, but in times of trouble.* ²⁶<u>*After*</u> *the sixty-two 'sevens,' <u>the Anointed One</u> will be <u>put to death</u> and will have nothing. The people of the ruler who will come will destroy the city and the sanctuary. The end will come like a flood: War will continue until the end, and desolations have been decreed...."* (Underlining is this author's emphasis)

Author's Note to Reader: Revision one of this book was precipitated by necessary changes in this Appendix B due to additional research.

CONTEXT AND DATE WRITTEN

Daniel, a prophet of God, and the Jews were in foreign captivity (first Babylonian, then Persian). Jerusalem and the first temple had been destroyed. Daniel was praying about the future of Israel when the angel Gabriel brought him the above message, recorded in Daniel 9.

Daniel's prophecy was written in the sixth century BC. Even the most biased critic cannot make a case for Daniel to have been written later than 250-150 BC, since the Greek Septuagint of the entire Old

Testament, including Daniel, had been completed by that time (Josh McDowell, Evidence that Demands a Verdict, Vol. I, p. 168).

DEFINITION OF TERMS

Sevens – The Hebrew word used is *shabua*, literally meaning "seven" or in this context "week of *years*," like *decade* means "ten years." In the case of the Messiah's appearance, it was to be "seven plus sixty-two" sevens, or "69 sevens," or 69 x 7 = 483 years. Note the below for further support that "sevens" means a week of years in this context:

- *Shabua* can mean either a "week of *days*" or a "week of *years*." For example, Leviticus 25:8 speaks of multiples of a "week of years."

- Daniel had been thinking in terms of years and multiples of seven in Daniel 9:1, 2.

- Israel was in captivity for 70 years since it had previously violated the God-ordained Sabbatical year (every seventh year) for 490 years (Leviticus 26:32-35; II Chronicles 36:21, and Daniel 9:24), which translates to 70 years for its captivity. This appendix focuses on the first 69 of the 70 "weeks" in Daniel 9:24.

- *Shabua*, as found in Daniel 10:2-3, means "week of *days*" or literally "three sevens of *days*." If Daniel had meant "sevens of *days*" in chapter 9, he would have used the same expression as in chapter 10 (*Ibid.*, p. 169).

THE MONTH OF NISAN AND PASSOVER

Nisan is the first month of the Jewish religious new year and is lunar-based (30 days/month). The first day of Nisan always falls on the day after the new moon (new moon = when the moon is totally dark facing earth) closest to the spring equinox of March 21 (Gregorian calendar) each year. Therefore, Nisan 1 typically falls in the March-April timeframe. The Jewish Passover always occurs on Nisan 15, a full moon.

Since it is lunar-based, from year to year Nisan 15 can occur on different dates and days of our Julian or Gregorian solar calendars.

DANIEL'S PROPHETIC PERIOD

Daniel's prophecy of 69 (7 + 62) weeks in Daniel 9:25 is 69 weeks of years as indicated above. Therefore, Daniel's prophetic period is 69 x 7 years for a total of 483 years. This number is widely agreed upon by scholars; no real debate exists about this number. The start of Daniel's prophetic period commences upon Israel's release from captivity, as the context makes clear.

DANIEL'S PROPHETIC PERIOD CONVERTED TO SOLAR YEARS

How many days per year was Daniel using in his prophetic period? The main view held by researchers and scholars appears to be 360 days (12 months x 30 days each month), which is called a "prophetic" or "biblical" year; it was lunar-based and used by many cultures at the time and for many centuries to follow. Islamic cultures still use a lunar-based calendar today. Every few years a "leap-month" was/is added to help the lunar calendar "catch-up" to the solar calendar.

Some scholars point out that the Bible utilizes the 360-day-per-year calendar elsewhere in Scripture. Therefore, it is maintained, the most reasonable view is that Daniel used 360 days as well. Two examples follow:

- In Genesis, the flood began on the seventeenth day of the second month (7:11) and ended by the seventeenth day of the seventh month (8:4), making a total of 5 months, which is said to be 150 days in the Genesis flood account. From these specifics, it would appear that the lunar month of 30 days (hence 360 days per year) was being used. Although a cursory read of chapters 7-9 may lead one to conclude that a lunar-based calendar was used, we cannot be certain that this was the case in that ancient time.

- In the Book of Revelation of the New Testament, the last half of Daniel's seventieth week is discussed and it clearly uses the 360-day prophetic year.

The best source this author has found on the 360-days-per-year view, as well as on the well-known view holding Artaxerxes's fourth decree as the starting point and March 30, 33 AD as the ending point of Daniel's prophetic period (see below), is *Chronological Aspects of the Life of Christ* by Dr. Harold W. Hoehner of Dallas Theological Seminary. Of course, this is not the only source available supporting this view.

An alternate position maintains that Daniel was thinking in terms of solar years and therefore was speaking of each year as 365.25 days, as in the Julian calendar, or 365.242222 days, using the revised Julian calendar.

The best source this author has found on the solar calendar view, and the position holding Artaxerxes's third decree as the starting point and 26 AD as the ending point of Daniel's prophetic period (see below), is the scholarly organization *Associates for Biblical Research (ABR)*. Their website is https://biblearchaeology.org. Several detailed articles on the entire subject being discussed in this appendix are located under "ABR Projects" and then "The Daniel 9:24-27 Project."

The significance of the 360- vs. 365.242222-days-per-year views will become clear later. Both views will be utilized without a resolution between the two as the subject is far too involved and complex to offer a full treatment here.

To convert Daniel's prophetic period of 483 years to our solar calendar years:

- Using the 360-days-per-year view:
  - » Multiply Daniel's 483 years x 360 days to give a total 173,880 days.
  - » Divide 173,880 days by 365.242222 (solar days per year) to equal 476.0676327 solar years.
  - » 476.0676327 years equals **476 solar years, 25 days (rounded)**

- Using the 365.242222-days-per-year view:

  » Multiply Daniel's 483 years x 365.242222 days to give a total of 176,412 days.

  » Using a solar year of 365.242222 days, the total equals **483 solar years, 00 days** (176,412 days divided by 365.242222).

DATES AND SPAN OF YEARS FOR THE REIGNS OF KINGS AND EMPERORS

Dating methods utilized:

- Dating Method No. 1: whether to include the first partial year or first full year of a reign (as king or emperor) in determining when the reign began.

- Dating Method No. 2: how to calculate the number of years in a span; for example, is 12-26 AD inclusive or not?

Concerning Dating Method No. 1:

At the time of the Jews' captivity under Babylon and Persia and subsequent Roman law, it appears that only the first full year of a king's or emperor's reign was counted as the "first year" of his reign. For example, if a king came to power sometime in the year of 500 BC after Nisan 1 (the beginning of the new year), his first official year of reign would begin on Nisan 1, 499 BC, thereafter being the first full year of his reign. This is the method, based on the burden of evidence, which will be used in this appendix, although its application in reality may not have been 100% consistent.

Therefore, per historical records and to avoid overly complex dating issues, the commonly held view is that 457 BC and 444 BC are the seventh and twentieth years of Artaxerxes's reign, respectively.

Concerning Dating Method No. 2:

In calculating the number of years in a span, is the first number included or not? In other words, assuming the first full year of a reign from 12 AD to 26 AD is 12 AD, should one count the first number (12) in the number of years in the span? In this case, would the span of years be 14 or 15? Roman tradition uses the inclusive approach; i.e., 12 would be included, and thus the span of years in this case would total 15.

A combination of the first and second dating methods will be used to determine the fifteenth year of reign for Tiberius Caesar (Luke 3:1-22). The Romans used the solar-based Julian calendar (with a new year starting on January 1).

The ascension (or partial) year of Tiberius Caesar's reign was either 11 AD or 14 AD, depending on whether one includes the time when Tiberius "co-reigned" as emperor with this father-in-law (Augustus) or only when he became sole emperor. Therefore, the first full (and official) year of his reign would have been either 12 or 15 AD, respectively. His fifteenth year of reign would have been either 26 AD or 29 AD, depending on whether Luke intended to include Tiberius's co-reigning period (some argue that 28 AD should be used instead of 29 AD since Tiberius had been emperor since his first full year of reign in 12 AD, albeit as co-emperor). It appears from the aforementioned dating methodologies that Luke was referring to the year 12 AD as Tiberius's first (full) year of reign; therefore, the fifteenth year of his reign would have been 26 AD. This conclusion aligns with other related information, as shown below.

START OF DANIEL'S PROPHETIC PERIOD

Daniel's prophecy begins with the decree to go and rebuild Jerusalem (Daniel 9:25):

> *"Know and understand this: From the time the word goes out to restore and rebuild Jerusalem until the Anointed One, the ruler, comes, there will be...."*

Two decrees from Artaxerxes I are starting possibilities for the above verse's action. The previous two decrees concerning the Jews, given in the years of 539 BC by King Cyrus and 519 BC by King Darius, clearly concerned only the rebuilding of the Jewish temple, not Jerusalem itself. The two possible decrees in the context of the Jewish captivity are as follows:

Third Decree from Artaxerxes I

The third decree from Artaxerxes I is in his seventh year of reign to Ezra in 457 BC (Ezra 7:11-28).

Some claim the year to be 458 BC rather than 457 BC.

Also, some researchers contend that Ezra was using the Nisan-based calendar, while others feel it was the Tishri-based calendar (the Jewish civic calendar). The Nisan calendar starts with the month of Nisan as the first month of the year, which is in the timeframe of March-April in our Julian/Gregorian calendars, whereas the Tishri calendar starts with the month of Tishri as the first month of the year, which is in the September-October timeframe. When discussing Jewish kings, the Nisan calendar was typically used. When discussing foreign kings the Tishri calendar was typically utilized.

The complexities of the issues cause scholars to disagree and will not be resolved here. However, because of some strong evidence that points to the 457 BC year, we will utilize that date here. The above-referenced source, *ABR*, states that their analysis indicates the third decree was on Tishri 1, 457 BC.

The purpose of Artaxerxes's third decree included the following:

- Financial provisions for temple sacrifices (v. 17);

- Besides the costs associated with the temple sacrifices, Artaxerxes said, "You and your fellow Israelites may then do whatever seems best with the rest of the silver and gold, in accordance with the will of your God" (v. 18);

- Anything else needed for the temple (v. 20);

- Appointment of magistrates and judges to administer justice and Old Testament laws to all the people (v. 25).

Proponents of this view hold that Daniel's prophetic period is an even 483 solar years.

Proponents of the third decree claim that the above purposes of this decree are, in effect, to order the rebuilding of Jerusalem, at least on a spiritual level. It could be argued that a physical rebuilding was also implicitly included by the decree's wording: *"You and your fellow Israelites may then do whatever seems best with the rest of the silver and gold, in accordance with the will of your God"* (v. 18). Besides, a spiritual rebuilding is more significant than a physical one. So goes the argument.

Further, the adherents of the 457 BC position point out that Ezra 7 specifically states that the letter of the king was a decree, whereas the letters for the fourth decree (discussed below) are not actually called a decree in the biblical text. This wording may or may not be significant.

Lastly, the *"restore and rebuild"* of Daniel 9:25 is argued to mean both spiritual *restoration* and physical *rebuilding*, whereas the fourth "decree" apparently involves only rebuilding, perhaps a valid and important point.

Fourth "Decree" (or Letters) from Artaxerxes I

The fourth decree is from Artaxerxes I in his twentieth year of reign to Nehemiah in 444 BC (Nehemiah 2:1-8).

One well-known past claim indicated that the twentieth year of his reign was 445 BC, but that view included the first partial year of Artaxerxes's reign. However, as stated above, the tradition at that time was not to include an initial partial year of a king's reign as the first year, but only the first *full* year. Therefore, we will use 444 BC. In addition, the year 445 BC, counting forward by the length of Daniel's prophetic period, does not work under this view because the period (173,880 days) would end in the year 32 AD. For reasons given later, 32 AD is not a candidate year for the end of Daniel's prophetic period.

The adherents to this view hold that Daniel's prophetic period is 476 solar years and 25 days.

The purpose of the decree or letters was to physically rebuild Jerusalem, as is made clear in Nehemiah 2.

Nehemiah states in verses 3 and 17 that Jerusalem was in ruins and its gates had been destroyed by fire. If the third decree, 13-14 years prior, had been to rebuild them, it had not happened by 444 BC! There-fore, the adherents to this view (173,880 days, or 476 solar years and 25 days) argue that the burden of proof reveals that the fourth "decree" in 444 BC should serve as our starting point. This idea is worth con-sidering, but does not come with an air-tight argument. It could be argued that Nehemiah was distressed since the rebuilding had not yet begun per Artaxerxes's third decree, or perhaps, it is argued, he was just distressed due to the fact that Jerusalem was still in ruins. This "fourth decree" point-of-view obviously assumes that Daniel meant a physical rebuilding of Jerusalem and not merely the start of a spiritual renewal and/spiritual rebuilding.

Nehemiah 2:1 is clear that the fourth "decree" was issued *"in the month of Nisan."* The custom of that day was that if the specific day of the month was not mentioned, the reference was to the first day of that month. In the Bible, only "in month of Nisan" is specified. There-fore, the evidence points to Nisan 1, although that conclusion is not 100% certain.

On what Julian calendar *equivalent* date did Nisan 1 occur in 444 BC? The Julian calendar actually started with Julius Caesar in the first century BC. The most referenced Julian-retroactive date for Nisan 1, 444 BC appears to be March 5, 444 BC. However, not all scholars agree; for example, one source this author encountered argued that March 5 was too early for Nisan 1. Generally, not much information is available concerning this aspect.

The Julian calendar date calculation for *within* 444 BC is quite complex due to various calendar issues: whether Nisan in 444 BC was preceded or not by a "leap-month" (probably not), the correct use of Sabbatical years, what solar calendar date Nisan 1 fell on, etc. The issues are far too complex and varied to fully examine here.

However, one source claimed that the use of stellar software shows March 5 as the correct day. This author tends to favor astronomical software over historical data, since the latter can be affected by many factors, such as the type of calendar used, calendar changes and tim-ing, even cultural factors, etc., whereas the movement of planetary and stellar bodies is constant.

ENDING OF DANIEL'S PROPHECY PERIOD

The event signaling the ending year of Daniel's prophetic period is the coming of Jesus as the Messiah, or as Daniel 9:25 states:

> *".... Until the Anointed One, the ruler, comes...."*

The *"Anointed One"* to the Jews meant *"the Messiah."* Following is a discussion of two New Testament events that could have been the fulfillment of Daniel's *"coming of the Anointed One."*

Event 1 (26 AD)

Event 1: *Either (i) when John the Baptist started his ministry of proclaiming the coming of the Messiah; or (ii) when John baptized Jesus, which was also the start of Jesus's ministry. These actions all occurred in the same year. The baptism of Jesus is where John proclaimed, "Look, the Lamb of God, who takes away the sin of the world!" (John 1:29).*

Proponents of 26 AD hold to the following two premises:

- The starting point of Daniel's prophetic period is Artaxerxes's third decree of Nisan 1, 458 BC or Tishri 1, 457 BC. As pointed out earlier, Tishri 1, 457 BC is being used in our discussion.

- Daniel's prophetic period is an even 483 years, 00 days (or 176,412 days).

Arguments that 26 AD is a realistic possibility:

- If you add the above 483 solar years to Tishri 1, 457 BC, you arrive at Tishri 1, 26 AD! (1 BC to 1 AD is only one year).

- Luke 3:1-22 states that the above one-year period wherein Jesus's baptism and the first year of Jesus's and John's ministries was the fifteenth year of Tiberius Caesar's reign, which would have been 26 AD based on the Julian calendar, as demonstrated earlier.

- Further supporting the 26 AD date is the fact that John 2:20 makes it clear that in Jesus's first year of ministry the temple had been under construction for 46 years (per historical records, said construction began in 20/19 BC under Herod). The forty-sixth year was 26 AD!

- Additional support is based on the known historical date of the death of King Herod Agrippa I in 44 AD. To make a very long analysis short, per the above-referenced organization *Associates for Biblical Research*: In Galatians 2:1, Paul states it had been 14 years since his (Paul's) conversion, which was within a few years of Christ's crucifixion, perhaps within 1-2 years (many scholars contend it was one year). Galatians 2:1 is in the context of Paul's return to Jerusalem, which can reasonably be determined to be 44 AD.

A further argument as to the validity of the 26 AD view is that it would also be consistent with a 30 AD crucifixion (which had to have taken place the day before a Passover occurring on a Saturday Sabbath). See the analysis below showing that during Jesus's ministry, only the years 30 and 33 AD had Passovers on a Saturday Sabbath. Note:

- Jesus's ministry was likely close to 3.5 years long, according to scholars.

- Adding the 3.5 years to the 26 AD date could easily bring us to the year 30 AD.

- In 30 AD, the Passover fell on Saturday, April 8.

- This would put the date of Christ's crucifixion on the preceding day, Friday, April 7, 30 AD.

- That would mean that Christ's day of triumphal entry occurred on either April 2 or 3. (Remember that according to this perspective, the day of triumphal entry is not considered the end of Daniel's prophetic period. See Event 2 below for that view.)

The information above reveals amazing agreement in the available information!

Certain dates within 26 AD for either the start of John the Baptist's ministry or Jesus's baptism and start of his ministry are not specifically given in Scripture, and neither is the specific date, as such, within 457 BC given. However, from 457 BC to 26 AD is definitely 483 solar years!

The previously-referenced *ABR* contends that their analysis of the biblical events has led them to conclude that the third decree was given on Tishri 1, 457 BC. If that is the case, the fulfillment would be on Tishri 1, 26 AD. Nevertheless, we can be certain that Event 1 was in 26 AD.

Event 2 (April 2-3, 30 AD or March 29-30, 33 AD)

Event 2: *The day of Christ's triumphal entry into Jerusalem on the back of a donkey (Zechariah 9:9), proclaiming himself Messiah (Matthew 21:1-11).*

The Zechariah 9:9 passage was well-known by the Jews of that time as an event that would proclaim the Messiah's coming. This event has two proposed years (and therefore possible end dates for Daniel's prophetic period): 30 or 33 AD. Christianity celebrates this event as Palm Sunday, an event that preceded Christ's crucifixion by 4-5 days.

Let us begin by determining the year and day of Christ's crucifixion. Christ was crucified on a Friday before a Saturday Sabbath that was also a Passover. A Passover falling on a Saturday Sabbath only occurred in the years 26, 30, 33, and 36 AD, during the 26 to 36 AD reign of Pontius Pilate, the one who sentenced Jesus to be crucified. No matter what assumptions or calculations one uses, the years 26 and 36 AD are out of the question for possible candidate years for Christ's crucifixion; that leaves us with either 30 or 33 AD.

In 30 AD the Saturday Sabbath Passover was on April 8, and in 33 AD it was on April 4 (Julian calendar). In light of these dates, Christ was crucified either on April 7 or April 3 in those respective years. This means the date of Jesus's triumphal entry, per the biblical timeline, had to occur 4-5 days earlier, on April 2 or 3, 30 AD or March 29 or 30, 33 AD.

The Gospels agree that Jesus died according to the following specifics:

- Christ was crucified on a Friday, called the "day of preparation" (for the next day, the Saturday Sabbath)
- In a year wherein the Passover fell on a Saturday Sabbath.

This position holds to the following premises:

- The starting date of Daniel's prophecy period is Nisan 1 (or March 5), 444 BC (the fourth "decree" of Artaxerxes).
- That Daniel's prophetic period is 476 (solar) years, 25 days.

An argument can be made that March 30, 33 AD is a realistic date for Event 2, considering the information below:

By Calculating the Date:

- Adding 476 years (solar) and 25 days to the starting date of Daniel's prophetic period of Nisan 1, 444 BC (March 5, 444 BC) results in the date of March 30, 33 AD!
- March 30, 33 AD is the fourth day prior to April 3, 33 AD, the date of Christ's Friday crucifixion!

From Biblical and Historical Data:

- Christ had to be crucified in either 30 or 33 AD since His crucifixion preceded a Passover that was on a Saturday Sabbath.
- That date would have to be April 7, 30 AD or April 3, 33 AD.
- That being the case, the day of the triumphal entry into Jerusalem would have to be either April 2-3, 30 AD or March 29-30, 33 AD.
- Calculating the date using Daniel's prophecy period of 476 years, 25 days results in a date of March 30, 33 AD when added to the March 5, 444 BC date of Artaxerxes's fourth

"decree." Therefore, it is argued, the year 30 AD is eliminated as a possibility.

It should be mentioned that up to the point when Christ rode on a donkey into Jerusalem, he discouraged his disciples from revealing that he was the Messiah, the Son of God, and he also prevented demons from doing so. However, Christ was now declaring his full identity by his action of riding on the back of a donkey into Jerusalem per Zechariah 9:9, a passage well known by the Jews. The above is a possible argument against Event 1 as the ending point of Daniel's prophetic period.

Some have promoted 32 AD as the year Christ died, but that is not possible since in 32 AD the Passover did not fall on a Saturday Sabbath!

In light of the above argument for the triumphal entry date being the end point of Daniel's prophetic period, Christ would have been crucified on April 3, a Friday. According to the Bible, he died at 3 p.m. Christ's triumphal entry into Jerusalem had to be either on the preceding Sunday or Monday per the biblical timeline leading up to his crucifixion. Monday was March 30, 33 AD! *The end date of Daniel's prophecy as determined above! Amazing consistency! Amazing prophecy!*

ADDITIONAL CONSIDERATIONS AND CONCLUSIONS

Any in-depth research will show differing analyses as to the proper year, month, and day that both started and ended Daniel's prophetic period. The numerous historical and calendar issues (types of calendars, changes, etc.) are quite complex, certainly beyond the scope of this appendix, and would require hundreds to thousands of hours of research to thoroughly deal with all of the viewpoints and their various nuances in a truly scholarly manner.

Although this author feels the above "summary-like" analysis is compelling, it is not necessarily 100% certain. The author has examined several possibilities and presented what he feels are the two most likely of those he personally encountered. Although completing considerable research, the author has not made a totally comprehensive and totally in-depth study of the topic.

What does appear to be certain is that the following points must be included in any theory:

- Daniel's prophetic period is either 476 solar years, 25 days or an even 483 solar years.

- Christ's crucifixion had to take place in either 30 or 33 AD.

- Depending on what event is considered the end of Daniel's prophetic period, 26, 28/29, 30, or 33 AD are the possible ending dates.

Although not 100% certain, the beginning point of the prophetic period would be 458 (or 457) or 445 (or 444) BC (this assumes the majority opinion as to when Artaxerxes's reign started and when the seventh and twentieth years of Artaxerxes's reign occurred).

This author prefers the choice of March 5, 444 BC to March 30, 33 AD, in part due to its precision to the 173,880ᵗʰ day! The second view of 457 BC to 26 AD is possibly valid, especially when one considers the death of King Herod Agrippa I in 44 AD and uses reverse chronology of events in the New Testament to arrive at 30 AD for the crucifixion. *If* the referenced King Herod/Paul analysis is ultimately correct from *ABR*, it would eliminate the possibility of 33 AD for Christ's triumphal entry (Event 2) and crucifixion; thus, Event 1 in 26 AD would be considered the better of the two possibilities.

A CRITICAL POINT

Regardless of how one calculates the date or what reasonable assumptions one makes, it is clear that the first appearing of the Messiah had to be <u>no later than</u> 33 <u>AD</u>!

This information should be of critical importance to those who are still looking for the <u>initial</u> coming of the Messiah! They need to read Daniel, Zechariah 9:9, the New Testament, and study relevant history.

BIBLE VERSES SHOWING JESUS CHRIST IS GOD

		Verses	TEXT of VERSES and/or Comments
DIRECT CLAIMS THAT JESUS IS GOD BY....	**God/God the Father**	Hebrews 1:8	*"But about the Son he* [the Father] *says, 'Your throne, O God* ['ho theos]...*"*
		Mark 9:7, Hebrews 1:8, etc.	The Father refers to Jesus as *"his/my Son."* "Son of God" is a Hebrew idiom meaning deity, that Jesus is God. Jesus was called "Son of God" many times by himself and others.
	Jesus Himself (also see below functions or activities Jesus does)	John 8:58-59	*"'Very truly I tell you,' Jesus answered, 'before Abraham was born I am!' [Ego Eimi]' At this, they picked up stones to stone him."* The Greek phrase for "I AM" is *Ego Eimi.* In Exodus 3:14, Jehovah God told Moses to tell the Israelites in Egypt that I AM [*Ego Eimi*] (referring to himself) sent Moses. Therefore, the Jews clearly understood Jesus's claim to being God, so they tried to stone him for what they wrongly thought was blasphemy (no other possibility here for stoning). See John 10:33 below.
		John 10:33	*"'We are not stoning you for any good work,' they replied, 'but for blasphemy, because you, a mere man, claim to be God.'"* Jesus did not deny their claim but affirmed it.
		Mark 14:61b-64	*"Again, the high priest asked him, 'Are you the Messiah, the Son of the Blessed one?' 'I AM'* [see John 8:58 above], *said Jesus. 'And you will see the Son of Man* [himself] *sitting at the right hand of the Mighty One and coming on the clouds of heaven.'"* His words, to the first century Jew, were a claim to being deity, so the high priest erroneously thought them to be blasphemy.
		John 14:9	*"Jesus answered: '...Anyone who has seen me has seen the Father.' "*
	Other	John 1:1,14	*"In the beginning was the Word* [Christ], *and the Word was with God,* **and the Word was God** ['theós eén ho Lógos'])... The Word became flesh and made his dwelling among us. We have seen his glory, the glory of the one and only Son, who came from the Father, full of grace and truth."*
		John 10:33	See above quotation of this verse.
		John 20:28	*"Thomas* [one of the twelve apostles] *said to him, 'My Lord and my God!' "* Jesus accepted Thomas's acclamation.
		Isaiah 9:6	A prophecy about the Messiah, the Christ; he is called *"Mighty God,"* etc.
		Isaiah 7:14	Matthew 1:23 references Isaiah 7:14 as referring to Christ, calling Christ "Immanuel" (God with us).

		Verses	TEXT of VERSES and/or Comments
JESUS DOES THINGS ONLY GOD DOES; HENCE, HE IS GOD	Creation	John 1:3	*"Through him all things were made; without him nothing was made that has been made."*
		Colossians 1:16-17	*"For in him all things were created: things in heaven and on earth, visible and invisible, whether thrones or powers or rulers or authorities; all things have been created through him and for him. He is before all things, and in him all things hold together."*
		Hebrews 1:10	*"He* [the Father] *also says, 'In the beginning, Lord, you* [Christ] *laid the foundations of the earth, and the heavens are the work of your hands.'"*
	Accepts Worship	Matthew 14:33, Matthew 28:9, John 9:38, Hebrews 1:6	A total of nine times in the New Testament, Jesus accepted worship [*proskuneo* in Greek]. In Revelation 19:10: when John went to worship [*proskuneo*] an angel, the angel said, *"Do not do it!... Worship* [*proskuneo*] *God!"* Ex. 34:14, etc. – only God is to be worshipped! *Hebrews 1:6 - "...God...says, 'Let all God's angels worship him* [Christ].'"*
	Forgives Sins Against God	Mark 2:5-12 Luke 5:20-26	Parallel passages. Jesus forgives the sins of the paralytic man. The Pharisees and teachers of the law stated *"who can forgive sins but God?"* Christ affirms he can forgive sins that only God can forgive and then physically heals the paralytic man as proof.
	Judges Sin	John 5:22	Only God judges sin, as sin is against God and his justice/holiness, etc. No created being, including an angel, could conduct such an activity.
	Omnipresent	John 14:23; Romans 8:9, I Cor. 3:16	Only God can be everywhere at once. Angels can only be at one place at any given time. These verses show Christ can be everywhere at once.

		Verses	TEXT of VERSES and/or Comments
TITLES ONLY FOR GOD ARE ALSO FOR JESUS	**First and Last**	Isaiah 44:6; 48:12 Revelation 1:8,11,17; 22:13	Only God is referred to as *"the first and the last"* and *"the alpha and the omega."* Jesus in the book of Revelation is referred to as *"the first and the last"* and *"the alpha and the omega."* In Revelation 2:8 the first and the last is stated to have died and is alive – only Jesus (God) did that!
	The Only Savior	Isaiah 43:11, 45:14; I Thess. 1:10	Several verses refer to God as "our Savior" and Jesus as "our Savior." However, these refer to God as our "ONLY" Savior and Jesus as our "ONLY" Savior. One cannot have two "ONLY" Saviors. Hence, they are one and the same.

Brief Analysis of Some Verses Incorrectly Used in Trying to Deny Christ's Deity

IMPORTANT NOTE: Christ always being fully God, upon his incarnation in Mary THEN ALSO became fully man (and was/ is still fully God). Some only look at his "humanity" verses, incorrectly stating he is not God; they ignore the above and other verses that clearly show him to be fully God. The Bible says he is both God and man. For example, in his "humanness" he prayed to the Father.

John 1:1: The Greek reads: *"God [theos] was the Word...."* Since "God" precedes the verb "was," Greek grammar does not need the definite article *[ho]* before "God" *[theos]* in order to capitalize it. Hence, God is capitalized, referring to the one true God.

John 14:28: Christ says, *"the Father is greater [meizon] than I."* The Greek word *meizon* is a comparison of function, not a comparison of the value of personage. Philippians 2 states that Christ voluntarily took on a subservient (servant) function while on earth.

Colossians 1:15-17: Christ is called *"firstborn [prototokos] over creation."* This does not mean he had a beginning. *Prototokos* can mean "priority or sovereignty over." Being Creator, Christ is sovereign over creation. See v. 16 (Christ is <u>before all things</u>). The Jews call Yahweh (God) the firstborn of all the world or of all creation. Christ is called that here. This is a Jewish idiom.

BIBLE VERSES ON HOLY SPIRIT'S IDENTITY/DEITY

Definition: Who Is the Holy Spirit?

According to the Bible, the Holy Spirit is:

- The one true God; he is fully and totally God.

- Often referred to as the "third member" of the Godhead; this is not a ranking of position or of lesser value as compared to the two other members (Father and Son) of the Godhead. They are co-equal, co-eternal, co-divine.

- The "Godhead" is simply the one true God of all that exists, consisting of three persons, Father, Son and Holy Spirit, *each equally and fully* the one same God (i.e, the "Trinity"). Although the word "Trinity" (meaning 3 in 1) is not found in biblical Scripture, it is a name used to succinctly and accurately describe the God of the Bible.

The Holy Spirit Is a Personage of Spirit and Not Some Kind of an Inanimate Force

The following characteristics/activities of the Holy Spirit show he is a Person, in addition to the consistent reference in the Bible to the Holy Spirit as "he" and "him")

Speaks, tells	Acts 8:29, 13:2; Revelation 2:11; Revelation 3:22; I Timothy 4:1; John 16:13		
Appoints/ Decides	Acts 20:28; I Corinthians 12:11	Forbids/ convicts	Acts 16:6-7; John 16:7-8
Can be Grieved/ Insulted	Ephesians 4:30; Isaiah 63:10; Hebrews 10:29	Sends/Helps, Intercedes	Acts 13:4; Rom. 8:26
Has a Mind/Will	Acts 15:28; I Corinthians 12:11	Leads	Rom. 8:14; Galatians 5:18

Various Names of Holy Spirit (Number in parentheses indicates number of times in the Bible.)			
Holy Spirit, Spirit	Spirit of God, Father	Spirit of Jesus	Names Showing Function
Holy Spirit (91)	Holy Spirit of God (1)	Spirit of Jesus (1-NASB)	Holy Spirit of Promise (1)
Spirit (104)	Spirit of God (12)	Spirit of Christ (2)	Spirit of Truth (3)
Eternal Spirit (1)	Spirit of your Father (1)	Spirit of Jesus Christ (1)	Spirit of Holiness (1)
		Spirit of his Son (1)	Spirit of Grace (1)
		Spirit of the Lord (4)	Spirit of Adoption (1)/Life (2)

The Deity of the Holy Spirit Is Shown by the Following: (*Continues on to next page.*)	
He Is Creator	Genesis 1:2 (only God created the heavens, earth, life – Malachi 2:10)
He Is Omnipresent	Romans 8:9; John 14:16-17; I Corinthians 3:16 (indwells all believers in the world)
Can Foretell Future	John 16:13 (only God can truly know the future)
Holy Spirit's Names	His names, shown above, clearly indicate his deity, that he is God. Just like a "spirit of a human" indicates it is a human spirit, similarly, the "Spirit of God," etc. indicates the Spirit is deity; he certainly is not a human spirit or an angelic spirit, demonic spirit, etc.
Can Be Blasphemed	Matthew 12:31 (only God can be blasphemed; Holy Spirit can be blasphemed)

The Functions of the Holy Spirit Also Show His Deity (marked with an *) and His Roles Some functions/activities of the Holy Spirit are given below.		
The Holy Spirit (Creator, Genesis 1:2) Points to the Father and Jesus		
Access to the Father: Ephesians 2:18	Glorifies Christ: John 16:14	Conceived Christ in Mary: Matthew 1:18, 20
In Support of the Above, the Holy Spirit Bears Witness to the Truth (Primarily of Salvation in Jesus)		
Testifies to truth: Acts 20:23, Romans 8:16; John 15:26	Guides us into truth: John 16:13	Searches all things*: I Corinthians 2:10
Truth (of Jesus) - The Holy Spirit Leads Us to Salvation		
Convicts men of sin, righteousness: John 16:7-8	Agent in new birth: John 3:1-8	Abides in all believers*: Romans 8:9, John 14:17; I Corinthians 3:16
After Saving Us, the Holy Spirit Sanctifies (Matures) Us		
Sanctifies Believers*: Romans 15:16; I Pet. 1:2	Gives Fruit of Holy Spirit*: Galatians 5:22-23	Gives Spiritual Gifts*: I Corinthians 12:4-11
The Holy Spirit's Sanctification of Believers Also Includes His Doing the Following		
Leads Believers: Galatians 5:18	Helps Men to Remember: John 14:26	Helps Men: Romans 8:26
Sends Men: Acts 13:4	Appoints and Decrees: Acts 20:28	Forbids: Acts 16:6-7
Convicts Men of Sin, Righteousness: John 16:7-8	Teaches: John 14:26; I Corinthians 2:13	Reveals Future: John 16:13

BIBLE VERSES
SHOWING THE TRINITY

Definition of Trinity: The one true God is three distinct personages who are *each equally and fully* the one, same, true God.			
BIBLICAL LOGIC REQUIRES IT	Deity of Father, Son, and Holy Spirit	Father	John 6:27; John 8:41; Romans 1:7; I Corinthians 1:3, 15:24; Galatians 1:1; Ephesians 6:23; Philippians 4:20; Colossians 1:2; Titus 1:4; II Peter 1:7; Jude 1; etc. Father is omnipresent (only God is) (John 14:23, etc.)
		Son	The Father calls the Son God (Hebrews 1:8-9); Jesus (the Word) is called God (John 1:1, 12, 13); Jesus Claims to be God (John 8:58 "I AM," etc.); he is Creator (John 1:3, Colossians 1:15-17, etc.); accepts worship 9 times (Matthew 14:33, John 9:38, Hebrews 1:6, etc.); forgives sins (Mark 2:5-12, Luke 5:20-26); Jesus is omnipresent (only God is) (John 14:23; Romans 8:9, I Corinthians 3:16). Limited space prohibits an extended discussion.
		Holy Spirit	The "Spirit of God"/"God's Spirit"- numerous times in Bible. Involved in creation (Genesis 1:2, hence is God); only God can be blasphemed/Holy Spirit is blasphemed (Matthew 12:31); he is omnipresent (only God is omnipresent) (Romans 8:9, John 14:16-17, I Corinthians 3:16); foretells future (only God can) (John 16:13); etc.
	Only One God!		Bible is filled with the fact that there is only one true God for all of existence and that this one true God is a living, personal being (not some impersonal force), who also loves, cares, etc. A few references: Isaiah 43-45; Deuteronomy 4:6, 39; Joel 2:27; James 2:19; I Corinthians 8:4-6. In the Bible, God is given all the attributes of a self-existent being with personality.
	Therefore, the Trinity		The Bible is plain: there is only one true God. The Bible is also clear that the Father is God, the Son is God, and the Holy Spirit is God. It is simplistic to say the Bible contradicts itself on such an obvious, basic train of logic. Common sense dictates the Bible is teaching a triune God: one God, who is three personages, who are each equally and fully the one true God. It is definitely a logical conclusion, though not fully comprehensible to our three dimensionally-limited minds.

Functions of Each of the Godhead Members (Father, Son, and Holy Spirit) Show Each Is God (*Note: only some functions shown here.*)
The Father
Creator (Genesis 1:1); forgives sins against God, which only God can do (Matt. 6:14); he sanctifies believers (Jude 1); plants, elects believers in Christ (Matthew 15:13; John 6:37, 17:24); sent Christ (John 5:37, 6:29, etc.) and the Holy Spirit (John 14:26); etc. The functions of the Father are many, but many of them tend to concentrate on his being the originator, sender, etc., hence the term *Father*.
The Son
Creator (John 1:3, Colossians 1:15-17, etc.); judgment (John 5:22, II Corinthians 5:10); forgives sins against God (only God can do that - Mark 2:5-12); Savior and Redeemer (Matthew 1:21, etc.); cleanses us from sin (I John 1:7-9); gives sanctification (I Corinthians 1:2); justifies (I Corinthians 6:11); peace with God through Jesus (Rom. 5:1); victory through Jesus (I Corinthians 15:57); preserves believers (Jude 1); plus many other "God only performs" functions. The functions of the Son are many, but a number of them tend to concentrate on his being the exact representation/expression of the Father (God), God in bodily form, the truth, etc., hence the term *Son* and the *Word* (John 1:1).
The Holy Spirit
Creator (Genesis 1:2); abides in all believers (Romans 8:9, John 14:16-17); distributes spiritual gifts (I Corinthians 12:4-11); gives love, joy, peace, etc. (Galatians 5:22-23); sanctifies believers (Romans 15:16, II Thess. 2:13); etc.
Only God Performs the Above Functions
Only God performs the above functions (and many more) according to the Bible. Consider just one of these functions: Creation. Genesis 1:26-27 states: "And God said, Let us make man in our image, after our likeness...' So God created man in his own image." Malachi 2:10 states, "Did not one God create us?" The above segment shows the Father is creator, the Son is creator, and the Holy Spirit was involved in creation. Therefore, the Father, Son and Holy Spirit must be God. Many more examples could be given, but space is limited.
Therefore, the Trinity
Only God performs certain functions (creation, judgment, forgives sins, accepts worship, distributes spiritual gifts, etc.). The Father/Son/Holy Spirit sometimes share functions that only God can do, and therefore each must be God. Only one or two of them perform some functions (*voluntarily, not by limitation*) that only God can do. Hence, for God to perform such functions (such as judgment, which only the Son does according to John 5:22), the Son must be God, or else God would not perform judgment, which would be ridiculous/contrary to Scripture.

In Light of the Above, the Following Further Shows the Trinity

John 1:1, 12-13: The Word (Jesus) was with God and the Word is God.

Isaiah 48:16: they show one member (God) of the Godhead talking to/about the other (God, Lord): "…from the time that it was, there am I [God]: and now The Lord GOD, and his Spirit, hath sent me [God]" (KJV). Hebrews 1:8 - The Father is talking to the Son, saying "Thy throne, O God…"

Deuteronomy 6:4 says "the Lord our God…is ONE" [*echad* in Hebrew – a composite unity; does not use *yachid* = singular unity]

Matthew 11:25; Philippians 2:10; 11; II Corinthians 3:17: Father/Son/Holy Spirit are each called "Lord." Bible says there's one Lord.

Psalm 106:21; Luke 1:47; I Timothy 4:10; Titus 1:3: Father/Son/Holy Spirit each called Savior. God is said to be our only Savior – Isaiah 43:11; Hosea 13:4.

John 14:14: Jesus said, "You may ask me for anything in my name, and I will do it" (if it is God's will, of course), and in John 16:23b Jesus said, "…my Father will give you whatever you ask in my name."

Matthew 28:19: Jesus said: "…baptizing them in the NAME of the Father and of the Son and of the Holy Spirit."

Matthew 1:18; John 1:14, 5:37: The Father/Son/Holy Spirit involved in virgin birth. Space prohibits other examples.

Philosophic and Scientific Analysis

By definition, the finite human mind cannot comprehend an infinite God. The Bible states that God is beyond our four dimensions (3 space, 1 time). Therefore, it is logical that God's nature is something beyond our comprehension. In 4 space dimensions, one *mathematically* can turn a basketball inside out without popping it. If string theory is correct, there are 10 dimensions (we only experience 4). Extra-dimensionality presents all sorts of interesting possibilities, and God is beyond all dimensions. A 3-dimension analogy: space is fully width, fully height, and fully depth; each is fully space; without any one of them, you no longer have 3D space (any 3D physical analogy by definition falls short of a perfect explanation).

APPENDIX F

CAN GOD BE A "SHE"?

The question of this appendix has only become a topic of discussion in the late twentieth century and the now twenty-first century. However, it is a legitimate question needing an answer.

Let us start with a passage from the apostle Paul, where he states:

> *There is neither Jew nor Gentile, neither slave nor free, nor is there male and female, for you are all one in Christ Jesus* (Galatians 3:28).

The obvious significance here is that God is nondiscriminatory regarding gender, race, or social status; he loves all equally.

As to the issue of the gender of God, we will look at each member of the one true God since God is a triune God. The Bible uses terms that are familiar to humans to help describe God's nature, including the personages of the triune Godhead:

- God the Father (first person of the trinity or Godhead): See Appendix E for a list of the "functions" of God the Father. These are best described with the human term *Father*, as we would characterize the first person of the Godhead. Jesus in the Bible says God (the Father) is Spirit:

God is spirit and his worshipers must worship in the Spirit and in truth (John 4:24).

Since God the Father is Spirit, he is without gender. Therefore, the term *Father* is a descriptive term that best describes the nature and functions of the first person of the Godhead and does not relate to gender. For example, sometimes our planet is called "Mother Earth," as earth is often depicted as the "source of life." The term *mother* best reflects this idea. Obviously, the earth has no sexuality.

- God the Son (Jesus Christ, second person of the Trinity, the Godhead): Before Jesus's incarnation in the virgin Mary, the second person of the Godhead was eternally a spirit and therefore was without any gender. In his few "pre-incarnate" appearances in the Old Testament, the second member of the Godhead did appear in male human form (for example, he was one of the three visitors to Abraham in Genesis; the term *Yahweh* [God or Lord] was applied to him). The second person of the Godhead did take on human form as a male called Jesus Christ per the historical record; he was/is God who took on being fully human (while still remaining fully God) and such cannot be changed.

- God the Holy Spirit (the third person of the Trinity, the Godhead): The Holy Spirit is a spirit and is therefore without any gender. However, the male personal pronouns are often used in referencing the Spirit. These are merely labels or terms of convenience, which, again, best describe the Holy Spirit's functions and roles. See Appendices D and E.

In the Bible male and female are equal, but not equivalent. They are equal as persons, but their roles are not always equivalent. Males are generally, obviously, the physically stronger, while females, generally, are more nurturing. And so on. Often their functions overlap.

It is true that in Genesis God set up the male to be the "lead" or "head" in the marriage relationship; any team has to have a leader, or there will be anarchy. The trouble is that men often do not carry out their roles in marriage the way they were intended by God as revealed in the Bible. Scripture is plain that the man in his marriage relationship is to use his leadership with love, giving up his life for his spouse and putting her needs and wants before his. The man is to give up his life for his wife as Christ gave up his life for the church (body of believers).

The man and woman are to be a "team" based on God's power, love, and direction. In I Corinthians 7:2-5, Scripture even says that the husband is to give the wife her sexual rights as a woman (unheard of in that culture!). Much more could be said on this, but that is the subject of another book…

A person may ask, "Why didn't Christ come in the form of a human female, rather than a male?" In this author's opinion, the answer is somewhat obvious. The culture of that time was male-dominated or patriarchal. That does not mean culture has always been "right" in how relationships between men and women were carried out. Since societies are more typically patriarchal in nature rather than matriarchal, God, in Jesus Christ, took on the male human gender and not a female one to best communicate authoritatively and effectively.

A good way to end this brief discussion is to go back to the beginning in Genesis chapter 1. Verse 27 states that both man and woman were made in God's image:

> *So God created mankind in his own image, in the image of God he created them; male and female he created them.*

BIBLIOGRAPHIES AND REFERENCES

BIBLIOGRAPHY

Axelrod, D.I. *Science* 128:7. New York: American Association for the Advancement of Science, 1958.

Bengtson, Stefan. *Nature* 345.765. United Kingdom: Nature Research (subsidiary of Springer Nature), 1990.

Bruce, F. F. *The Books and Parchments: How We Got Our English Bible.* Old Tappan, N.J.: Fleming H. Revell Co., 1950, Reprints: 1963, 1984.

Cashmore, Anthony R. "The Lucretian Swerve: The Biological Basis of Human Behavior and the Criminal Justice System." In *PNAS [Proceedings of the National Academy of Sciences of the United States of America].* Washington, DC: official journal of the publisher United States National Academy of Sciences (NAS), March 9, 2010 (10) 4499-4504.

Clark, Austin Hobart. "The New Evolution." In *Zoogenesis, orig. 1923, multiple eds.*

Collins, Francis S. *The Language of God.* New York: Free Press, 2006.

Corner, E.J.H. *Contemporary Botanical Thought.* Chicago: Quadrangle Books, 1961.

Darwin, Charles. *Descent of Man and Selection in Relation to Sex.* New York: D. Appleton and Company, 1872.

Darwin, Charles. *On the Origin of Species by Means of Natural Selection.* London: John Murray, 1860 edition as found in The Project Gutenberg EBook, Sept. 2007, EBook #22764.

Darwin, Charles. Chapter IX, "On the Imperfection of the Geological Record," *On the Origin of Species by Means of Natural Selection.* London: John Murray, 1869 ed.

Davies, Paul. "The Anthropic Principle," *Science Digest.* New York: Hearst Corporation, 191, No. 10, October 1983.

Davies, Paul. *Superforce*. New York: Simon and Schuster, a Touchstone Book, 1985.

Davies, Paul. *The Cosmic Blueprint*. West Conshohocken, PA: Simon and Schuster, Templeton Foundation Press, 1988, reprint 2004.

Davidson, Samuel. *The Hebrew Text of the Old Testament*. London: 1856. Quoted in Norman L. Geisler and William E. Nix, *General Introduction to the Bible*. Chicago: Moody Press, p. 89.

Dawkins Richard. *The Blind Watchmaker*. New York: W. W. Norton, 1987.

Dawkins, Richard. *River out of Eden: A Darwinian View of Life*. New York: Basic Books, 1995.

Dawkins, Richard. "The Ultraviolet Garden," In a Royal Institution Christmas Lecture (No. 4, 1991), quoted in Vinoth Ramachandra, *Subverting Global Myths: Theology and the Public Issues Shaping Our World*. 2008, p. 187.

Drane, John. *Introducing the New Testament*. San Francisco: Harper and Row, 1986.

Eckhardt, Robert. *Scientific American* 226 [1]: 94. England: Springer Nature, 1972.

Ehrman, Bart. *Jesus: An Apocalyptic Prophet of the New Millennium*. New York: Oxford University Press, 1999.

Einstein, Albert. *The Expanded Quotable Einstein*. Edited by Alice Calaprice. Princeton, NJ: Princeton University, 2000.

Eldredge, Niles. *The Monkey Business: A Scientist Looks at Creationism*. New York: Washington Square Press, 1982.

Flew, Antony with Roy Abraham Varghese. *There Is a God: How the World's Most Notorious Atheist Changed His Mind*. New York: HarperCollins Publishers, 2007.

Fox, Douglas. "Primordial Soup's On: Scientists Repeat Evolution's Most Famous Experiment," In *Scientific American*, Mar 28, 2007.

Futuyma, Douglas. *Evolutionary Biology*, 2nd ed. Sunderland, Mass.: Sinauer Associates, Inc., 1986.

Geisler, Norman and William E. Nix. *General Introduction to the Bible*. Chicago: Moody Press, 1968 (orig.), Revelation 1986 (quoting from *The Hebrew Text of the Old Testament* by Ira Maurice Price).

Goldschmidt, R. B. "The Material Basis of Evolution." In *American Scientist* 40:97. Research Triangle Park, North Carolina: Sigma Xi, 1952.

Gould, S. J. "Evolution's Erratic Pace," In *Natural History.* Manhattan, NY: American Museum of Natural History, 86 (5):13, 1977.

Gould, S. J. and Niles Eldredge. "Punctuated Equilibria: The Tempo and Mode of Evolution Reconsidered," *Paleobiology,* Vol. 3, No. 2. Cambridge University Press. Spring, 1977.

Graham, Philip L. "Is Man a Subtle Accident?" In *Newsweek,* New York, November 3, 1980.

Greenstein, George. *The Symbiotic Universe.* New York: William Morrow, 1988.

Harris, Sam. *Free Will.* New York: Free Press (A Division of Simon and Schuster, Inc.), 2012.

Harrison, Edward. *Masks of the Universe.* Cambridge, United Kingdom: Cambridge University Press, July 31, 1985 (also August 5, 2003, November 24, 2011).

Hawking, Stephen. *A Brief History of Time.* New York, NY: Bantam Dell Publishing Group, 1988 (originally published; multiple subsequent eds.).

Hoehner, Dr. Harold W. *Chronological Aspects of the Life of Christ.* Grand Rapids, MI: Zondervan Academic, 1978.

Hingora, Q.I. *The Prophecies of the Holy Qur'an.* Sh. Muhammad Ashraf, January 1, 1964.

Hoyle, Sir Frederick. *The Intelligent Universe.* London: Michael Joseph Ltd, 1983.

Isaacson, Walter. *Einstein: His Life and Universe.* New York: Simon and Schuster, 2008.

Islam Fatwa Number 41409, dated 7-5-1421, or Aug 8, 2000.

Jastrow, Robert. *God and the Astronomers.* New York: W. W. Norton and Co., 1978, 2000.

Jones, J. S. and S. Rouhani. "How Small Was the Bottleneck?" In *Nature* 319. England: Springer Nature Limited, 6 February 1986.

Kenyon, Sir Frederic. *Our Bible and the Ancient Manuscripts.* London: Eyre and Spottiswoode, 1896 (2nd ed.).

Kitts, David B. "Paleontology and Evolutionary Theory," *Evolution: International Journal of Organic Evolution.* Hoboken, New Jersey: John Wiley and Sons, 28:467, 1974.

Krauss, Lawrence M. "The End of the Age Problem and the Case for a Cosmological Constant Revisited," *Astrophysical Journal* 501 (July 10, 1998): 461, doi:10.1086/305846.

Leakey, Mary. *Disclosing the Past.* New York: McGraw-Hill, 1984.

Luckhoo, Sir Lionel. The Question Answered: Did Jesus Rise from the Dead? Lionel Luckhoo, publisher, back page.

Macbeth, N. *American Biology Teacher.* Los Angeles, CA: University of California Press, November 1976.

Mackay, Alan Lindsay (quoting Salvador Dali). *A Dictionary of Scientific Quotations.* Routledge; 1 edition, January 1, 1991, p. 66.

Martin, R. "Man Is Not an Onion," *New Scientist.* London, August 4, 1977.

Martyr, Justin. *Dialogue with Trypho,* chapter 108.

Martyr, Justin. *First Apology,* XLVIII (c. 150 AD).

Martyr, Justin. *First Apology,* XXXV (c. 150 AD).

Maududi, Sayyid Abul A'La. *The Meaning of the Qur'an,* Vol. 3.

McDowell, Josh and Sean. *Evidence of the Resurrection, What It Means for Your Relationship with God.* Grand Rapids: Baker Books, 2009.

McDowell, Josh. *Evidence that Demands a Verdict.* Vol. I. San Bernardino, CA: Here's Life Publishers, Inc., 1979.

McDowell, Josh. *The New Evidence that Demands a Verdict.* Arrowhead Springs: Campus Crusade for Christ, 1999.

Morowitz, Harold. *Energy Flow in Biology.* New York: Academic Press, 1968.

Nabeel Qureshi. "Do the Roots of Jihad Lie in the Qur'an," *Huffington Post,* Apr 4, 2016, updated Apr 05, 2017.

Nature, Vol. 294, No. 5837 (quoting Sir Frederic Hoyle). United Kingdom: Nature Research (subsidiary of Springer Nature), Nov. 1981.

O'Collins, Gerald. *Interpreting Jesus.* London: Paulist Press, 1983 (orig.); revised – Wipf and Stock, publisher, Oct. 2002.

Parker, Barry. *Creation—the Story of the Origin and Evolution of the Universe.* New York and London: Plenum Press, 1988.

Penrose, Roger. From the Stephen Hawking-related movie *"A Brief History of Time."* Burbank, CA: Paramount Pictures, Inc., 1992.

Pilbeam, David. "Patterns of Hominoid Evolution," In *Ancestors: The Hard Evidence.* Hoboken, New Jersey: Wiley-Liss, 1985.

Pilbeam, David. "Rearranging Our Family Tree," In *Human Nature.* New York, NY: Springer Nature, June 1978.

Ross, Hugh. *Creation as Science*. Colorado Springs, CO: NavPress, 2006.

Ross, Hugh. *Why the Universe Is the Way It Is*. Grand Rapids, MI: Baker Books (a division of Baker Publishing Company), 2008.

Sahih Bukhari. 4:54:430 (an Islamic Hadith).

Stafford, Timothy. "Cease-fire in the Laboratory," *Christianity Today*. Carol Spring, Illinois: Christianity Today International, 3 April 1987.

Stoner, Peter W. and Robert C. Newman. *Science Speaks*. Chicago: Moody Press, Nov. 2005 (revised online edition).

Strauss, Stephen. "An Innocent's Guide to the Big Bang Theory: Fingerprint in Space Left by the Universe as a Baby Still has Doubters Hurling Stones." In *The Globe and the Mail*. Toronto, 25 April 1992.

Toledoth Yeshu (a Jewish document, sixth century).

Warren, Rick. *The Purpose Driven Life* (quoting Philosopher Bertrand Russell). Grand Rapids, MI: Zondervan, 2002. Ultimate source is letter to Hugh Moorhead from Bertrand Russell, January 10, 1952.

Wilford, John Noble. "Sizing up the Cosmos: An Astronomer's Quest," In *New York Times*, 12 March 1991.

Woodruff, David. (Review of Steven Stanley's "Macroevolution Pattern and Process," In *Science 208:716*, 1980.

E-LINK BIBLIOGRAPHY

(all e-links current and working as of final check thereof)

Associates for Biblical Research.

    (https://biblearchaeology.org)

Bear, Dick, and Jim Robertson. *False Prophecies of Joseph Smith*. Concerned Christians, January 1, 1999.

    (https://amazon.com/False-Prophecies-Joseph-Smith-Dick/dp/B003P777HY).

Bharati, Bharata. *Thighing – Muslim Scholars*, October 11, 2011.

    (https://bharatabharati.in/2011/10/11/fatwa-number-41409-thighing-muslim-scholars/).

"Dark Energy" (article). Simple English Wikipedia (from Wikipedia, the free encyclopedia)

    (https://simple.wikipedia.org/wiki/Dark_energy).

Darwin, Charles. Letter to John Fordyce (May 7, 1879). *Darwin Correspondence Project*. University of Cambridge.

    (https://darwinproject.ac.uk/DCP-LETT-12041).

Drake, Gordon W.F. "Entrophy." *Britannica*.

    (https:// britannica.com/science/entropy-physics).

Geisler, Norman L. *I am Put Here for the Defense of the Gospel: Dr. Norman L. Geisler: A Festschrift in His Honor*, edited by Terry L. Miethe. Pickwick Publishers, 2016.

    (https://normangeisler.com/category/reliability-of-the-bible/).

Habermas, Gary R. *History, Philosophy, and Christian Apologetics: Specializing in Resurrection-of-Jesus Research*.

    (https://garyhabermas.com/).

"List of Killings Ordered or Supported by Muhammad" (article). *WikiIslam, the Online Resource on Islam.*

(https://wikiislam.net/wiki/List_of_Killings_Ordered_or_Supported_by_Muhammad).

Mol, Arnold Yasin. Article "Aisha (ra): The Case for an Older Age in Sunni Hadith Scholarship." Irving, TX: Yaqeen *Institute for Islamic Research*, Oct. 3, 2018.

(https://yaqeeninstitute.org/arnold-yasin-mol/aisha-ra-the-case-for-an-older-age-in-sunni-hadith-scholarship/).

Qureshi, Nabeel, Article "Nabeel Qureshi in The Huffington Post: Do the Roots of Jihad Lie in the Quran?" @ RZIM Website.

(https://rzim.org/read/rzim-global/nabeel-qureshi-in-the-huffington-post-do-the-roots-of-jihad-lie-in-the-quran).

Above article originally appeared in *The HuffPost*, April 5, 2017

(https://www.huffpost.com/ entry/is-the-quran-the-roots-of-jihad_b_9594484).

Rana, Fazale. Article "New Challenge to the Bird-Dinosaur Link," April 1, 2000.

(https://reasons.org/explore/publications/connections/read/connections/2000/04/01/new-challenge-to-the-bird-dinosaur-link, which in turn references Alan Feduccia, *The Origin and Evolution of Birds*, second ed. New Haven: Yale University Press, 1999).

Rana, Fazale. Article "Tetrapod Transitions: Evidence for Design," January 1, 2010.

(https://reasons.org/explore/publications/nrtb-e-zine/read/nrtb-e-zine/2010/01/01/tetrapod-transitions-evidence-for-design).

Ross, Hugh. Article "Fine-Tuning for Life on Earth," updated June 7, 2004.

(https://reasons.org/explore/publications/tnrtb/read/tnrtb/2004/06/07/fine-tuning-for-life-on-earth-updated-june-2004).

Ross, Hugh. Multiple Articles on Fine Tuning by Hugh Ross, plus others.

(https://reasons.org/search-results?searchQuery=fine   %20Tuning%20%20%20&mode=0).

Ross, Hugh. Article "RTB Design Compendium (2009)," November 16, 2010

(https://reasons.org/explore/publications/tnrtb/read/tnrtb/2010/11/16/rtb-design-compendium-2009).

Siegel, Ethan. "Ask Ethan: Have We Finally Found Evidence for a Parallel Universe?" *Forbes Magazine*, May 22, 2020.

(https://www.forbes.com/sites/startswithabang/2020/05/22/ask-ethan-have-we-finally-found-evidence-for-a-parallel-universe/#6f44f98342fc).

Stoner, Peter W. and Robert C. Newman. *Science Speaks*, Online Edition, Nov. 2005.

(sciencespeaks.dstoner.net).

Thakur, Vishal. Article "How Many Atoms Are There in the Universe?" Jan 13, 2020 @ *Science ABC*.

(https://scienceabc.com/nature/universe/how-many-atoms-are-there-in-the -universe.html).

Wallace, J. Warner. "Can We Trust the Prophecies of Joseph Smith?" *Cold-Case Christianity*, 2014.

(https://coldcasechristianity.com/writingsresources-to-help-you-respond-to -mormonism/).

Weldon, John. "False Prophecy in the Watchtower Society," *John Ankerberg Show*, Sept. 2005.

(https://jashow.org/articles/false-prophecy-in-the-watchtower-society).

"What Is the Big Bang?" (Article). SpacePlace: NASA

(https://spaceplace.nasa.gov/big-bang/en/)

RECOMMENDED
REFERENCES

The below references are in addition to those listed in the bibliography, but are not specifically quoted. These are but a few of the many valuable resources available.

Scientific-Related Books and Material

- **Reasons to Believe** (RTB) at www.reasons.org. This link is the easiest to access and best single source for showing how science supports the Bible and the latest related scientific findings. Multiple books and materials are available from their website. The president is astrophysicist Dr. Hugh Ross, and the vice president is biochemist Dr. Fuz Rana, with additional scientific scholars on staff and as "guest scholars." Their research and facts are first-class.

- **Illustra Media** at www.illustramedia.com. The best source for full-length DVDs and other video "shorts" for showing the harmony of the Bible and science. Excellent information and production quality.

- **Discovery Institute** at www.discovery.org. While the Discovery Institute covers a wide range of topics, the "Intelligent Design" area is of special interest. Excellent source of information. The general subject area of "Intelligent Design" sometimes has inputs (not necessarily related to Discovery

Institute) from well-meaning proponents of a "young earth/universe" perspective.

General Apologetics (Bible reliability, the resurrection, etc.)

- **Gary Habermas** at https://www.garyhabermas.com/. World's foremost expert on Christ's resurrection. Some of his books include: *The Case for the Resurrection of Jesus; Did Jesus Rise from the Dead? The Resurrection Debate; The Historical Jesus: Ancient Evidence for the Life of Christ; Did the Resurrection Happen? A Conversation with Gary Habermas and Antony Flew*, etc.

- **Josh McDowell Ministry** at https://www.josh.org/resources/. Formerly a skeptic, Josh has written over 150 books, with the majority of them on apologetics. He is one of Christianity's best apologists. A few of his books include: *Evidence that Demands a Verdict, Life-Changing Truth for a Skeptical World* (this is the latest and most up-to-date edition of the several *Evidence that Demands a Verdict* books), *Evidence for the Resurrection* (with Sean McDowell, his son), *The Resurrection Factor, More than a Carpenter*, and so many more.

- **Lee Strobel** books and DVDs at www.leestrobel.com. Formerly a skeptic, he is now an excellent Christian apologist. With a Harvard law degree, he was a former legal editor and investigative journalist for the *Chicago Tribune*. Some of his books/DVDs include *The Case for Faith, The Case for Christ, The Case for a Creator, The Case for Christianity Answer Book, The Case for Miracles*.

- **J. Warner Wallace** at https://coldcasechristianity.com/. A former police detective in murder investigations, J. Warner's professional investigative work has received national recognition; his cases have been featured more than any other detective on NBC's Dateline, and his work has also appeared on CourtTV and Fox News. He also appears on television as an investigative consultant. Formerly a skeptic, his books include (but are not limited to): *Cold-Case Christianity, God's Crime Scene,* and *Forensic Faith.*

Other Belief Systems Compared to Christianity (and general apologetics):

- www.Equip.org. The Christian Research Institute (CRI) was founded by Dr. Walter Martin, perhaps the most prominent expert on world religions, cults, and the occult. The current president is Hank Hanegraaff (many leaders/scholars in mainline Christianity disagree with some of Hank's views of eschatology [study of end times] and of Israel, so caution is recommended on these two topics). Some of Dr. Martin's books include *Kingdom of the Cults, Jehovah of the Watchtower, The Christian Science Myth, The Rise of the Cults, Mormonism, Essential Christianity: A Handbook of Basic Christian Doctrines, The Maze of Mormonism, The Riddle of Reincarnation, Walter Martin's Cults Reference Bible, The New Age Cult,* etc. Some of the current CRI's President, Hank Hanegraaff's books: *Christianity in Crisis, The Bible Answer Book, The Complete Bible Answer Book* - Collector's Edition, *Has God Spoken?: Proof of the Bible's Divine Inspiration, Resurrection: The Capstone in the Arch of Christianity, MUSLIM: What You Need to Know about the World's Fastest Growing Religion,* etc.

ABOUT THE AUTHOR

John T. Davis, MBA, has researched, written, and taught on Christian apologetics for over fifty years, with an emphasis on cosmology and other scientific disciplines, as well as on the cults and occult.

John is retired after 40 years at the Jet Propulsion Laboratory (JPL), an operating division of NASA, winning multiple performance awards.

He is a volunteer apologist with the Christian think tank *Reasons to Believe* (president and astrophysicist Dr. Hugh Ross) and has conducted 15 years of public skeptics forums, where people were encouraged to ask questions regarding the Bible, science, and related issues. John also led a biblical apologetics group for 20 years, and has written two previous books and numerous Christian tracts.

John attended *The First Presbyterian Church of Hollywood* for 21 years, where he served as both a deacon and teacher. For fifteen years he attended Dr. Hugh Ross's Sunday School class, "Paradoxes," at *First Congregational Church of Sierra Madre*, where he also periodically substituted as a teacher in Dr. Ross's absence. He is currently attending *The Church at Rocky Peak* in Chatsworth, California, where he has fellowshipped for over 15 years.

John and his wife Gloria have been married since 1985 and have one son, Joshua. They reside in Los Angeles, California.

The author may be contacted at jtdavispx@gmail.com.

Made in the USA
Middletown, DE
24 July 2022